Poverty Rebels

JUSTICE, POWER, AND POLITICS

Heather Ann Thompson and Rhonda Y. Williams, editors

Editorial Advisory Board

Dan Berger
Peniel E. Joseph
Daryl Maeda
Barbara Ransby
Vicki L. Ruiz
Marc Stein

The Justice, Power, and Politics series publishes new works in history that explore the myriad struggles for justice, battles for power, and shifts in politics that have shaped the United States over time. Through the lenses of justice, power, and politics, the series seeks to broaden scholarly debates about America's past as well as to inform public discussions about its future.

A complete list of books published in Justice, Power, and Politics is available at https://uncpress.org/series/justice-power-politics.

Poverty Rebels
Black and Brown Protest in Post–Civil Rights America

Casey D. Nichols

The University of North Carolina Press CHAPEL HILL

© 2025 Casey D. Nichols
All rights reserved
Set in Merope Basic by Westchester Publishing Services
Manufactured in the United States of America

Library of Congress Cataloging-in-Publication Data
Names: Nichols, Casey D., author.
Title: Poverty rebels : Black and brown protest in post-civil rights America / Casey D. Nichols.
Other titles: Justice, power, and politics.
Description: Chapel Hill : The University of North Carolina Press, [2025] | Series: Justice, power, and politics | Includes bibliographical references and index.
Identifiers: LCCN 2024044991 | ISBN 9781469684666 (cloth) | ISBN 9781469684673 (paperback) | ISBN 9781469684630 (epub) | ISBN 9781469687377 (pdf)
Subjects: LCSH: Anti-poverty movements—United States—History—20th century. | African Americans—Relations with Hispanic Americans. | Poverty—Government policy—United States. | Economic assistance, Domestic—United States—History—20th century. | African Americans—Economic conditions—20th century. | Hispanic Americans—Economic conditions—20th century. | BISAC: SOCIAL SCIENCE / Ethnic Studies / American / African American & Black Studies | SOCIAL SCIENCE / Activism & Social Justice
Classification: LCC HC110.P63 N53 2025 | DDC 362.5/524097309046—dc23/eng/20241026
LC record available at https://lccn.loc.gov/2024044991

Cover art: "Los Angeles area anti-poverty workers picketing Federal building in protest over funding cuts, 1966," Los Angeles Times Photographic Archive, UCLA Library Special Collections, uclalat_1429_b584_234417. The Regents of the University of California. Licensed under CC BY 4.0: https://digital.library.ucla.edu/catalog/ark:/21198/zz0002vbzp.

An earlier version of Chapter 6 was previously published in the *Pacific Historical Review* and is used here with permission. Casey D. Nichols, "'The Magna Carta to Liberate Our Cities': African Americans, Mexican Americans, and the Model Cities Program in Los Angeles," *Pacific Historical Review* 90, no. 3 (August 2021): 377–98.

For Dewahn J. Brooks Jr.

Contents

List of Illustrations ix
Acknowledgments xi

Introduction 1
Tracing the Historical Roots of Black-Brown Relations

CHAPTER ONE
Black and Brown Los Angeles 12

CHAPTER TWO
Black Noise, Brown Invisibility 33

CHAPTER THREE
The Economic Opportunity Generation 59

CHAPTER FOUR
Black and Brown at the White House 82

CHAPTER FIVE
Su Lucha Es Mi Lucha (Your Battle Is My Battle) 107

CHAPTER SIX
The Magna Carta to Liberate Our Cities 128
African Americans, Mexican Americans, and the Model Cities Program in Los Angeles

Epilogue 153
The War on Poverty's Legacy in Black and Brown America

Notes 159
Bibliography 179
Index 193

Illustrations

FIGURES

Augustus Hawkins, 1964 20

Edward Roybal, 1953 22

Rena, Marquette, and Ronald Frye, 1965 43

Two buildings on fire during the Watts Rebellion, 1965 46

Mexican American students' walkout at Garfield High School, 1968 65

Audience listening to Lyndon Johnson's commencement address at Howard University, 1965 67

Tommy Jacquette, 1967 70

Lyndon Johnson signing the Economic Opportunity Act, 1964 87

Black activists meet with Lyndon Johnson at the White House, 1968 93

Lyndon Johnson meeting with Mexican American activists, 1966 99

East Los Angeles buildings on fire, 1970 142

Chicano moratorium, 1971 144

MAP

City of Los Angeles, ca. 1970 7

TABLES

Table 1. African American and Mexican-Origin city population, 1920–40 19

Table 2. African American and Mexican-Origin city population, 1950–70 28

Acknowledgments

When I started this book, I never imagined the amazing community that would grow alongside each research trip, chapter, and revision. The biggest lesson I learned is that it takes a village to write an academic book. Although some of my strongest advocates did not reach the end of the publication journey with me, my nephew Dewahn Brooks Jr., and my grandparents Nell, Sam, and Rosetta, they remain my motivation and inspiration as guardian angels. Although I cannot name everyone who has been a part of this book's journey, I am grateful to each individual person who supported my work.

I am grateful for the generous guidance offered by archivists and their staff at the California State Archives, Los Angeles City Archives, Huntington Library, Stanford University's Special Collections, Young Research Library's Department of Special Collections at UCLA, National Archives at College Park, and Lyndon Baines Johnson Presidential Library. I am especially thankful to the LBJ Library and Huntington Library for awarding me research fellowships that aided the completion of my book. My time in the archives introduced me to a diversity of historical actors and issues that helped bring *Poverty Rebels* to life.

Colleagues and students have provided invaluable research and professional support over the past several years. At Texas State, Ana Romo, Jeff Helgeson, Dwight Watson, John Mckiernan-González, and Dwonna Goldstone read chapters and/or offered guidance throughout the publication process. Conversations with student researchers Alejandra Magallon and Trinity Taylor have helped me think critically about historical significance as I prepared this book. Outside of Texas State, I am grateful to Lori Flores, Ula Taylor, Premilla Nadasen, Jane Dabel, Shana Bernstein, and Michael Green for sharing their insights about the publication process and/or reading chapters.

This research is supported by generous grants. The offices of research at California State University, East Bay, and Texas State University provided funding that allowed me to visit archives to complete this book. I am grateful for the Institute for Research on Poverty at the University of Wisconsin, Madison, whose Emerging Poverty Scholars Fellowship provided research funding and community during the final stages of this project. I thank

Katherine Magnuson, Rebecca Schwei, Dana Connelly, Judith Siers-Poisson, and my fellowship cohort.

The University of North Carolina Press has taken great care with this project and its development over the past several years. My editor, Dawn Durante, has offered expert guidance and careful feedback throughout the review and publication process. Brandon Proia, the editor who first procured my work, believed in this project since our first meeting at the American Historical Association's annual conference in 2017. I am grateful that Brandon and Dawn not only saw my work as a great fit for UNC Press, but that they brought my project to Rhonda Williams and Heather Ann Thompson for the Justice, Power, and Politics series. I am thankful for the anonymous reviewers whose expert feedback helped make my book stronger. I am grateful for UNC Press's editorial team, who honored my vision and answered numerous questions and helped me get this project to the finish line.

As a first-generation scholar, I was provided with a critical community by Stanford University that allowed me to develop my craft as a historian. Campus community centers offered welcoming spaces for social and intellectual engagement. I thank Frances Morales, Elvira Prieto, Margaret Sena, and Faith Kazmi. Chris Golde and Anika Green from Stanford's Vice Provost for Graduate Education remain avid supporters. My graduate school advisors, Quintard Taylor, Paulla Ebron, Allyson Hobbs, and Al Camarillo, created space for me within the historical profession and nurtured my interests in Black-Brown relations. My doctoral advisor, Al, believed in my scholarly potential since I first emailed him during my junior year as an undergraduate student at California State University, Long Beach. Al understood the significance of Black-Brown relations as a fellow Southern Californian and remains a mentor and advocate.

I am grateful for friendships that have allowed me to build a family away from home. This book was completed with the support of writing groups over the past several years that included Maneka Brooks, Rebecca Taylor, Maribel Santiago, Tadashi Dozono, Tristan Ivory, Derisa Grant, Naila Smith, Pascale Guiton, Kimberly Thomas McNair, Tammy Owens, and Aimee Roundtree.

I am grateful for my family's love, encouragement, and support. To my siblings, Chanell, Melody, Steve, Ian, and Gabriel, who have supported me through every step of this journey. My mother, Yolanda, who taught me that I matter and remains my biggest advocate. To my partner, Kevin, for his support, motivation, and sacrifices. Finally, to my nieces and nephews, whom I hope understand that my journey has been to expand opportunities for their futures.

Poverty Rebels

Introduction
Tracing the Historical Roots of Black-Brown Relations

In an April 1971 letter to US congressman Augustus F. Hawkins, the first Black person elected to represent Los Angeles in the US House of Representatives, constituent Linda Rodriguez expressed her sincere appreciation for Hawkins's commitment to growing the US federal government's War on Poverty reform program. Rodriguez's letter gently and enthusiastically urged Hawkins to continue advocating for additional funding from policymakers to extend the War on Poverty into the 1970s. Rodriguez even identified Los Angeles as a "model city" for policymakers, arguing that Angelenos effectively used federal funding to institute successful antipoverty programs throughout their neighborhoods. Like Rodriguez, numerous Angelenos wrote Congressman Hawkins during the War on Poverty, especially after Lyndon Johnson's presidency, when legislators aggressively cut the federal antipoverty program budget in response to pressure from conservative politicians and their constituents. While the War on Poverty took off nationally in 1964, Los Angeles poverty rebels like Congressman Hawkins drew on three decades of economic and political activism that originated with New Deal coalitions to establish Los Angeles as a priority location for federal antipoverty dollars.[1]

The three decades leading up to President Lyndon Johnson signing the Economic Opportunity Act in 1964, which allocated funding for the War on Poverty, marked a period when Black and Brown Angelenos joined a national shift to the Democratic Party. Although African Americans and Mexican Americans emerged as some of President Johnson's staunchest supporters, liberal democratic policies designed to address race and class inequality often fell short of radically altering US society. For instance, the Economic Opportunity Act emphasized neighborhood program development and individual responsibility even though institutional factors that excluded people of color from business, real estate, and education contributed to poverty. In addition, the US federal government's public relations campaigns to promote the War on Poverty emphasized the economic status of Black urban residents, leading to claims of neglect by Mexican Americans who had also built movements in concert with liberal democratic policies. Black-Brown relations in Los Angeles demonstrates the centrality of race and place in shaping how Mexican Americans and African Americans recognized the limits of Johnson-era civil rights and social policy. Through the War on Poverty, they harnessed existing social justice movements, community programs, and political engagement to adapt federal antipoverty policy into the next stage of struggles for racial equality.[2] Poverty rebels included politicians, activists, youths, professionals, and local people who redefined the War on Poverty into an informal economic justice clause to the Civil Rights Act of 1964.

Poverty Rebels explores Black-Brown relations in Los Angeles, California, with a specific focus on how the US federal government's War on Poverty and Model Cities programs brought these two groups into closer social and political proximity. President Lyndon Johnson signed the Economic Opportunity Act just one month after passing the Civil Rights Act of 1964. As a US federal government mandate, bill supporters throughout the United States rightly heralded the Civil Rights Act as a social justice triumph due to the legislation's ability to lift deep-rooted historical barriers to "discrimination or segregation on the ground of race, color, religion, or national origin."[3] Unfortunately, the Civil Rights Act lacked economic class consciousness, and, as a result, legislators needed to pass additional legislation to address the unique ways that race and class impacted people of color who lived below the poverty line. Black and Brown Angelenos represented the activists, local people, and political actors in communities throughout the United States who implemented War on Poverty programs to solve the Civil Rights Act's limited capacity to fight poverty in communities of color. Examining the War on Poverty from the vantage point of a racially diverse city like Los Angeles reveals the role of Angelenos in cultivating and contributing to a critical national debate about how to conceptualize federal policy with a view toward racial, regional, and class inclusion. A historical analysis of the War on Poverty, its impact on Black-Brown relations, and its intersections with social justice movements uncover an important story about civil rights, economic justice, and democracy in the post–civil rights United States.

Race, Policy, and Inclusion

At the core of Black-Brown relations between 1964 and 1979, whether collaboration, constellation, or conflict, existed a desire to make social justice policy more inclusive. The War on Poverty reflects a period in US history when Mexican Americans critically compared their struggle for local and national recognition to the Black Freedom movement. Several scholars have explored significant examples of tension between African Americans and Mexican Americans around efforts to share space socially, politically, and economically. However, tension reflects one dimension of a multifaceted history of Black-Brown race relations in the United States. *Poverty Rebels* aims to peel back the layers of collaboration, conflict, and constellation in Brown-Black histories to uncover critical debates about the Civil Rights Act's effectiveness as a national policy designed to protect all constituents.[4] When criticism or calls to collaborate arose between Mexican Americans and African Americans during the War on Poverty, these struggles represented a desire to create a more democratic vision for US society inclusive of Mexican Americans and African Americans. Closely examining the relationship between African Americans and Mexican Americans within the context of antipoverty policy provides an opportunity to decenter whiteness as an analytical framework and to understand better how Blackness and Brownness were mutually constituted around movements for economic justice.

I build on research completed over the past twenty-five years by scholars who have published numerous writings inspired by long-debated questions about whether allyship or competition is the essence of African American and Mexican American relations.[5] Academics have found compelling examples for both. For instance, several scholars have published insightful research arguing that Mexican Americans and African Americans have an important history of coalition and community-building rooted in a shared experience of residential segregation.[6] Others have turned their attention to multiracial civil rights, focusing on how Black and Brown Angelenos channeled their political power to fight against mutual and group-specific forms of discrimination.[7] While some scholars within this thread of analysis argue that multiracial civil rights activism profoundly impacted local and state institutions, some posit that identity politics constantly undermined multiracialism during the second half of the twentieth century.[8] Debates that emerged through the War on Poverty reveal that neglect from government officials sat at the core of Mexican Americans' tensions with African Americans during the 1960s and 1970s, in contrast to the powerful anti-Blackness white society exploited to violate Black people.

Several historians have crafted compelling analyses of the War on Poverty and Black-Brown relations in Los Angeles, Texas, and the broader United States.[9] Much of this work focuses on local-level activism, community institutions, and grassroots organizing.[10] I trace key moments in African American and Mexican American history to describe how their stories intersected and ran parallel during a critical moment in US policymaking history. While civil rights scholarship often emphasizes monumental legislation, including *Brown v. Board of Education of Topeka*'s decision in 1954, Civil Rights Act of 1964, and Voting Rights Act of 1965, these political accomplishments represent the beginning of a much larger national quest for economic justice centered on US cities after 1964, when people of color gradually desegregated US institutions.[11] The period 1964-79, the beginning decades of the post–civil rights United States, delineates a time when African Americans and Mexican Americans advocated to refine existing legislation, and in doing so, ushered their movements into a new phase of social justice activism that emphasized closing loopholes in civil rights policies. The War on Poverty, and later Model Cities, helps to conceptualize economic justice as an effort to strengthen US federal government social reforms and to develop community institutions that allowed poor African American and Mexican American city residents to thrive as the United States entered a new phase of racial integration.[12]

New Deal Democrats, including congressmen Augustus F. Hawkins and Edward Roybal, played vital roles in advocating for the War on Poverty and Model Cities programs in Los Angeles. As political representatives for Black and Brown Angelenos, Hawkins and Roybal fought for their constituents at both the national and local levels by using their political expertise to promote community involvement in antipoverty programs. For example, both Roybal and Hawkins joined a coalition of Congress members to challenge Los Angeles mayor Sam Yorty, who attempted to bring complete control of War on Poverty programs under municipal government jurisdiction. Several politicians throughout California and the nation became poverty rebels because the post–civil rights decades marked a period when Black and Brown Angelenos earned political office and used this newfound institutional power to advocate for their communities. With so much change taking place at the federal government level, African American and Mexican American politicians, along with their white allies, were vital figures in the history of antipoverty activism in the 1960s and 1970s United States.[13]

Antipoverty activism included diverse movements and individuals who often maintained different social justice philosophies.[14] When civil disobedience advocates Martin Luther King Jr. and Bayard Rustin visited Los Angeles following the Watts Rebellion of 1965, many African American residents did not respond enthusiastically to King. In addition, many Mexican American and African American poverty rebels who met with President Johnson to discuss civil rights were educated, middle class, and typically espoused respectability politics. At the same time, young leftists sought to foster community self-determination through their antipoverty activism. Collectively, Black and Brown Angelenos, with support from their allies outside California, demonstrate the importance of US federal policy in advancing social justice movements in western cities initially overlooked in national civil rights campaigns. Democratic politics brought this complex group of historical actors into the same local and national debates about race and economic justice during the post–civil rights decades.

The twenty years following the Civil Rights Act of 1964 and the Voting Rights Act of 1965 saw the proliferation of movements designed to strengthen these triumphant pieces of legislation. Los Angeles's identity as a haven for African Americans, when compared to the violent Jim Crow South, helped conceal the unique forms of discrimination that Black Angelenos faced over the first half of the twentieth century. Some historians have even argued that Los Angeles's multiracial composition spread white aggression throughout the city and brought some relief to African Americans who migrated from the South.[15] The War on Poverty gave Black and Brown Angelenos a federal policy framework to articulate their unique experiences as western urban residents.[16] Between 1964 and 1979, the Black Freedom and Chicano movements continued to progress alongside existing activist campaigns to fight for economic justice.[17] This moment in US history brought previously overlooked groups and regions into civil rights activism to help ensure that policies reached the most economically vulnerable communities in the United States.

Los Angeles as a Case Study

Although Black and Brown communities in Los Angeles had a history of economic justice that can be traced back to the 1930s, poverty rebels responded to fundamental changes in US cities that took place immediately after World War II. African American and Mexican American city dwellers were overwhelmingly isolated into central city neighborhoods as the United States transitioned from a rural to an urban society after 1945.[18] Furthermore, postwar hypersegregation created barriers to shared community spaces between Mexican American and African American Angelenos. As Black Americans became isolated into South Central Los Angeles neighborhoods and Mexican Americans into East Los Angeles residential areas after World War II, their communities faced widespread neglect from the local government. When federal officials passed legislation targeting Black and Brown urban populations, officials often supported punitive measures related to juvenile delinquency and social welfare.[19] Poverty rebels understood economic reform as an opportunity to create programs that pushed back the tide of neglect by underfunded schools, insensitive landlords, and declining community institutions. Unequal policy decisions created their urban realities, and poverty rebels sought to play a defining role in implementing antipoverty legislation in ways that improved their material lives.[20]

The Watts Rebellion of 1965 laid bare patterns of discrimination that prevented many Black and Brown Angelenos from thriving in US cities. When African Americans took to the streets in August of 1965, their frustration, anger, and exhaustion shattered long-term myths about the state of race relations in California.[21] While racial violence and discrimination in the Jim Crow South far outweighed life in the City of Angels, poor treatment toward African Americans, Mexican Americans, and communities of color more broadly, remained an urgent concern for Angelenos. The Watts Rebellion brought Los Angeles into the nation's more prominent Black Freedom movement and helped further establish the place of economic justice as an essential next step in struggles for racial equality. For instance, well-known labor activist A. Philip Randolph even proposed that the US national government establish a "Freedom Budget" in response to the Watts Rebellion. From the perspective of Randolph and Martin Luther King Jr., a dedicated government fund might address issues affecting central city African American residents.[22] The uprising in Watts also helped establish the Model Cities program as a brief but crucial second phase within the US federal government's efforts to reduce widespread poverty. Most significantly, the uprising helped inspire youth activists who came of age after World War II and who centered advocacy around economic divestment from their communities. Antipoverty programs contributed to the work of youth activists and gave rise to a younger generation of poverty rebels who continued their community work into the new millennium.

The Watts Rebellion also motivated and inspired Mexican Americans. The Chicano movement grew into a national campaign during the post–civil rights decades when events like the Watts Rebellion pushed legislators to consider the class limitations of federal civil rights policies. Although organizations including the GI Forum, Mexican American Political Association, and the Political Association of Spanish-Speaking Organizations, predated the mid-1960s rise of what became the Chicano movement, an amalgam of Mexican American activists increasingly pointed to the Watts Rebellion as a protest strategy that gained Black Los Angeles necessary attention from policymakers.[23] Legal scholar Ian Haney López identifies the mid-1960s as a turning point in Mexican American protest history, when unequal treatment

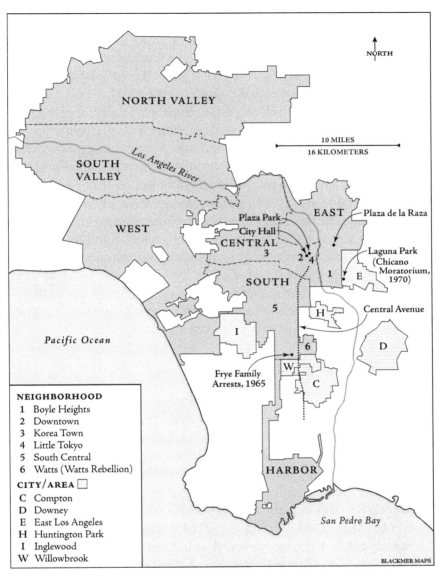

City of Los Angeles (shaded) with reference to neighborhoods, cities, and historical markers, ca. 1970.

in the justice system motivated Mexican Americans to abandon earlier strategies that emphasized their classification as white in their calls for fair treatment. Both an older guard of activists and youth experienced this critical transition in Mexican American civil rights and political history. By the end of the 1960s, the Chicano movement in Los Angeles had fully cultivated a set of social justice demands around Brownness to acknowledge their history of colonization and exclusion while celebrating cultural pride.[24]

Federal government policies in the 1960s profoundly shaped Mexican American and African American activist movements and how these groups understood one another's struggle for economic justice. Post-1964 national policy and social justice movements fostered new social and political conditions that helped further cultivate relationships between African Americans and Mexican Americans in Los Angeles. Although Brown and Black Angelenos faced similar social, economic, and political discrimination, post–World War II hypersegregation created geographical barriers to cross-racial organizing. Still, the War on Poverty pushed African Americans and Mexican Americans to consider how and why their lives intersected around race and class inequality in the United States after 1964.

Multiracial Los Angeles and the United States

The War on Poverty takes readers on a journey from Black and Brown Los Angeles to the national sphere and back. Drawing on historical sources, including manuscript collections, government records and reports, newspapers, oral histories, and activist organization papers, *Poverty Rebels* is organized into six chapters designed to narrate the interconnections between local struggles and national policy debates. The first three chapters examine the War on Poverty's impact on bringing nationwide attention to race relations in Los Angeles and the centrality of California to the history of federal antipoverty policy. These chapters are designed to uncover the impact of politics on galvanizing African Americans and Mexican Americans, especially under the leadership of congressman Augustus F. Hawkins. Chapter one examines how Los Angeles grew into a robust western metropolis throughout the twentieth century and the economic and educational opportunities that propelled African Americans and Mexican Americans into political activism. Chapter two explores Los Angeles's demographic shifts as the city's total population nearly doubled between 1950 and 1970, when southerners and northerners made their way west. Focusing on the Watts Rebellion of 1965, this chapter argues that when African Americans rebelled against discrimination in August of 1965, they drew increased attention to racial discrimination in Los Angeles and brought the city into conversation with the Black Freedom movement taking place in the US North and South. The uprising—and state, media, and community responses to it—set the tone for constructing African American and Mexican American relations over the remainder of the twentieth century. Chapter three examines intersections between the War on Poverty and youth activists in Los Angeles. This chapter shows that as future African American and Mexican American community leaders, young people took seriously President Lyndon Johnson's claim that antipoverty programs established the nation's next stage in the struggle for racial equality. However, young poverty rebels faced criticism from an older guard of activists, reformers, and policymakers, who exploited hysteria about Black-Brown conflict to discredit young community leaders.

The final three chapters describe the significance of Lyndon Johnson's presidency in bringing Black-Brown relations into national debates about racial inequality and policy. These chapters elaborate on politics' critical role in shaping economic justice struggles during the 1960s. Chapter four explores the interconnected history between the To Fulfill These Rights Conference on the status of civil rights for African Americans held in 1966 and the Hearings of the Inter-Agency Cabinet Committee on Mexican American Affairs in 1967 as examples of how Black and Brown middle-class activists worked with state and federal officials in an effort to make policy more effective. The conversations, questions, and conflicts that emerged from To Fulfill These Rights and the Inter-Agency Cabinet Committee on Mexican American Affairs provide insight into the role officials played in shaping and mediating Black-Brown relations during the 1960s, especially as Mexican Americans articulated a civil rights agenda around Brownness. Chapter five examines the Poor People's Campaign, the largest and most diverse national campaign led by poverty rebels. The Poor People's Campaign was a multiracial antipoverty movement organized by the Southern Christian Leadership Conference. Comprising Indigenous groups, Puerto Ricans, African Americans, Mexican Americans, and poor white Americans, the Southern Christian Leadership Conference recruited hundreds of participants to join mass demonstrations in Washington, DC, during the summer of 1968 to demand a more profound commitment to the War on Poverty. The Poor People's Campaign, this chapter demonstrates, reveals how western racial politics influenced the work of moderate African American activists connected to the White House.

Chapter six transitions to the Model Cities program to trace the War on Poverty's evolution into new policies implemented primarily after Lyndon

Johnson's presidency. Administered by the Department of Housing and Urban Development, Model Cities emerged as an additional pool of antipoverty funding explicitly earmarked for cities. This chapter delves into the Chicano moratorium demonstrations between 1969 and 1971, which offer insight into how Mexican American activism grew in concert with the Black Freedom movement. While Black Angelenos and the Watts Rebellion reflected the beginning anchor of the War on Poverty in Los Angeles, the Chicano moratorium and Model Cities program ushered in the decline of Los Angeles's direct contact with federal authorities through antipoverty initiatives. Model Cities was unique when compared to the original War on Poverty because organizations with an outwardly radical identity gained access to funding through Model Cities. However, Richard Nixon quickly went to work restructuring antipoverty programs by instituting a new system known as revenue sharing, which empowered local and state governments eager to modify the War on Poverty and prevent constituents from leading community-level programs. National policy debates about the Civil Rights Act, Economic Opportunity Act, and Demonstration Cities and Metropolitan Development Act reflect a period in US history when Blackness and Brownness entered new conversations around economic inequality that had a long-term impact on Los Angeles and the nation.

Historicizing Black-Brown Relations

This book traces several episodes in African American and Mexican American history during a period when terms used to identify these groups shifted and changed. Terms, including African American and Black, are used interchangeably to identify African-descended historical actors throughout this text. Mexican Americans began utilizing several terms between 1964 and 1979, including Chicana/o and Brown. These terms also appear interchangeably to describe the experiences of Mexican-descended historical actors. At times, I distinguish between Mexican Americans and Mexicans when describing demographic shifts in Los Angeles over time to reflect periods when Mexican-descended Angelenos migrated from other parts of the United States while others immigrated directly from Mexico. Latina/o is used periodically to describe periods when immigration from Mexico and Central America demographically transformed historical Mexican American and African American communities in Los Angeles. To foreground African Americans and Mexican Americans as central characters in this story, I capitalize Black and Brown throughout each chapter. At times I use Los Angeles's nickname,

City of Angels, and the term Angeleno to describe residents. As a collective, terminology used in this text is designed to acknowledge identification terms Black and Brown people have used since the twentieth century.

This research focuses on antipoverty policy, experiences within lower socioeconomic neighborhoods the US government classified as "poverty areas," and how activist movements emerged to target economic inequality. I use terms such as poverty, impoverished, and poor to highlight the centrality of class in post–civil rights Black and Brown struggles. Activists, politicians, and writers used this terminology in popular debates designed to bring awareness to class inequality in the United States. The term "poor" became a rallying cry and political position for several movements, especially the Poor People's Campaign in 1968. Using poor to articulate a political position demonstrates how activists and everyday people used this terminology for empowerment and resistance. Combined, poverty, poor, and impoverished reflect the time periods covered and acknowledge the economic and political activism Black and Brown Angelenos cultivated between 1964 and 1979.

Poverty rebels emerged throughout the 1960s and 1970s, when communities of color did not simply accept the US federal government's approach to civil rights. Brown and Black Angelenos called on officials to refine existing legislation to reach some of the most economically vulnerable people, making the city of Los Angeles foundational to this historical moment. As westerners and city dwellers, they helped transform the War on Poverty into the country's next stage in the fight for equality, where class foregrounded understandings of what it meant to be Black, Brown, and urban in the United States. The intertwined experiences of African Americans and Mexican Americans reveal a complex history of race and rights in the United States. When examined side by side through the lens of African Americans and Mexican Americans, post–civil rights activism becomes a fuller national story filled with city dwellers, westerners, and efforts to cross political boundaries. Los Angeles is a place where Black and Brown residents have historically attempted to understand how their experiences intersect as two groups with similar political and economic profiles. At times, these efforts did indeed result in conflict derived from misunderstanding. Most significantly, the dynamics of Black-Brown relations facilitated struggles to reconsider and strengthen policy.

CHAPTER ONE

Black and Brown Los Angeles

> To be sure, Los Angeles is no Paradise, much as the sight of its lilies and roses might lead one to believe. The color line is there and is sharply drawn.
>
> —W. E. B. DU BOIS, "Colored California"

> Those who shall prefer to remain in the said territories may either retain the title and rights of Mexican citizens, or acquire those of citizens of the United States. But they shall be under the obligation to make their election within one year from the date of the exchange of ratifications of this treaty; and those who shall remain in the said territories after the expiration of that year, without having declared their intention to retain the character of Mexicans, shall be considered to have elected to become citizens of the United States.
>
> —Treaty of Guadalupe Hidalgo, Article VIII, 1848

Future US congressmen Augustus F. Hawkins and Edward Roybal arrived in Los Angeles as children during the early twentieth century and represent migrants who shaped the city's social justice history. Like many newcomers to Los Angeles during this migration and community formation period, Roybal and Hawkins found their new hometown in the throes of rapid economic, demographic, and cultural change. Migrants settled into neighborhoods, schools, and community institutions where Asians, Asian Americans, Mexicans, Mexican Americans, ethnic white groups, and African Americans comingled. Although the insidious nature of Jim Crow spanned every corner of the United States by the early twentieth century, small windows of opportunity in real estate, education, and politics available to African Americans and Mexican Americans in Los Angeles set the stage for their long-term contribution to local and national social justice movements.

As African Americans migrated to a city formerly belonging to the Republic of Mexico, Black newcomers tended to find residence in areas where Mexicans and Mexican Americans lived.[1] The Treaty of Guadalupe Hidalgo, which ended the US-Mexico War and ceded former Mexican territory throughout the Southwest to the United States, politically and socially defined Mexican American life in the early twentieth-century United States. As historian

William Deverell argues in his research about Mexican Americans after California transitioned from a Mexican to a US state, "Mexicans were not Americans, even though they were."[2] While the US national government legally classified Mexican Americans as white for much of the early twentieth century, residential segregation, violence, and lynching made clear that Mexican Americans were "nominally white," as historian Albert Camarillo argues. However, by the 1960s, Mexican Americans transformed their "nominal whiteness" into a rallying cry for Brown Power. They organized a national civil rights movement designed to tell their history of violence, exclusion, and discrimination in the United States. As Mexican Americans increasingly defined themselves and their unique discrimination through the lens of Brownness after 1964, questions about how their history intersected with African Americans became even more pronounced.[3] The US federal government's War on Poverty emerged at this historical juncture and provides a novel case study about the intertwined history between Black and Brown Los Angeles.[4]

The history of African Americans and Mexican Americans in Los Angeles before 1964 is essential for understanding the formation and construction of Black-Brown relations later in the twentieth century for two significant reasons. First, as a US-Mexico borderland city, local officials imposed racially discriminatory laws and practices onto people of Mexican descent immediately after the US-Mexico War ended in 1848. For instance, as historian Kelly Lytle Hernández argues in her research about California's long history of mass incarceration, the United States opened a local jail as one of the very first Los Angeles institutions during the city's transition to the United States.[5] Racialized criminal justice practices emerged almost immediately as a form of control against Mexican Americans' mobility and to define their position within the United States' racial stratagem as not entirely white. In addition, white supremacist organizations like the Ku Klux Klan and incidents of racial aggression led to lynching and violence against Mexicans and Mexican Americans throughout the Southwest as an additional method of social control.[6] This brutal experience as residents in a settler-colonial city became the foundation for Chicano movement activism in the 1960s and helped bring awareness to deep structural inequities that connected Blackness and Brownness as US-based constructions of racial identity.[7]

The US West had a long history of race-making that started with sixteenth-century Spanish colonization. As Indigenous peoples, enslaved Africans, and Spaniards bore mixed-race offspring, Spain responded by establishing a racial hierarchy system known as *sistema de castas* (society of castes), which defined social status based on one's proximity to whiteness. *Sistema de castas* attempted to define every potential identity derived from multiracial children, including mestizo (Indigenous and Spanish), mulatto (African and Spanish), and *pardo* (Indigenous and African.)[8] In fact, Spaniards of African heritage made up the majority of the group charged with establishing the city of Los Angeles in 1781.[9] This longer history of racial identity construction and formation reveals some of the ideas that shaped how Mexicans and Mexican Americans understood themselves and race more broadly as they increasingly encountered African American migrants. However, upon California's successful admission to the United States in 1850 as a free state, Angelenos of Mexican descent entered the United States' stringent system of racial stratification anchored by whiteness at the top and Blackness at the bottom. In her analysis of New Mexico's transition from a Mexican to a US state in the nineteenth century, historian Laura Gómez argues that Mexicans' multiracial background led white Americans to define people of Mexican descent as "off-white" when compared to Indigenous groups and African Americans.[10] Mexican Americans' experience with being legally classified as white but socially defined as racially inferior set the foundation for their later feelings of invisibility during the civil rights era.

California's admission to the United States as a free state inspired African Americans to conceptualize Los Angeles as a geography of hope when they began migrating to northern and western states by the late nineteenth century. As historian Douglas Flamming argues in his research about early Black Los Angeles, African Americans did not naively expect to live in an antiracist society upon moving to Los Angeles.[11] However, the region's history as a Republican stronghold where African Americans voted, purchased property, and avoided daily racial terror, made Los Angeles a more desirable choice when compared to southern states. Los Angeles's transition from a Mexican to a US city is essential to understanding Black-Brown relations. While Mexican Americans built a civil rights movement to reveal their reality of life in a settler-colonial city where the United States expanded its internal nation-state following the war with Mexico, African Americans' advocacy centered around Los Angeles living up to its expectations as a safer environment. Historians Pekka Hämäläinen and Samuel Truett describe the unique nature of borderland cities as "remote from empire, self-reliant, cultural and politically fluid, and rooted in face-to-face relations that often took precedence over the market forces of the Atlantic world. Instead of simply setting the stage for a subsequent Anglo-American ascendancy, early America now appears as a patchwork of cultures and polities, grounded in local relationships that point to future nations in only the most tenuous ways."[12] They go on to argue that borderlands research often "subordinates" relationships among communities of color. How African American and Mexican American Angelenos started their journeys in US California further establishes Los Angeles as a meeting ground where the city's connection to colonialism, exclusion, and national growth sits at the core of Black-Brown relations.

During the first half of the twentieth century, African Americans and Mexican Americans formed multiracial coalitions designed to address their shared experiences of discrimination. As historian Shana Bernstein argues in her research about multiracial civil rights and political alliances in Los Angeles before 1964, cross-racial movements fostered an ethos of survival during this early period.[13] One example of multiracial organizing included the Sleepy Lagoon Defense Committee (SLDC). Founded in 1942, the SLDC comprised African Americans, Mexican Americans, and Jewish Americans and garnered support for a group of seventeen Mexican American youths in Los Angeles who faced trial for the murder of José Díaz. After local authorities found Díaz's body brutally beaten and stabbed, his death made front-page news. It sparked hysteria across Los Angeles with rumors of an increase in Mexican American gangs and juvenile delinquency. In response to Díaz's death, local police questioned some 600 African American and Mexican American youths. The SLDC represents the urgency of multiracial collaboration during the first half of the twentieth century and Los Angeles's rich history of intergroup activism.[14]

Many activists, especially Edward Roybal and Augustus Hawkins, maintained earlier commitments to Black-Brown collaboration and brought them into the War on Poverty. However, by the 1960s, California had increasingly become one of the most dynamic western locations for the Black Freedom movement. While organizations like the National Association for the Advancement of Colored People, the National Urban League, and the National Association of Colored Women's Clubs founded active branches in Los Angeles, antiracist activism expanded as a younger generation of African American Angelenos built movements designed to bring awareness to structural and institutional racism.[15] Mexican American movements for social justice expanded by 1964 as well. Organizations including the GI Forum, Mexican American Political Association, and Political Association of Spanish-Speaking Organizations set the groundwork for Mexican American civil rights activism throughout Los Angeles.[16] In addition, youth-led organizations like the Brown Berets, United Mexican American Students, and Movimiento Estudiantil Chicanx de Aztlán emerged to bring awareness to the unique ways that racism impacted their daily lives as city residents. The activism that grew throughout Brown and Black communities in Los Angeles, and California more broadly, transformed the region into a central location for the Black Freedom and Chicano movements. Hawkins and Roybal took on the task of trying to create coalitions necessary to build bridges with varied and diverse activist collectives during the second half of the twentieth century.

Los Angeles's multiracial neighborhoods began to disintegrate after World War II, creating a geographic and political barrier to coalition-building. Eastside communities separated African Americans, Mexican Americans, Mexicans, Asian Americans, Asians, and ethnic white groups from Anglo residents on the westside during the first half of the twentieth century. Although one specific racial or ethnic group made up majorities in some eastside neighborhoods, they still fostered cross-racial friendships, marriages, churches, schools, and other institutions. As migration to Los Angeles increased after the Second World War, African Americans increasingly settled into South Central area neighborhoods, and Mexicans and Mexican Americans moved into East Los Angeles.[17] Because the War on Poverty sought to provide federal funding through neighborhood grants, the program made it inherently difficult to build the type of coalitions that existed early on. As historians Johanna Fernández and Robert Self have demonstrated in their work on the growth of post–civil rights era militant movements, community politics became a vital organizing strategy for city residents of color by the late 1960s.[18] Although the War on Poverty emerged during a complicated time for cross-racial collaboration, Hawkins and Roybal worked diligently to bring their congressional districts together through the War on Poverty.

Since 1910, African Americans, Mexican Americans, and Mexicans have critically and consciously considered how to share space, institutions, and access as racially marginalized groups in Los Angeles. By the time Lyndon Johnson's presidential administration passed a groundbreaking civil rights act in 1964, Black-Brown relations had endured immense social, cultural, and political change. As the United States entered a new phase where federal policy lifted some barriers to discrimination, a desire to craft a nation-state that felt truly equal greatly influenced relationships between Mexican Americans and African Americans. Although African Americans migrated to Los Angeles starting in the late nineteenth century in search of lives that felt closer to freedom, they forged a community in a settler-colonial city alongside Mexicans and Mexican Americans. As Mexicans became American, they increasingly joined forces with their Black neighbors to form coalitions and collaborations that created social, political, and economic opportunities for their communities. However, post–World War II urban transformation forged geographic barriers that intensified both groups' unique experiences of discrimination in Los Angeles and within the United States. When the War on Poverty arrived in Los Angeles during the mid-1960s, multiracial neighborhoods had undergone significant changes due to hypersegregation. Post–World War II residential changes established a context that required Brown and Black Angelenos to consider how their experiences intersected as they faced increased segregation from one another.

Migration and Community Development

Black Los Angeles grew as the city's economic and real estate boom motivated a diverse array of migrants to move west starting in the 1880s. On any given day, migrants from southern and northern states boarded trains destined for Los Angeles. Some migrants, such as Charlotta Bass, moved to Los Angeles hoping the city's warm weather and sunshine might improve her health. Others, including future Harlem Renaissance writer Arna Bontemps's family, fled Jim Crow violence. While African Americans migrated to Los Angeles for a variety of reasons during the late nineteenth and early twentieth centuries, these relocations represented an urgency to find freedom and safety.[19] Journalist Isabel Wilkerson sums up the mass exodus that characterized Black life in the United States starting in the late nineteenth century. "What binds these stories together was the back-against-the-wall, reluctant yet hopeful search for something better, any place but where they were. They did what human beings looking for freedom, throughout history, have often done. They left."[20] Black migrants arrived in Los Angeles determined to forge secure lives for themselves, their families, and their communities. A grave desire for a safer and economically stable existence also influenced how African American Angelenos engaged with the War on Poverty decades after the first Great Migration began.

Los Angeles became an important hub for Mexican and Mexican American migrants throughout the Southwest starting in the early twentieth century. Many Mexicans and Mexican Americans moved to Los Angeles from California's agricultural regions in the Imperial and San Joaquin Valleys. Immigrants from Mexico also joined migrations to California during the first half of the twentieth century and often settled in Los Angeles. Railroad hubs including El Paso, Texas, linked the Mexico-US border and sometimes resulted in eventual relocation to the City of Angels. In addition, a ten-year revolution that started in 1910 led thousands of Mexicans to accept invitations from labor recruiters to move to the United States for work. As Mexicans and

Mexican Americans began to urbanize in more significant numbers between 1920 and 1940, many migrants moved to California from other parts of the United States, including Texas, New Mexico, and Arizona. During the first half of the twentieth century, Los Angeles experienced profound demographic growth that shaped the city's culture, society, and politics as Los Angeles became a meeting ground for Black and Brown people.[21]

Los Angeles's transition from a Mexican to a US city set the stage for its growth as a multiracial and multiethnic region starting in the mid-nineteenth century. As historian Kelly Lytle Hernández argues in her research on mass incarceration, peopling Los Angeles fostered "systems, structures, and practices that wove Anglo American invasion into the fabric of everyday life in the new US West."[22] As a result, while residents of Mexican descent made up 80 percent of Los Angeles's population in 1850, their numbers decreased to 20 percent by the 1880s as the region grew into a US city of 11,183 residents. Still, companies that earned contracts to build California's infrastructure recruited laborers from China, the Philippines, and Mexico and as a result, further expanded Los Angeles's multiracial and multiethnic communities. Boosters and recruiters even published advertisements in Black-owned newspapers and helped attract a steady stream of Black migrants to Los Angeles over the first two-thirds of the twentieth century. By 1940, Los Angeles's population climbed to over 1.5 million. Collectively, post-1880 migrants established multiracial and multiethnic communities that became a key feature of Los Angeles's unique culture and contribution to US social justice movements.[23]

Los Angeles's diverse neighborhoods exemplified a pervasive history of restrictive real estate covenants in the state of California, which shut people of color and non-Anglo white immigrants out of westside neighborhoods. At the same time, social, political, and economic inequalities that created racially segregated neighborhoods fostered cross-racial interactions and collaborations between African Americans and Mexican Americans. Government programs like the Home Owners' Loan Corporation upheld residential segregation by characterizing multiracial and multiethnic neighborhoods in Los Angeles as "melting pot areas" as a signal to white property buyers when a neighborhood included a diverse demographic and to label these districts "undesirable."[24] Historian Keeanga-Yamahtta Taylor argues in her recent work on African Americans and federal housing policies that homeownership has remained a definitive marker of US citizenship and privilege.[25] African Americans and Mexican Americans saw the War on Poverty as an opportunity to revitalize and equip their neighborhoods with resources to thrive politically and economically. However, the

TABLE 1 African American and Mexican-Origin population in the city of Los Angeles, 1920–40

	1920	1930	1940
African American	15,579	38,894	66,774
	(3%)	(3%)	(4%)
Mexican-Origin	30,000	97,000	107,680
	(5%)	(8%)	(7%)
Total Population	576,673	1,238,048	1,504,277

Sources: Quintard Taylor, *In Search of a Racial Frontier: African Americans in the American West, 1528–1990* (New York: W. W. Norton and Company, 1998), 223, 254; George Sánchez, *Becoming Mexican American: Ethnicity, Culture, and Identity in Chicano Los Angeles, 1900–1945* (New York: Oxford University Press, 1993), 90; Albert Camarillo, "The Racial Borderhoods of America: Mexican Americans and the Changing Ethnic/Racial Landscapes of Cities, 1850–2000" (New York: in press), based on Table 7.1.

legacy of housing discrimination had an important impact on the formation of Black-Brown relations as African Americans and Mexican Americans worked to build coalitions later in the twentieth century across geographic divisions.[26]

Los Angeles's multiracial and multiethnic neighborhoods often maintained a visible majority of one specific racial/ethnic group that developed important community institutions. Augustus Hawkins's family settled into Los Angeles's thriving Black community known as the Central Avenue District. In a neighborhood described as the "most beautifully housed group of colored people in the United States" by scholar and activist W. E. B. Du Bois in 1913, Black Angelenos established newspapers, hotels, restaurants, theaters, and professional offices along Central Avenue. Even though the Black press characterized African American communities like the Central Avenue District as "full of push and energy," Black residential districts also grew as a result of exclusionary practices and unrelenting violence.[27] The devastating race riot that destroyed Greenwood, a prominent African American neighborhood in Tulsa, Oklahoma, in 1921, demonstrates the vulnerability of majority Black communities like the Central Avenue District during the early half of the twentieth century. Although Black Los Angeles's early successes brought great pride to the community, Central Avenue also reveals how African Americans across the United States turned inward during the late nineteenth and early twentieth centuries to shield themselves from incidents of racial terror designed to curtail Black progress.[28]

Representative Augustus F. Hawkins (*center*) with Dr. Christopher Taylor and Dr. H. Hartford Brookins at a "get-out-the-vote" program. Ambassador News Conference, September 23, 1964. *Los Angeles Times* Photographic Archive, UCLA Library Special Collections, uclalat_1429_b536_225963. Licensed under CC BY 4.0: https://digital.library.ucla.edu/catalog/ark:/21198/zz0002sqgv.

One's ability to thrive in a city that felt at least "half-free," as historian Douglas Flamming argues in his analysis of early Black Los Angeles, led families like Hawkins's to migrate from Shreveport, Louisiana.[29] Historian Natalia Molina's research on race in Los Angeles reveals that the sense of half-freedom African Americans felt derived from sharing white supremacist aggression with Mexican Americans and immigrant groups.[30] Like many African Americans who joined early migrations to Los Angles, Hawkins's family fared well in Shreveport, where his father worked as a pharmacist and later ran a local transportation agency. Prospects for a better education and access to greater professional opportunities led Hawkins's father to move his family west. Relocating to Los Angeles connected Hawkins to opportunities that sometimes led to harassment, death threats, and violence in the Jim Crow South. For instance, Hawkins enrolled at the University of California, Los Angeles, to study economics and to build a strong reputation as a young leader among his peers. Such rare achievements for African Americans of Hawkins's generation demonstrate some of the possibilities for upward mobility in Los Angeles that led the Black population to increase by nearly 30,000 between 1930 and 1940. The presence of various racial and ethnic groups in Los Angeles and the need to develop California as a US state created several significant opportunities for African Americans, allowing people like Hawkins to make a long-term impact on Los Angeles and the United States.[31]

Areas with significant Mexican and Mexican American residents in Los Angeles grew from efforts by white politicians, business owners, and residents to define these groups as inferior to Anglos after the US-Mexico War. Although the US government legally classified Mexicans and Mexican Americans as white, they still faced widespread discrimination, violence, and exclusion based on race and national origin. As US Los Angeles increasingly defined Mexicans and Mexican Americans as laborers, they were sometimes housed near railroads and other places of employment. In some cases, Mexicans and Mexican Americans developed shanty towns and small communities in unincorporated areas east of the Los Angeles River.[32] The persistence of residential segregation continued to shape Mexican and Mexican American life throughout the first half of the twentieth century, with population increases resulting in East Los Angeles's growth as a center of Mexican American life and culture during the 1960s. Still, however, Mexican and Mexican American populations found housing in more areas when compared to their African American counterparts, who have faced the most sustained residential segregation of any racial group in the United States.[33] While Mexican Americans and African Americans occupied unique positions within the United States' racial and citizenship hierarchies, their nearly identical economic, residential, and political experiences created opportunities for cross-racial dialogue and interactions.

While Mexican Americans have been largely omitted from the history of twentieth-century migrations, historian James Gregory's research shows that Mexican Americans also contributed to the United States' transition from a rural to an urban society during the 1960s.[34] The Roybal family's decision to leave Albuquerque, New Mexico, for Boyle Heights in 1922 is one example of how Mexican Americans participated in the Great Migration. A majority Jewish neighborhood by the 1920s, Boyle Heights increasingly grew into a

City councilman Edward R. Roybal with Rev. H. H. Collins, Los Angeles, California, 1953. *Los Angeles Daily News* Negatives, UCLA Library Special Collections (uclalat_1387_b180_60653_1). Licensed under CC BY 4.0: https://digital.library.ucla.edu/catalog/ark:/21198/zz0002pg81.

historic Mexican American district over the second half of the twentieth century. The Roybals' son, Edward, took full advantage of educational and career opportunities available in Los Angeles after graduating high school. Like Hawkins, Edward Roybal attended the University of California, Los Angeles, and later attended Southwestern University Law School. He served as director of health education with Los Angeles County's Tuberculosis and Health Association. Roybal's ability to take advantage of the educational and professional opportunities in Los Angeles set the foundation for his ascent into local and national politics later in the twentieth century. Roybal's political career and active civic engagement set him apart from other young Angelenos and reveal a long history of racial justice work that shaped Black and Brown lives before 1964. Access to education helped further establish ties between middle-class Mexican Americans and African Americans like Roybal and Hawkins, who wanted to create more opportunities for Black and Brown Angelenos to thrive socially, politically, and economically.[35]

Los Angeles's transition from a Mexican to a US city led to the formation of multiracial and multiethnic neighborhoods that defined life for Black and Brown Angelenos. Demographic shifts reveal one critical example of how African Americans and Mexican Americans moved into closer proximity during the first half of the twentieth century. As Los Angeles grew into a US city, the United States' racial hierarchy engulfed African Americans, Mexican Americans, and relationships between these groups. By the 1930s, Black and Brown Los Angeles developed the community strength to articulate their difficulties as Angelenos of color. Economic justice and politics emerged as some of the most pressing issues that shaped pre-1964 Black and Brown activism, both monoracially and interracially.

Economic Justice and US Democracy

Los Angeles's fight for economic justice started in the 1930s when the Great Depression and New Deal profoundly impacted local activist organizations and disrupted long-standing myths that defined California as a land of opportunity. Although Los Angeles's real estate, agricultural, and industrial booms brought thousands of newcomers to the city, the Great Stock Market Crash of 1929 and the New Deal laid bare economic limitations for Black and Brown residents.[36] As unemployment set in for approximately one-third of the workforce, economic conditions uncovered deep connections between race and class in the United States. According to African American labor history scholars, Black men and women most often found employment in household, maintenance, and janitorial labor before the 1930s.[37] White families who employed African American maids, laundresses, cooks, and chauffeurs increasingly laid off their household employees.[38] In some cases, white employers fired their Black staff in order to hire white workers during the Depression. Still, African American southerners continued to make their way to Los Angeles. Although 1930s economic conditions devastated African American Angelenos, they transformed these experiences into advocacy by fighting for access to New Deal programs.[39] African Americans increasingly developed a public-facing critique of their labor experiences in an industrialized economy. However, one of the most significant challenges to economic equality African Americans faced by the 1960s was a presumption that service and menial labor were inherently Black. As poverty in Black communities garnered more attention during the 1960s, US federal government debates about social welfare often assumed that poverty in Black communities resulted from so-called laziness and a lack of work ethic.[40] Black- and Brown-led programs provided opportunities to challenge these assumptions through the War on Poverty.

White Californians claimed scarce job opportunities as their birthright and labeled Mexicans and Mexican Americans a burden to social welfare programs. White factory and construction laborers increasingly replaced workers of Mexican descent. In addition, local and federal authorities targeted Mexicans and Mexican Americans for deportation and repatriation schemes as the Great Depression intensified. Between 1930 and 1935, approximately 30 percent of Los Angeles's Mexican-descended residents experienced voluntary or forced deportation to Mexico. Local officials even diverted some Depression-era relief funds to cover repatriation train fare, arguing that deportation lowered welfare costs. Such examples of racism and xenophobia during the Great Depression reveal how Los Angeles created its own version of Jim Crowism that impacted Mexican Americans in unique ways around race and citizenship. The constant reminder that Mexicans and Mexican Americans resided in a settler-colonial city played a central role in the formation of the Chicano movement thirty years later.[41]

The Great Depression expanded economic justice advocacy in communities throughout the United States.[42] Many African Americans found an activist home in the Communist Party USA during the Depression, demonstrating just how much class activism grew among Black Americans. In Los Angeles, labor organizing became one avenue for redress in Black and Brown communities. While Black Americans remained excluded from many locals affiliated with mainstream unions such as the American Federation of Labor and the Congress of Industrial Organizations (these organizations later combined to become the AFL-CIO), African Americans developed their own unions. For example, the Red Cap Station Porters Federal Local 18329 of the Southern Pacific Railroad and a local branch of the Brotherhood of Sleeping Car Porters emerged to advocate for improved work hours, wages, and labor conditions. Unions offered protection from some of the most exploitative and violent conditions African American workers experienced.

Augustus Hawkins even described African Americans as "becoming pro-labor" during the 1930s, demonstrating how this period became a turning point in developing an economic justice agenda.[43] The War on Poverty mapped onto these earlier efforts and created more opportunities to bring the longer struggle for Black economic justice into national policy debates about civil rights during the 1960s.[44]

Mexicans and Mexican Americans gained affiliation in mainstream labor unions at greater rates than their African American neighbors. National unions including the AFL and Industrial Workers of the World developed relationships with Mexican American laborers and helped organize strikes in agricultural and industrial sectors. For example, in 1933, representatives for the International Ladies Garment Workers Union helped Mexican American women organize a dressmaker's strike to call for improved work hours and wages that aligned with recent government regulations under the New Deal. Mexican Americans faced employment discrimination, and employers often relegated workers of Mexican descent to factory and agricultural positions. Unions helped facilitate opportunities for Mexican Americans to advocate for better working conditions as they struggled through the 1930s economic downturn. When the experiences of African Americans and Mexican Americans are placed side by side, the history of the Great Depression and New Deal demonstrates why Los Angeles became so important to post–civil rights debates about how to actualize equality of opportunity for the country's most economically vulnerable residents. The economic justice work that shaped early twentieth-century Black and Brown activism set the stage for Los Angeles's rise as an important region for post–civil rights activism.[45]

The Great Depression also facilitated historic political shifts in African American and Mexican American communities, which expanded their political engagement with the Democratic Party. As historian Alan Brinkley argues in his research about the New Deal's impact on US society, 1930s economic reforms improved people's daily lives and fueled US state-building. For Black Americans, New Deal programs harkened back to a strong central government reminiscent of federal protections passed during Reconstruction.[46] In response to widespread unemployment, decline in consumerism, and bank closures, New Deal policies offered emergency relief for each level of the US economy. During the New Deal's first phase, reforms like the National Industrial Recovery Act, Banking Act, and Agricultural Adjustment Act made minor but recognizable changes. Even though the New Deal purposefully included stipulations that excluded agricultural jobs primarily held by African Americans and Mexican Americans to appease southern

Democrats, Black and Brown Angelenos still saw great potential in a strong central government.[47] Mexican Americans and African Americans received the War on Poverty in a similar fashion.

Black and Brown Angelenos transformed their support for the New Deal into advocacy that increased political representation, ultimately shaping the War on Poverty. Augustus F. Hawkins's political career exemplifies the national shift from the Republican Party to the Democratic Party among Angelenos and how this transition shaped economic justice throughout the twentieth century. In 1934, Hawkins ran for California's State Assembly as a New Deal Democrat and utilized his relationships with labor unions to develop a multiracial coalition that successfully secured his election. Hawkins became the second African American to reach this political benchmark, and he represented a group of young Black Angelenos who sought to disrupt African Americans' loyalty to the Republican Party.[48] With support from labor unions, including the Brotherhood of Sleeping Car Porters, Hawkins won his first campaign for California's State Assembly in 1934 at the age of twenty-seven. He later credited the Great Depression with this victory, stating, "And you still had, as I say, that Republican loyalty that we had to overcome. But then things began to change rapidly because of the Depression."[49] Hawkins remained in California's statehouse until his election to Congress in 1962. As Hawkins's campaign for State Assembly reveals, African Americans combined political mobilization with struggles for economic justice during the 1930s. Hawkins continued to build on this momentum as a US congressman during the War on Poverty.[50]

Edward Roybal's political career also grew from New Deal–era political transitions, and his election to the city council became a significant victory for Mexican Americans. Roybal first ran for the Los Angeles City Council in 1947. Although Roybal lost, his campaign committee sprang into action and prepared for the 1949 council race. Roybal's campaign not only garnered multiracial support but also mobilized the United Steel Workers, International Ladies Garment Union, and other labor advocacy groups. This monumental coalition secured Roybal's win in 1949, making him the first Mexican American to hold a seat on the Los Angeles City Council since 1881. Roybal's political career moved to the national level with his election to Congress in 1962, representing Los Angeles's Twenty-Fifth Congressional District and joining his friend Augustus Hawkins. Drawing on their successes with multiracial and labor coalition-building in California politics, Hawkins and Roybal came together throughout the War on Poverty to advocate for African Americans and Mexican Americans. They also created opportunities for

Black and Brown Angelenos to join forces through antipoverty programs. Roybal's and Hawkins's experiences as New Deal Democrats directly influenced their ability to organize with African Americans and Mexican Americans during Lyndon Johnson's presidency.[51]

An increase in organizing during the 1930s politically transformed African Americans and Mexican Americans in Los Angeles. Both groups joined organizations that asked vital questions about the intersections of race and class in shaping their histories of inequality in the United States. As the New Deal mobilized Black and Brown Angelenos, their historic transition to the Democratic Party inspired both groups to layer political engagement atop economic justice. While much of the research on Black-Brown relations in California emphasizes the post–World War II decades, revisiting the Depression and New Deal reveals that the War on Poverty represented a much longer history of economic justice. Historian William Clayson's research on the relationship between the War on Poverty and the civil rights movement explores the "long War on Poverty" by describing the broader impact of antipoverty legislation on local communities. *Poverty Rebels* extends this framing by identifying the New Deal as an important anchor in Black and Brown economic justice histories.

Color Lines

World War II solidified Los Angeles's position as the nation's West Coast metropolis when wartime manufacturing growth caused the city's population to skyrocket. Los Angeles experienced an economic boom that provided people across racial and ethnic lines access to industrial employment and laid the foundation for the city's future as a major urban center. Los Angeles joined cities nationwide that gained federal contracts to expand the defense industry, making Los Angeles the second-largest industrial manufacturer during World War II. Government contracts allowed Los Angeles shipbuilding and aircraft companies to soar, creating employment opportunities for men and women throughout the region. Other industries grew in concert with war production, including food processing and automobile industries, which helped facilitate Los Angeles's transition into an influential US city by the 1950s. Opportunities for economic mobility during and after the Second World War initiated what historian Josh Sides characterizes as a "moment of possibility" to challenge patterns of racial inequality in the City of Angels. Companies in Los Angeles, a major industrial employer, provided African Americans and Mexican Americans with access to middle-class wages at an

TABLE 2 African American and Mexican-Origin population in the city of Los Angeles, 1950–70

	1950	1960	1970
African American	171,209 (9%)	334,916 (15%)	503,606 (18%)
Mexican-Origin	157,067 (8%)	260,389 (10%)	518,791 (18%)
Total Population	1,970,358	2,479,015	2,816,061

Sources: Quintard Taylor, *In Search of a Racial Frontier: African Americans in the American West, 1528–1990* (New York: W. W. Norton and Company, 1998), 254, 286; Albert Camarillo, "The Racial Borderhoods of America: Mexican Americans and the Changing Ethnic/Racial Landscape of Cities" (New York: in press), based on Table 7.1; US Bureau of the Census, *1970 Census of Population: General Social and Economic Characteristics, California,* US Department of Commerce (Washington, DC, US Government Printing Office, 1972), based on table 96: General Characteristics of Persons of Spanish Language or Spanish Surname.

unprecedented rate starting in World War II. With Los Angeles's long history of economic justice, many people heralded access to middle-class positions as a victory for Black and Brown Angelenos and the nation more broadly.[52]

Migration intensified as the war production industry expanded, and movement into Los Angeles continued for three decades.[53] For African Americans, the Second World War facilitated a significant demographic shift as Black southerners fled the rural South by the thousands and settled into US cities. By 1960, Los Angeles's total population doubled to nearly 2.5 million. Between 1940 and 1970, the African American population in Los Angeles increased from 63,774 to 503,606 and caused overcrowding in majority African American neighborhoods. Black migrants even crowded into Little Tokyo during the war, replacing Japanese and Japanese American residents forced to abandon their homes for US government–enforced internment camps. The city's Spanish-surname population grew substantially after World War II from 157,067 in 1950 to an estimated 260,389 residents by 1960.[54] These large-scale demographic changes helped further define Los Angeles as a multiracial metropolis. Historian James Gregory has identified this mass movement as the "southern diaspora" to capture how Black, Brown, and white southerners not only moved to US cities but also shaped the culture, policies, and practices in their new hometowns.[55]

Black Americans settled into US urban centers in record numbers between 1940 and 1970. During this period, many African American southerners migrated to northern and western cities, including Cleveland, Detroit, Seattle, Chicago, and Los Angeles. African Americans who moved to Los Angeles hailed primarily from Texas, Louisiana, Mississippi, Arkansas, Oklahoma, Georgia, Alabama, Missouri, Tennessee, and Kansas.[56] The 1960 US census listed Los Angeles's total African American population at 334,916, and Black newcomers became increasingly isolated in South Central Los Angeles neighborhoods. A special census published in 1965 revealed that approximately 40 percent of Los Angeles County's African American population resided in South Los Angeles, which included the neighborhoods of Watts, Willowbrook, Avalon, and Florence. These neighborhood and demographic changes required more work to build ties with Mexican American Angelenos after 1964.

World War II also saw a rise in civil rights activism and increased hostility toward communities of color. For instance, builders, brokers, and real estate agents refused to sell or rent to African Americans well into the 1950s, even though the Supreme Court struck down racial discrimination in housing through *Shelley v. Kraemer* in 1948 and the *Barrows* decision in 1953. Los Angeles journalist and lawyer Loren Miller took the lead in trying these two cases that ultimately outlawed restrictive real estate covenants. Throughout the first half of the twentieth century, property owners added restrictive covenants to deeds, which stipulated the specific racial groups who could own or rent their properties. In the first case to strike down restrictive covenants, *Shelley v. Kraemer* in 1948, California's Supreme Court argued that restrictive covenants violated the Fourteenth Amendment. The final challenge to restrictive covenants occurred in 1953 when the US Supreme Court case of *Barrows v. Jackson* addressed significant loopholes in *Shelley* and finally outlawed all racially restrictive covenants. African Americans have remained the most residentially segregated population in US cities.[57] When middle-class African Americans earned opportunities to move into suburbs, they often found homes in emerging Black middle-class communities in Compton and Baldwin Hills. As these changes demonstrate, postwar Los Angeles began to look different from the Central Avenue District Hawkins lived in among an economically diverse group of African Americans.[58]

Los Angeles's Mexican American population grew over the first half of the twentieth century. Mexican Americans began to urbanize in large numbers during the 1920s, and by the 1940s, they had increasingly settled in cities throughout California, Texas, New Mexico, and Arizona. Mexican

Americans settled further west, with cities like Denver and Chicago developing smaller, visible communities during the twentieth century.[59] Mexican and Mexican American migrants to California settled in Los Angeles, San Francisco, San Jose, and San Bernardino, among other cities.[60] According to the 1960 US census, Los Angeles's native-born Spanish-surname population totaled 195,268, while the foreign-born Spanish-surname population climbed to 65,121.[61] The Spanish-surname population of South Los Angeles decreased by the 1960s from about 10 percent in Watts to 8 percent in 1965. As the Mexican American population in East Los Angeles expanded, a small number of African American residents, primarily residing in Boyle Heights, declined by a few thousand. However, in contrast to African Americans, some Mexican Americans moved into white suburbs, including Huntington Park, Inglewood, and Downey, during the post–World War II decades. These demographic changes critically shaped Mexican Americans' experiences as urban residents and helped to define their social justice movements in the post–civil rights United States.[62]

As Los Angeles's total population soared, communities of color faced increased hostility from white Angelenos, officials, and law enforcement. For instance, US military officials declared Japanese and Japanese Americans living along the United States' West Coast a threat to national security following Japan's bombing of Pearl Harbor on December 7, 1941, forcing residents of Japanese descent out of their homes, jobs, and businesses for internment camps.[63] In addition, Mexican Americans faced violent repression during World War II through the Zoot Suit Riots of 1943. On June 3, white service members and civilians descended on downtown Los Angeles and eastside neighborhoods, brutally beating and stripping young Mexican American men (and some African Americans). Japanese internment and the Zoot Suit Riots reflected how World War II heightened anxieties in Los Angeles as white supremacy's more brutal nature surfaced during wartime. As Black and Brown populations increased throughout the city, white officials, politicians, and residents tended to treat African Americans and Mexican Americans with hostility. Such changes to Los Angeles's racial climate intensified after the war and further shaped residential segregation based on race and class.[64]

After World War II, hypersegregation became one of the most pressing racial justice issues in Los Angeles as neighborhood boundaries determined access to adequate public schools, hospitals, public transportation, and even middle-class jobs. Local law enforcement reinforced hypersegregation by overpolicing Black and Brown communities and reinforcing stereotypes that white suburbs required protection from so-called dangerous African American and Mexican American outsiders. After World War II, federal funding to boost real estate development and homeownership significantly increased residential segregation and economic inequality. First, the Federal Housing Authority and the Veterans Administration heavily subsidized new suburban developments on the outskirts of Los Angeles. Redlining, a process instituted by the Home Owners' Loan Corporation during the New Deal, used maps and demographic descriptions to demarcate areas that included African Americans, Mexican Americans, and other racial and ethnic groups as "risky" for real estate investment and homeownership. In some cases, African Americans who purchased homes in primarily white suburbs faced harassment, property destruction, and picketing on their front lawns. When real estate developers received federal housing subsidies for Black and Brown communities, they prioritized constructing public housing projects. These post–World War II housing patterns gave rise to community politics that created fractures in Black-Brown relations that challenged the cross-racial community work African Americans and Mexican Americans participated in earlier in the twentieth century.[65]

US federal government funding also facilitated white retreat to suburban communities through continued funding for aircraft and aerospace industries, which relocated to the outskirts of Los Angeles with white residents. In the postwar period, Los Angeles became one of the largest regions for aircraft development, providing some of the most desirable blue-collar salaries in the city. However, when these companies moved to new suburbs, white Angelenos typically received priority for employment. For central city Black and Brown residents, blatant exclusion from jobs in aircraft and aerospace companies, a lack of transportation, and continued exclusion from suburban neighborhoods limited their access to economic mobility that overwhelmingly came to characterize the lives of Los Angeles's white residents after World War II. The decline in available middle-class jobs, especially for African Americans, demonstrates just how short-lived post–World War II economic successes were for Black Angelenos. As white residents and the aircraft industry moved to suburban areas, Black employees often faced termination, harkening back to the inequities that plagued employment opportunities during the Great Depression. The War on Poverty offered a chance to bring employment training to these communities. It ignited further momentum to continue advocacy around economic inequality in the post–civil rights United States.[66]

Los Angeles on the Eve of the Poverty War

As a settler-colonial city, Los Angeles experienced rapid demographic and geographic change in the first half of the twentieth century. National and international migrants made their way to Los Angeles, where they joined Mexicans and Mexican Americans. As African Americans settled into districts that became increasingly multiracial during the first few decades of the twentieth century, they understood cross-racial collaboration as an important means of survival in the City of Angels. Over time, geographic divisions made cross-racial organizing much more difficult as African Americans became primarily concentrated in South Central Los Angeles and Mexican Americans in East Los Angeles.

On the eve of the War on Poverty, Los Angeles had undergone widespread social, political, and economic change. Pre-1964 multiracial neighborhoods gave African Americans and Mexican Americans opportunities to grow together as neighbors, friends, collaborators, and sometimes competitors. The growth of post–World War II hypersegregation created a geographic boundary between the city's African American and Mexican American populations. While South Central Los Angeles helped cultivate Black activism and political engagement, East Los Angeles became the same for Mexican Americans. Still, the legacy of pre-1964 multiracial organizing, especially under the leadership of Hawkins and Roybal, fostered opportunities to collaborate as Los Angeles grew geographically divided. The growth of residential barriers required Los Angeles's African American and Mexican American populations to now reach across social, political, and residential boundaries to join forces in the decades following World War II. Federal civil rights and antipoverty policies brought the excitement and challenges of organizing across residential and racial boundaries to the fore in 1964.

CHAPTER TWO

Black Noise, Brown Invisibility

> Our conclusions and recommendations are the distillation of the information received from these sources, together with our own observations of existing physical and sociological conditions. We wish to emphasize that, in compliance with your directive, we have been absorbed in the study of the problems in our Negro community. However, we are deeply conscious that the Mexican-American community, which here is almost equal in size to the Negro community, suffers from similar and in some cases more severe handicaps than the Negro Community.
> —Governor's Commission on the Los Angeles Riots, 1965

> The Los Angeles riot, the worst in the United States since the Detroit riot of 1943, shocked all who had been confident that race relations were improving in the North, and evoked a new mood in the Negro ghettos around the country.
> —National Advisory Commission on Civil Disorders, 1967

Los Angeles became one of the highest-funded cities for the US federal government's War on Poverty program following the Watts Rebellion of 1965. The intimate relationship between the Watts Rebellion and the War on Poverty shaped Black-Brown relations in Los Angeles and the United States more broadly after 1964. As "Black noise" rang through Los Angeles for six days from August 11 to August 16, 1965, African American Angelenos carved out a space for themselves within Black resistance movements that took place throughout the United States.[1] One unexpected debate that emerged from Mexican Americans during the Watts Rebellion's aftermath were claims that officials tended to disregard the plight of Mexican Americans in political debates about racial inequality in Los Angeles. While Mexican Americans' claims of exclusion and invisibility can be traced back to the New Deal, these assertions intensified under President John F. Kennedy.[2] Historian Julie Pycior's research showcases the critical impact Mexican American voters throughout the Southwest had on electing John F. Kennedy and Lyndon Johnson to national office in 1960. Mexican Americans' ability to increase voter turnout for Kennedy's presidential campaign cultivated political organizing momentum that continued well beyond the 1960s.[3] Following Kennedy's election, Mexican American civil rights groups, including the Mexican American Political Association, Political Association of Spanish-Speaking Organizations, and League of United Latin American Citizens, called for equal representation in federal offices and civil rights initiatives alongside African Americans. Coveted Los Angeles Times reporter Rubén Salazar pinned an article in 1963 that exemplified Mexican Americans' calls for equal access to US federal government programs. Salazar's article described African Americans as "well organized, overly publicized, and [know] how to apply political pressure" to explain their recent civil rights victories and ability to garner attention from policymakers.[4] As African American Angelenos ascended into the Black Freedom movement and Mexican Americans into a national Chicano movement, federal government policy became an important meeting ground for the development of Black-Brown relations in post–civil rights United States as both groups pushed for greater federal protections.

The Economic Opportunity Act (EOA), signed by President Lyndon Johnson on August 20, 1964, revealed that policymakers envisioned the War on Poverty as a program to "eliminate the paradox of poverty in the midst of plenty in this Nation by opening to everyone the opportunity to work, and the opportunity to live in decency and dignity."[5] With $947 million allocated to fund the development of local programs that provided job training, work-study, and other Community Action Programs (CAPs) in low socioeconomic neighborhoods across the United States, Angelenos responded to the War on Poverty enthusiastically.[6] Unfortunately, Los Angeles mayor Sam Yorty spent the EOA's first full year engaged in a tense conflict with local African Americans, Mexican Americans, and their allies over Title II of the EOA, which authorized local people to actively participate in developing CAPs in their neighborhoods in what officials believed would result in "an attack on poverty."[7] Title II of the Economic Opportunity Act stipulated that local people best understood the unique types of CAPs that might help people in their neighborhoods thrive. According to the EOA, giving residents a voice in the War on Poverty allowed specific neighborhoods to play a role in how CAPs were "developed, conducted, and administered with the maximum feasible participation of residents of the areas."[8] Including Title II in the Economic Opportunity Act empowered Brown and Black Angelenos to fold CAPs into existing advocacy for racial equality.

Community Action Programs comprised a variety of local resources and institutions designed to improve economic, education, and health outcomes for residents in low socioeconomic neighborhoods. For example, historian Crystal Sanders's analysis of Head Start, a national preschool program, argues that Black women who administered EOA-funded early childhood education in Mississippi understood their antipoverty work as an extension of the civil rights movement.[9] In addition to Head Start, CAPs consisted of tutoring and literacy programs, job training, youth enrichment, health care clinics, and multiservice centers established to help low-income communities thrive with the assistance of baseline resources. Like Mayor Yorty, city and state officials throughout the United States resisted CAPs because they placed federal funding in the hands of local people, especially African Americans and Latinas/os. With battles over Jim Crow and racial discrimination still raging on when President Johnson signed the Economic Opportunity Act, Mayor Yorty represented numerous local and state politicians who resisted Title II of the EOA by arguing that community participation made the War on Poverty vulnerable to influence from activists. Yorty's efforts to block Title II took place for a year until the Watts Rebellion curtailed Yorty's attempts to create a city government–controlled War on Poverty.

The Watts Rebellion brought international attention to Los Angeles's Black population. While pre–World War II Los Angeles saw the development of several cross-racial alliances and commitments to multiracial activism, the Watts Rebellion offered African American Angelenos opportunities to collaborate with Black activists throughout the United States and to incorporate Los Angeles into broader social justice movements. Scholars of multiracial Los Angeles have identified pre–World War II coalitions as a vital survival strategy during a period when state booster rhetoric presented Los Angeles as a safer alternative to southern states for Black migrants.[10] African American, Mexican American, Mexican, Asian, Asian American, and ethnic white residents often shared neighborhoods, churches, and schools in Los Angeles before World War II. Racially diverse communities and institutions resulted in several multiracial coalitions founded to advocate for youth of color and to elect local Brown and Black officials.[11] However, the Watts Rebellion impacted multiracial coalitions as influential activists from across the United States and critics around the globe directed their attention to Black Los Angeles. Although African American Angelenos continued to organize with other racially marginalized groups, they no longer needed multiracial coalitions to place pressure on policymakers because influential movement leaders, including Martin Luther King Jr., identified the Watts Rebellion as Los Angeles's entry into the Black Freedom movement. The Watts Rebellion set the stage for Black-Brown relations in the post–civil rights

United States because the War on Poverty helped foster meaningful conversations about the Black Freedom movement, the Chicano movement, and their intersections around US federal government policy.[12]

Black and Brown Political Power

The growth of Black and Brown political power in Los Angeles since the New Deal took the War on Poverty by storm. Recent historical research about the War on Poverty in Houston, Louisiana, and Los Angeles has emphasized the Economic Opportunity Act's impact on politicizing lower socioeconomic communities throughout the United States. Los Angeles is a unique case study because the city had several politicians in Congress who influenced debates about the federal antipoverty policy, including Edward Roybal and Augustus Hawkins.[13] By 1965, Roybal and Hawkins were neophyte congressmen in Washington, DC, where they championed legislation that advanced civil rights and economic justice. Locally, Los Angeles elected three Black men to the city council in 1963, further demonstrating increased support for Black candidates and the impact civil rights activism had on their ability to influence political affairs.[14] Congressman Hawkins, whose political career began with the support of ground-breaking multiracial coalitions, emerged as the most outspoken politician for Angelenos during the War on Poverty. As a Black congressman who built his political career on liberal democratic policies during the New Deal, Hawkins began preparing for Los Angeles's place in the War on Poverty as policymakers drafted and debated the Economic Opportunity Act. Drawing on his experience with multiracial coalitions, Hawkins assembled his local congressional colleagues from districts that included identifiable African American and Mexican American populations into a group known as the Community War on Poverty Committee (CWPC). This group, led by congressmen Hawkins, Roybal, James Roosevelt, Charles Wilson, and George Brown, first worked together in an organization known as the Economic Development Agency that focused on youth employment, housing, and voter education. An April 1964 *Los Angeles Sentinel* article titled "Hawkins Program Two Years Ahead of LBJ" characterized the Economic Development Agency as a precursor to the US federal government's War on Poverty.[15] As a New Deal Democrat with a long history of activism in Los Angeles, Hawkins tied the War on Poverty to existing priorities and helped create space for Black and Brown Angelenos in congressional debates. His work reveals Los Angeles's critical role in the War on Poverty nationally and the city's centrality to post–civil rights struggles for economic justice.

The Community War on Poverty Committee announced plans to create a local War on Poverty screening agency that prioritized African Americans and Mexican Americans during an April 1964 press conference. Called by Congressman Hawkins, the press conference served as an opportunity to convey a message to Mayor Yorty that Hawkins and his congressional allies stood united in their fight to ensure that residents who resided in lower socioeconomic neighborhoods earned leadership roles in the city's administration of the War on Poverty. During the press conference, Hawkins reinforced the Economic Opportunity Act's focus on community involvement, asserting, "We are attempting to coordinate the efforts of major action agencies as these agencies will be responsible for the initiation and implementation of the Anti-Poverty Program on the community level."[16] By rallying the CWPC along with Los Angeles area Congress members, Hawkins attempted to consolidate congressional districts comprised of Black and Brown Angelenos. Drawing on Los Angeles's history of multiracial action since the New Deal, Hawkins hoped to harness collective political power to shape the War on Poverty in ways that served some of the most economically vulnerable Los Angeles residents. The War on Poverty's ability to boost existing political momentum in economically neglected neighborhoods across the United States, especially in poor African American and Mexican American communities, helps expand the traditional civil rights narrative.[17] As a collective, the War on Poverty, Civil Rights Act, and Voting Rights Act pushed the struggle for racial equality beyond a narrow focus on integration to using policy to address the grave issue of economic inequality. In Los Angeles, elected officials played an essential role in these efforts and demonstrates how legislators of color have used their position to advance social justice priorities.

State and local government officials throughout the United States, including Mayor Yorty, firmly objected to the Economic Opportunity Act's requirement that poor residents actively participate in developing, approving, and administering antipoverty programs. Historian William Clayson describes how this process took place in Texas, a state second to California in the amount of funds allocated for the War on Poverty. According to Clayson, Texas governor John Connolly resisted the Civil Rights and Economic Opportunity Acts. As President Lyndon Johnson's former campaign manager, Connolly's refusal to comply with the EOA's requirement that residents in areas served by the War on Poverty help to create local programs reflected the complicated identity of the Democratic Party in 1964. Because the Democratic Party helped birth white supremacy following the US Civil War, politicians who disagreed with racial justice, desegregation, and liberal policies still actively participated in the party.[18] Although a California Democrat, Mayor Yorty approached the War on Poverty similarly to his southern colleagues by refusing to support the Community War on Poverty Committee's interest in serving as Los Angeles's citywide antipoverty program screening agency. In this capacity, the CWPC would screen, approve, and disburse funds for local antipoverty programs. Yorty responded to CWPC by proposing the Youth Opportunities Board (YOB), an organization he established within the mayor's office to oversee programs funded by President John F. Kennedy's Committee on Juvenile Delinquency and Youth Crime, as the centralized agency in charge of disbursing War on Poverty funds. By administering the War on Poverty through the YOB, Mayor Yorty's office sought to control the flow of funding into Los Angeles and to prevent social justice–oriented Angelenos of color from leadership roles in administering federal dollars. By proposing that Los Angeles run the War on Poverty through an organization founded initially in concert with federal government policies that unfairly targeted Black and Brown youth through the criminal justice system, Mayor Yorty perpetuated unsubstantiated claims about widespread criminality in African American and Mexican American urban communities to advocate for control of federal antipoverty dollars.[19]

While Mayor Yorty's office joined a national movement of politicians who resisted community-level involvement in administering the War on Poverty, African American and Mexican American Angelenos also joined a nationwide response to the War on Poverty. Across the United States, people impacted by class inequality and their allies used Title II of the Economic Opportunity Act to challenge city and state officials who desired complete jurisdiction over the War on Poverty. This policy's galvanizing power demonstrates the significance of politics and policy in US social justice movements. Black and Brown people's responses to the EOA indicate that these communities had a profound understanding of how actions by the federal government helped to initiate access to power and upward mobility. African Americans and Mexican Americans seized this opportunity to exert their vision for community advancement through policy. A July 21, 1964, Senate report released by the Committee on Labor and Public Welfare reflected some of the ways antipoverty program supporters within the federal government described Title II of the EOA: "The central core of the poverty program is the community action program, which relies upon the traditional and time-tested American methods of organized local community action to help individuals, families, and whole communities to help themselves. Each of the other programs authorized by this bill will contribute to and reinforce the efforts of the community to strike at poverty at its source."[20] The Economic Opportunity Act's Title II empowered Black and Brown Los Angeles to articulate their vision and priorities for the War on Poverty. It helped shape post-1964 activism around the dual effects of race and class in the United States.

As leader of the Community War on Poverty Committee, Congressman Hawkins helped draft a screening agency proposal that supported the growing Black Freedom movement and a burgeoning Mexican American civil rights movement. In the meantime, other organizations stepped in to protest Mayor Yorty's determination to oversee the War on Poverty. In 1965, an organization led by middle-class African Americans, known as the Economic Opportunity Foundation (EOF), emerged in opposition to Yorty's plan by advocating for Black residents to participate in Los Angeles's antipoverty program screening agency. Socially and politically moderate African American civil rights groups, including the National Association for the Advancement of Colored People, National Urban League, and Congress of Racial Equality, made up the EOF's leadership. Unexpectedly, the Office of Economic Opportunity, the federal government agency that administered the War on Poverty nationally, suggested that the EOF and Youth Opportunities Board merge to create one organization. When Mayor Yorty opposed this compromise, EOF leadership turned to the city's history of coalition politics, as described in a *Los Angeles Times* article from May 1965. "If the city won't accept the merger, we will ask the other government agencies in the YOB to go ahead without the city," an EOF representative stated. "And if they won't, we will begin talks with Mexican-American groups and others to form an agency ourselves that will meet federal requirements for screening antipoverty projects here."[21] As this interview demonstrates, African American activists understood the political power inherent in Black-Brown coalitions. Activists saw collaboration as necessary during the 1960s because combining congressional districts might yield long-term changes to local, national, and federal politics. Yorty eventually agreed to a merger between the YOB and EOF, and combined, both organizations became known as the Economic and Youth Opportunities Agency of Greater Los Angeles (EYOA) in April of 1965. This new organization prioritized job training, youth programs, and neighborhood revitalization to improve Los Angeles's economic conditions. Since Black civil rights organizations that advised President Johnson mainly made up the EOF's leadership, this might explain why the

Office of Economic Opportunity suggested a merger with the Youth Opportunities Board and not with the Community War on Poverty Committee. Still, infighting continued between the EOF and Yorty. At the same time, Mexican Americans began to argue that federal officials prioritized African Americans in the quest to create a local War on Poverty screening board.[22]

Congressman Hawkins remained steadfast in his pursuit of a local antipoverty screening agency centered on the needs of Mexican Americans and African Americans. For Hawkins, running the War on Poverty through the city mayor's office did not reflect the true spirit of community action. Activists, including Manuel Ruiz, reached out to Congressman Hawkins for support in securing a place for Mexican Americans in the War on Poverty. Although Ruiz transitioned to conservative politics later in his career, he and Hawkins built reputations as community leaders during the 1930s and 1940s. Ruiz penned a telegram to Hawkins in March of 1965 that called attention to his oversight in informing Mexican American civil rights organizations about a public hearing Hawkins convened to discuss the War on Poverty in Los Angeles. "The Mexican American Political Association (MAPA) and the War on Poverty Council, A Non-Profit California Corporation, and numerous other organizations and leaders of the Mexican American community," Ruiz wrote, "protest their exclusion from the current public hearing taking place under your chairmanship."[23] Given Hawkins's long history of coalition-building, including within the War on Poverty, his failure to communicate with Mexican American organizations may have surprised Ruiz. Hawkins responded to Ruiz's telegram the following month and encouraged him to propose suggestions about how the War on Poverty might better serve Mexican Americans by inviting Ruiz to meet during one of Hawkins's visits to Los Angeles.[24] Ruiz's decision to contact Hawkins demonstrates how the War on Poverty preserved lines of communication between Black and Brown Angelenos who began their activist careers during the New Deal and Second World War. While Ruiz penned his telegram out of frustration, his correspondence still demonstrates a desire to keep a Black official accountable to his supporters throughout Los Angeles. Such lines of communication demonstrate how even though federal officials outside of Los Angeles thought of these groups as divided, their history of coalition-building played a tremendous role in local battles over the War on Poverty.

Hawkins elaborated on his commitment to fostering collaboration in an interview with the *Los Angeles Times* in June 1965. "We feel it is our responsibility to provide what leadership we can in order to get the most out of whatever programs are developed and to insure [sic] cooperation rather than competition among the various agencies and groups," Hawkins stated.[25] As someone with a long history of navigating multiracial and class-diverse coalitions in Los Angeles, Hawkins's interview reflects his experiential knowledge of how to consider Black-Brown relations when implementing new funding streams and how local leadership might help to prevent federal officials from upsetting the local culture. The Community War on Poverty Committee's efforts to create more space for African Americans and Mexican Americans in the organization's proposed antipoverty screening agency represents an extension of pre–World War II efforts to unite communities of color. Federal government officials even took notice of Hawkins's work. In a memorandum written to provide President Johnson with background information on Hawkins, federal officials characterized him as "a leader in the fight to obtain greater representation for Negroes and Mexican American groups."[22] While most Black and Brown activists organized protests at the local level, post-1964 struggles for equality also included a small cohort of African American and Latina/o elected officials in local, state, and federal government offices. Hawkins's continued engagement with Black and Brown Angelenos as a congressman shows that local people increasingly developed connections to the political sphere through their elected officials and how constituents of color actively rallied to vote for candidates who included social justice in their platforms. The War on Poverty came at an opportune time for Black and Brown urban communities because of their ability to lean on elected officials and to use their power as voters to hold politicians accountable for meeting the needs of their constituents.

As the fight for control over the War on Poverty between Yorty and Hawkins continued, the Community War on Poverty Committee pushed on during the summer of 1965. It proposed an antipoverty program screening agency inclusive of Black and Brown Angelenos. Representatives from poor neighborhoods made up most of the agency's board members, with sixteen spots. In addition, one member from a Mexican American and an African American organization would sit on the board. Finally, the CWPC consciously limited the number of government agency representatives to ten seats, reaffirming the central focus of creating a board that prioritized poor residents as the best advocates for their communities. By June 1965, congressmen Hawkins, Roybal, Roosevelt, and Brown wrote the Office of Economic Opportunity to request that the CWPC serve as a centralized antipoverty program screening board for Los Angeles. This eclectic group of politicians, activists, and local people is an example of how African American and Mexican American communities in Los Angeles used the War on

Poverty in inventive ways that pushed beyond how the US federal government tended to conceptualize racial inequality as a Black, white, and southern issue. African Americans and their Brown neighbors involved in earlier political coalitions played an essential role in developing a War on Poverty screening agency uniquely tailored for Los Angeles.[26]

Although the Community War on Poverty Committee galvanized poor residents, community activists, and even state representatives, the US federal government decided not to designate this momentous grassroots movement as Los Angeles's central antipoverty program screening agency. In doing so, federal officials fell short of understanding what made Los Angeles unique compared to other cities and placed decision-making power about the War on Poverty in the hands of local officials with little interest in the type of coalition politics that led to Hawkins's and Roybal's political careers. Hawkins and his colleagues attempted to create an antipoverty screening agency representative of Los Angeles culture and that sought to include the city's two most politically neglected groups. As Angelenos, they best understood how to construct a screening agency aligned with local priorities, but Mayor Yorty's office strongly resisted the group's emphasis on economic justice. Still, the CWPC provides a window into how African Americans and Mexican Americans came into greater contact around economic and political inequality by the mid-1960s. When Congressman Hawkins united his congressional allies and endorsed a community-centered War on the Poverty screening board, collaboration between Los Angeles Congress members reflected an effort to reach across political districts to integrate poor residents into leadership roles over programs designed to meet their needs. As an organization led by politicians who represented Black and Brown Los Angeles, the CWPC demonstrates how the city's unique history of multiracial organizing became an asset in advocacy for African American and Mexican American communities during a pivotal time for federal policy designed to address economic inequality. Although the War on Poverty placed Los Angeles officials and residents into a tense struggle with mayor Sam Yorty for an entire year, their efforts reveal why the city's history of Black-Brown organizing is historically significant to the War on Poverty.

The Watts Rebellion of 1965

The Watts Rebellion of 1965 ended a year-long stalemate between Mayor Yorty, Hawkins's coalition, and local people over control of Los Angeles's War on Poverty. The Watts Rebellion began on the evening of August 11, 1965,

"Attorney A. L. Wirin with Rena Frye and Her Sons, Ronald and Marquette at Los Angeles Courthouse, 1965," *Los Angeles Times* Photographic Archive, UCLA Library Special Collections, uclalat_1429_b557_230015. Licensed under CC BY 4.0: https://calisphere.org/item/ark:/21198/zz0002twqb/.

when California Highway Patrol officer Lee W. Minikus stopped a vehicle driven by twenty-one-year-old Marquette Frye with his brother Ronald in the passenger seat. Minikus stopped Frye and administered a sobriety test, which Frye failed. Since Frye's arrest took place close to his home, Ronald fetched their mother, Rena, to claim her vehicle from arresting officers. According to Minikus, Rena arrived and scolded Marquette for drinking. Allegedly frustrated by his mother's chastisement, Marquette resisted, and a struggle ensued between police and all three members of the Frye family. At some point during the scuffle, Minikus drew his firearm, and Rena jumped onto his back. Once backup officers arrived, police arrested Marquette, Ronald, and Rena.

Rumors that police brutalized both Rena and a pregnant bystander added volatility to an already frustrated crowd who had gathered to watch. The Watts Rebellion began within hours of the Frye family's arrests.[27] As African Americans across South Central Los Angeles rose in rebellion, they responded to decades of frustration with local, state, and federal officials who failed to address the impact of post–World War II municipal change on their lives. Overpolicing, hypersegregation, white hostility, and a lack of funding for essential resources made Black Angelenos feel isolated and unjustly criminalized. Passage of the 1964 Civil Rights Act made the continuation of discrimination even more disheartening for African Americans.

The incident between Los Angeles police officers and the Frye family that led to the Watts Rebellion reflected Los Angeles's failure to live up to the expectations of migrants who moved to the city in search of better material lives, like Rena Frye. After leaving her native Oklahoma for Wyoming when Marquette was just six months old, Rena Frye settled in Los Angeles with her husband. The Fryes represented discriminatory practices many African Americans in Los Angeles faced after World War II, which were often concealed by popular mythology that characterized Los Angeles as a haven for Black migrants. Even though Rena headed westward early in Marquette's life to establish a better life for her family, Marquette suffered under post–World War II era state repression against African American and Mexican American youth throughout California. Marquette had dropped out of high school and accumulated a juvenile criminal record by the time of his arrest in August of 1965, revealing how discriminatory practices had shaped his childhood.[28] When compared to Hawkins's experience growing up in Los Angeles before the New Deal, Marquette Frye's story demonstrates how a city that gave rise to some of the first Black politicians since Reconstruction continued to perpetuate grave injustices against African Americans.

Young men with similar personal backgrounds to Marquette Frye represented the most prominent participants in the Watts Rebellion of 1965. A summary of the rebellion compiled by Federal Bureau of Investigation (FBI) officials offered insight into the Watts Rebellion's first two nights. When Los Angeles police chief William H. Parker dispatched officers into Watts, local African American community leaders encouraged Parker to retreat under assumptions that demonstrations would subside without much intervention. However, demonstrators refused to back down, and the rebellion intensified as they looted businesses, set buildings on fire, and fought back against police aggression. Watts resident Lacine Holland described her eyewitness account of looting forty years later. "You'd witness people running with furniture, food, liquor, and anything they could grab. It was horrific," she described. A witness named Stan Diamond, whose father owned Nat Diamond Empire Furniture, recalled fleeing his father's store just as demonstrators threw a Molotov cocktail near the front door.[29] The Watts Rebellion laid bare the frustration and financial challenges many African American Angelenos faced by the mid-1960s. As many Watts residents raided stores for groceries, clothing, shoes, and furniture, they revealed that recent legislation had not effectively reduced economic inequality. Looting for basic daily necessities dominated during the Watts Rebellion, demonstrating further why policy that took the relationship between race and class seriously sparked so much interest during the War on Poverty. Looting and the broader economic aspects of the Watts Rebellion showed the increasing economic gap between Black and white Angelenos.

The presence of the National Guard and police during the Watts Rebellion revealed a longer history of local and national officials deploying force against Black and Brown people. California's governor, Edmund Brown, was on vacation when the uprising began, placing lieutenant governor Glenn Anderson in charge of deciding how to address demonstrators best. By the rebellion's third night, Anderson called in California's National Guard to assist Los Angeles Police Department (LAPD) officers in halting the uprising. Federal Bureau of Investigation reports characterized the Watts Rebellion as all-out warfare between residents and local authorities. Official reports stated that participants raided pawnshops for guns, made Molotov cocktails, and placed false emergency phone calls to lure police officers into Watts. Tommy Jacquette, an uprising participant and long-time Watts activist, offered insight into how his generation of emerging grassroots activists understood their actions. A Los Angeles native, Jacquette participated in the Watts Rebellion at just twenty-one years old. "I was throwing as many bricks, bottles and rocks as anybody," he recounted. "My focus was not on burning and looting. My focus was on the police."[30] Jacquette's account reflected the frustration and contempt African Americans had for local authorities due to years of harassment and brutality. Still, focusing on conflicts between police and demonstrators tended to overshadow economic underpinnings as a core reason behind the Watts Rebellion.

The Los Angeles Police Department, led by chief William Parker, bore much of the blame once Watts Rebellion demonstrators returned home and Angelenos began recovering from six difficult days of unrest. Throughout South Central Los Angeles, residents pointed to police harassment as a constant in Black neighborhoods. As historian Max Felker-Kantor argues in his

Aerial view of two buildings on fire during the Watts Rebellion, Los Angeles, California, August 15, 1965. *Los Angeles Times* Photographic Archive, UCLA Library Special Collections, uclalat_1429_b556_229847. Licensed under CC BY 4.0: https://digital.library.ucla.edu/catalog/ark:/21198/zz0002twdp.

analysis of Los Angeles area policing over the second half of the twentieth century, the Watts Rebellion helped to expand the dialogue about racism in local police forces.[31] In doing so, the uprising built on anti–police brutality activism led by Mexican Americans since the 1940s.[32] When the Watts Rebellion took place, Parker had served on the LAPD for thirty-eight years and rose to chief in 1950. Like his African American and Mexican American counterparts, Parker moved to Los Angeles during the wave of twentieth-century migrations that brought newcomers to the City of Angels when he moved to Los Angeles from South Dakota as a child. As a white migrant, Parker had the privilege of shaping Los Angeles institutions in ways that directly challenged the work of people like Hawkins and Roybal. *Life Magazine* even named Parker second on their list of the country's most respected law enforcement officers in 1966. Under Parker, African Americans argued that police brutality ran rampant among LAPD officers, and the Watts Rebellion grew from a long history of ignoring police misconduct against Black and Brown Angelenos.[33]

After mobilizing California's National Guard, local authorities gained control of the uprising by day five, when Lieutenant Governor Anderson implemented an 8:00 P.M. curfew throughout Los Angeles. The governor's office also averted Mayor Yorty's requests to declare Los Angeles a disaster zone because Yorty did not have a legal basis to request such a declaration from the White House. As uprising participants returned home, California state and federal government officials assessed how an alleged routine stop by highway patrol led to a rebellion that resulted in thirty-four deaths, 1,032 injuries, 3,952 arrests, and $40 million in property damage, all of it primarily restricted to the business strip in Watts.[34] In days following the uprising, discussions ensued about what caused African Americans to respond to the Frye family's arrest in mass resistance and how Los Angeles might recover from the trauma of an urban uprising. When many Angelenos blamed their frustrations on conflicts surrounding the War on Poverty, President Lyndon Johnson finally intervened in the stalemate among Yorty, local politicians, and residents that prevented Los Angeles from fully implementing a local War on Poverty.

Just days after African Americans rose in rebellion, President Johnson sent LeRoy Collins, director of the federal Community Relations Service, to help residents and politicians reach an agreement over their local War on Poverty screening agency. Collins's reputation as a "New South" governor from Florida who promoted integration led Johnson to appoint Collins as Community Relations Service director after signing the 1964 Civil Rights Act. In this capacity, Collins represented Johnson during mass desegregation protests throughout southern states, including the march on Selma in 1965. However, by dispatching a federal official with a background in Black-white race relations in the US South to multiracial Los Angeles, President Johnson's approach fell short of acknowledging that both African Americans and Mexican Americans had advocated for antipoverty resources before the Watts Rebellion.[35] When Collins landed in Los Angeles just days after the uprising ended, he set out to unify feuding factions by helping them reach a compromise over the War on Poverty. Upon meeting local and state government officials, community leaders, journalists, and Watts residents, Collins quickly learned that conditions in Los Angeles were much more complicated than he had anticipated. According to Collins's official report to President Johnson, "When I landed in Los Angeles shortly after noon on Wednesday, August 18," Collins described, "the air was more filled with tension than smog. Everyone was criticising [sic] and blaming everyone else. Even reporters at the airport were abrasive in their questioning. No one had a good word to say for anyone—except about you, for having done something about what was obviously a worsening situation in which no cohesive leadership in Los Angeles was emerging."[36] Collins's report reflected the fear, anger, and hysteria in Los Angeles after the Watts Rebellion.

Collins's immediate task included meeting with Mayor Yorty, whom Collins characterized as "a most difficult man" and "harder to work with than a tomato seed on a plate."[37] For instance, the very same day Collins landed in Los Angeles, Yorty demonstrated his inability to cooperate with mediations by writing Vice President Hubert Humphrey to request the release of funds while the mayor's staff developed an adequate proposal. "Why can't we be treated the same as other cities and have funds released while we try to meet criteria?" Yorty wrote. He went on to say, "We are certainly trying, but it is frustrating."[38] Yorty's letter even blamed the national director of Community Action Programs and California Congress members for the city's antipoverty stalemate, revealing the magnitude of interpersonal conflicts Collins expected to resolve during his brief trip to Los Angeles. Yorty's decision to resist federal intervention that did not favor his interests demonstrates some of the local government barriers that poor communities faced when actively participating in the War on Poverty. Although the Economic Opportunity Act explicitly mandated that communities served by the War on Poverty join in developing and administering programs, Yorty refused to relinquish control of federal funding. Even after the Watts Rebellion, Yorty remained steadfast in pursuing a local government-controlled War on Poverty for Los Angeles.

Black Angelenos did not offer Collins much reprieve during a Watts community forum on his final day in Los Angeles. Collins regretted his decision to schedule a meeting with residents at the end of his trip. "I should have gone straight out to the Watts area and listened and let people know that someone (in this instance their President) wanted to know what was hurting them and cared about them," he later wrote to President Johnson. Collins provided Johnson with details from the community forum, where Watts residents "tore my hide off," Collins asserted, as he listened to grievances directly from African American community members before departing Los Angeles. Although Watts residents represented one Los Angeles faction set to benefit primarily from the War on Poverty, Collins did not prioritize their perspective as part of his mediation with Yorty's office. During the forum, attendees blamed Yorty, the LAPD, and middle-class Black leadership for issues that led to the Watts Rebellion. Black Angelenos pointed to a series of frustrations they shared with Black central city residents across the United States. Even outside of the Jim Crow South, state and local government officials often ignored African American neighborhoods, except to increase resources to police these areas. Working-class and poor Black city residents often felt as though middle-class leaders did not include them in discussions and decision-making about their communities, which often created a lack of cohesiveness among African Americans. The uprising represented frustration with white supremacy, as well as a desire to have a voice alongside their middle-class counterparts through the War on Poverty. Still, Collins failed to include those who rebelled in his mediations and final recommendations in meaningful ways.[39]

By the time Collins boarded a plane for Washington, DC, Los Angeles authorities had successfully reached a compromise and sent their plans for a citywide War on Poverty program screening agency to Sargent Shriver, national director for the Office of Economic Opportunity. Los Angeles's new War on Poverty screening board, known as the Economic and Youth Opportunities Agency, included twenty-five members from across Los Angeles County. Twelve representatives from the city and county government, Los Angeles Unified School District, Los Angeles City Junior College District, and Los Angeles County Superintendent of Education, would be selected to sit on Los Angeles's new antipoverty screening board. In contrast to Yorty's original plan to run the War on Poverty through his office, the EYOA included four Los Angeles city residents and three county residents to represent antipoverty program recipients. Lastly, the final six EYOA board members came from social support agencies and labor unions, including the Welfare Planning Council, United Way, and the American Federation of Labor-Congress of Industrial Organizations. After a year of internal conflict, culminating in one of the most unexpected uprisings of the era, Los Angeles finally settled on an antipoverty screening agency to recover from the Watts Rebellion of 1965.[40]

The future of Mexican Americans within the War on Poverty remained ambiguous upon Collins's departure, and his final report to Johnson focused on the complicated relationship between local government officials and African Americans. Although Collins's report made minimal mention of Mexican Americans, they had played an essential role in local debates about antipoverty funding before the uprising. They only entered the final proposal that created the Economic and Youth Opportunities Agency as community representatives. According to the screening agency proposal Los Angeles submitted to Shriver, "an agreed-upon committee of outstanding citizens composed of five Negroes, five Mexican-Americans, one Anglo-American and a non-voting convener of the committee" would select a pool of candidates to undergo screening by the mayor and County Board of Supervisors to serve as community representatives for the city's antipoverty program screening board.[41] Within a few short days after Shriver received Los Angeles's proposal, he wrote LeRoy Collins with official approval for the EYOA. While including Mexican Americans in the process of selecting community representatives on Los Angeles's citywide screening board can be seen as a win for this group, their erasure from other aspects of Collins's mediation reflects a tendency by federal officials to ignore Mexican Americans. Collins's visit to Los Angeles epitomizes the impact of the War on Poverty on existing discourses about Brown invisibility. Federal policymakers, including those who supported civil rights, tended to address racial inequality as a standard universal category of Black-white relations rather than a complex web of discriminatory practices influenced by national origin, age, gender, class, and language, among other demographic characteristics. While Congressman Hawkins's coalition offered an opportunity to create a Los Angeles War on Poverty screening board that included both Mexican Americans and African Americans, Collins's visit and a desire to quickly resolve the Watts Rebellion prevented him from understanding the unique aspects of racism in Los Angeles. Collins's departure back to Washington, DC, marked an increase in debates about Black visibility and Brown invisibility.

Congressman Hawkins continued to consult Collins about the need for a more inclusive board after he returned to Washington, DC. Hawkins argued that Los Angeles's approved proposal fell short of representing the goals of the Economic Opportunity Act. As a congressman who actively contributed to federal conversations about the War on Poverty, Hawkins believed he best understood the goals and potential impact of implementing the War on Poverty as originally planned with the support of local people. He lamented that allowing public agencies to play such a prominent role in the primary screening board went against the vision for community action. Instead of seeing Hawkins as an official with the necessary experience to help Collins work with Los Angeles, Collins encouraged Hawkins to support the post–Watts Rebellion compromise. Collins wrote President Johnson to say, "I had a long personal talk with Congressman Hawkins and his reaction was surprisingly cooperative. He said he would not carry on any battle against the new board."[42] By September 1965, the OEO had allocated a $29 million grant for antipoverty programs in Los Angeles.[43] Although Los Angeles had an approved board when Collins completed his mission to mediate the tensions between local people and Mayor Yorty's office, Collins exemplifies federal officials' role in shaping Black-Brown relations since 1964.

Examining Mexican American and African American relations through the vantage point of US federal government policy debates, demonstrate how the relationship between these two groups was constructed over time. Struggles to establish a citywide War on Poverty screening board for Los Angeles revealed the challenges inherent in federal policies shaped by assumptions that civil rights were a Black, white, and southern issue. After President Johnson signed the Economic Opportunity Act in 1964, Black and Brown Angelenos emerged as some of the most vocal residents in favor of the War on Poverty and community involvement in local programs. Leroy Collins's brief visit to Los Angeles failed to consider several months of advocacy carried out by local people, demonstrating the critical impact government actors had on constructing the trajectory of Black-Brown relations over the rest of the twentieth century. Mexican Americans increasingly identified their experience with racial discrimination and economic inequality as invisible in response to the US federal government's emphasis on Black-white relations. Although Collins did not have time to fully understand Los Angeles's unique racial history, California's state government attempted to consider both Mexican Americans and African Americans in their official response to the Watts Rebellion.[44]

The McCone Commission

The Governor's Commission on the Los Angeles Riots attempted to present a more complicated analysis of race in Los Angeles that included both African Americans and Mexican Americans. Assembled by California governor Edmund "Pat" Brown in August 1965, the Governor's Commission on the Los Angeles Riots' primary mission focused on investigating the Watts Rebellion and composing a list of recommendations to improve conditions through the War on Poverty programs.[45] This commission stands out when compared to other mid-1960s urban uprisings and subsequent government studies because the Governor's Commission on the Los Angeles Riots included Mexican Americans in their final recommendations. According to the commission's opening remarks in their published findings, "In this report, our major conclusions and recommendations regarding the Negro problem in Los

Angeles apply with equal force to the Mexican-Americans, a community which is almost equal in size to the Negro community and whose circumstances are similarly disadvantageous and demand equally urgent treatment. That the Mexican-American community did not riot is to its credit; it should not be to its disadvantage."[46] Although the commission proposed to research and prepare a report that aligned with the city's history of Black-Brown organizing, the preceding quotation demonstrates that the commission considered Mexican Americans on a secondary level as a reward for not rising up. In doing so, the Governor's Commission on the Los Angeles Riots reinforced Black noise and Brown invisibility by characterizing African Americans as volatile and Mexican Americans as passive. Such claims undermined the previous three decades of activism by Brown and Black Angelenos and represented a significant example of how officials increasingly compared these two groups. A critical examination of the Governor's Commission on the Los Angeles Riots and their final report further demonstrates the role of government officials in imposing competitive rhetoric on the development of Black-Brown relations around the War on Poverty.

The Governor's Commission on the Los Angeles Riots earned the nickname "the McCone Commission" after the group's leader, John A. McCone. A retired Central Intelligence Agency (CIA) director and California native, McCone entered politics through his successful career as an engineer for the war production industry and his appointment to the Air Policy Commission under President Harry S. Truman. McCone served as chairman of the Atomic Energy Commission for President Dwight Eisenhower and later directed the CIA under President John F. Kennedy. McCone resigned from his CIA duties early in Lyndon Johnson's administration, claiming that Johnson underutilized CIA agents. The McCone Commission's remaining members included health care professionals, church leaders, educators, and police department officials. Even though congressman Edward Roybal asked for a Mexican American appointee, California's governor failed to include any Mexican Americans or African American women on the McCone Commission.[47] While the commission's mission statement created an opportunity to provide a voice for Black and Brown Angelenos, Governor Brown's decision to omit Mexican American representatives reinforced claims of Brown invisibility and brings to light the vital role white officials played in upholding assumed racial boundaries between African Americans and Mexican Americans.

While the McCone Commission did not appoint any Mexican Americans to lead their group, the commission's final report still attempted to take a more nuanced approach to examining racial inequality in Los Angeles that included African Americans and Mexican Americans. For example, the commission's report included a summary letter to Governor Brown that described how they incorporated Mexican Americans into their investigations. According to the letter, "We wish to emphasize that, in compliance with your directive, we have been absorbed in the study of the problems in our Negro community. However, we are deeply conscious that the Mexican-American community, which here is almost equal in size to the Negro community, suffers from similar and in some cases more severe handicaps than the Negro community. Also, we are mindful that there are many others within our community living in conditions of poverty and suffering from unemployment and incapacity. In designing programs to assist the Negro, the needs of others must not be overlooked."[48] As a California-based group, the McCone Commission understood that a plan for Black Los Angeles must also include Mexican Americans. However, the commission's tone reinforced competitive race relations by arguing that efforts to address inequality in Black communities must acknowledge that Mexican Americans suffer "from similar and in some cases more severe handicaps." At the same time, the McCone Commission's efforts to include African Americans and Mexican Americans in their report reflect the legacy of Black and Brown organizing in Los Angeles. The commission sought to craft a report that highlighted interconnections between the experiences of African Americans and Mexican Americans, especially around urban inequality. While portions of their final report demonstrate a tendency to compare and emphasize differences between Black and Brown Angelenos, the McCone Commission's work represents the first attempt by a political body to assess discrimination in both African American and Mexican American communities in Los Angeles. Although complex, moments like this demonstrate why mid-1960s policies facilitated a transformative moment for Black-Brown relations.

In December 1965, the McCone Commission released its final report detailing some of the causes behind the Watts Rebellion. It offered recommendations for a host of issues affecting African Americans and Mexican Americans in Los Angeles. The commission based its findings on a series of interviews with local residents, institutions, and officials to understand conditions that led to the Watts Rebellion. For example, the report spent significant time examining community and police relations, describing interviews with African Americans who revealed that harassment and excessive force by LAPD fostered widespread mistrust of the local police department. Even though Mexican Americans had a long history of police harassment in Los Angeles, the commission's final report did not specifically highlight interviews to show Mexican Americans' unique perspectives on race and policing.[49] Still, the McCone Commission's final recommendations for how best to reform police and community relations included both African Americans and Mexican Americans by encouraging the LAPD to hire more Black and Brown people through creating exploratory programs that allowed potential recruits to learn more about careers in law enforcement.[50] As the commission's investigations of community and police relations show, the Watts Rebellion created an opportunity to assess overpolicing in communities of color. However, the McCone Commission's final recommendations emphasized hiring practices and community education, which fell short of critically assessing how the LAPD contributed to the repression and isolation of African Americans and Mexican Americans in mid-1960s Los Angeles. While the McCone Commission developed a report that had the potential to address a series of inequities shared by Brown and Black Angelenos, their recommendation to further expand police influence through community programs reflects some of the commission's shortcomings as a body assembled to improve Brown and Black lives.

In addition, the McCone Commission did not consider the history of policing around crime and citizenship for Mexican Americans in the United States. As historian A. K. Sandoval-Strausz argues in his analysis of Latinas/os in US cities, the Immigration and Nationality Act of 1965 created numerous challenges for Latinos immigrating to the United States, especially Mexicans.[51] He states, "The result was that labor migration across the Rio Grande, largely taken for granted for many years, was increasingly redefined as unlawful." He argues, "Migration from Mexico in particular was thus transformed from a widely accepted stream of seasonal workers into a problem."[52] While Mexican Americans and Mexicans faced scrutiny and profiling for alleged unlawful entry into the United States, the Governor's Commission on the Los Angeles Riots did not explore questions about citizenship and border patrol in their investigations about policing. The McCone Commission's decision to employ a limited scope in their research about local police failed to address how debates about citizenship might look different for both groups.[53]

Social-scientific ideas about race and dysfunction loomed large in post–World War II political debates throughout the United States. They guided the McCone Commission's examination of unemployment in Black and Brown Los Angeles. According to the commission's final report, unemployment facilitated a "cycle of poverty" among African Americans that most likely affected "an equal number of unemployed Mexican Americans."[54] Investigators focused on unemployment rates among men, reinforcing distorted gender ideologies that associated men with family leadership and women with household labor. According to the commission's report, unemployment fostered feelings of despair among men who subsequently passed a similar disposition to their children. The McCone Commission proposed developing employment programs to restore men to an idealized role as breadwinners and authorities over their families. Within the context of 1960s social-scientific debates, the commission applied a set of pejorative assumptions associated with the "culture of poverty" debate and romanticized gender norms for Black Angelenos. The "culture of poverty" thesis, first introduced by anthropologist Oscar Lewis in a study about poor Mexican families published in 1959, used family units he observed to argue that generational poverty resulted in cultural traits passed down to children. The "culture of poverty" thesis is an important example of the intertwined history between African Americans and their Latina/o counterparts because Lewis's idea gained further popularity in the United States when secretary of labor Daniel Patrick Moynihan adapted the "culture of poverty" to craft a federal study about Black city residents.

While numerous critiques of the "culture of poverty" thesis existed, the McCone Commission, like most governing bodies, ignored scholarly critiques. For instance, scholar Ernesto Galarza's 1966 essay, "LA Mula No Nacio Arisca" (The mule isn't born stubborn, he's made stubborn), challenged claims that culture served as a legitimate framework for analyzing why many Black and Mexican Americans lived in economically depressed conditions. Like poverty rebels throughout the United States, Galarza argued that economic conditions in Brown and Black communities reflected deeply entrenched inequality in US society. The McCone Commission ignored expert critiques and used the "culture of poverty" thesis to inform their analysis of life in Los Angeles. McCone and his colleagues failed to understand the deeply rooted historical, social, and political processes that created poverty in the United States. The Watts Rebellion offered an opportunity to listen to Mexican American and African American residents empathetically and to understand better how economic inequality impacted their lives. However, the McCone Commission relied on studies that perpetuated racial stereotypes about Black and Brown city residents in its report.[55] The use of problematic social-scientific frameworks to assess Mexican American and African American Angelenos is important to how the relationship between these two groups developed since the 1960s, because efforts to disentangle their communities from these ideas further undermined Los Angeles's multiracial activist past. For instance, a *Los Angeles Sentinel* article published in 1974 claimed that Mexicans and Mexican Americans benefited from civil rights and social welfare policy more than other groups in the United States. According to the article, "Blacks have been citizens for generations without benefits and have sat back and watched Chicanos who are not citizens come on over and get benefits denied them for years," demonstrating how efforts to distance African Americans from stereotypes facilitated some anti-Mexican sentiment.[56]

Geographical divisions defined racial identity politics in post–World War II United States. While previous scholars have examined the role of residential segregation in Black-white relations since 1945, few have considered how neighborhood boundaries shaped Black-Brown relations during this time.[57] The McCone Commission confronted geographical divisions between African Americans and Mexican Americans in their research on education in South Central and East Los Angeles neighborhoods. The commission investigated predominately African American schools in South Central and Mexican American schools in East Los Angeles. According to the commission's final report, schools in lower socioeconomic neighborhoods had lower test scores, temporary teaching staff, and a lack of pedagogical resources. In addition, overcrowding often created larger class sizes, double-session school days, and limited counseling services to accommodate students. To improve these conditions, the McCone Commission suggested that schools develop plans to improve literacy rates and make early childhood education more readily available. Because federal officials enthusiastically encouraged Head Start, especially in the Office of Economic Opportunity, the commission's report showed a direct link between federal government priorities and Los Angeles. Still, the McCone Commission fell short of examining the unique educational experiences of Mexican Americans, even when an opportunity presented itself in their investigation of local public schools. In doing so, the commission reinforced Black visibility and Brown invisibility throughout their entire report.[58]

Like most uprising and riot studies commissioned by government officials during the 1960s, some of the McCone Commission's recommendations appeared in youth programs, school tutoring, and community police forums. Still, they failed to address the deep institutional and structural processes that led to the Watts Rebellion. The McCone Commission also set an ambitious goal by attempting to create recommendations for Brown and Black Los Angeles. While creating an agenda to investigate inequities experienced by both African Americans and Mexican Americans harkened back to the pre-

World War II coalitions that resulted in local political change, the McCone Commission did not go far enough to challenge the trope of Brown invisibility and Black visibility in their final report. Investigators assumed that a plan for African American Los Angeles automatically extended to Mexican American residents, who faced inequities unique to their racial and ethnic group. Even within a statewide context, Brown invisibility continued to challenge efforts by Mexican American activists to address race and poverty alongside African Americans.

The Power of Urban Rebellion

The Watts Rebellion of 1965 brought international attention to race relations in Los Angeles. The uprising placed African Americans at the center of discussions about racial inequality in Los Angeles, even though Mexican Americans were building a civil rights movement as well. In addition, the Watts Rebellion helped place Black Angelenos into context with civil rights movements taking shape nationally. As the McCone Commission reveals, officials who attempted to address social, political, and economic inequality shared by African Americans and Mexican Americans often relied on Black-white race relations in the United States as their framework. While Congressman Hawkins attempted to bring African Americans and Mexican Americans together in the year before the rebellion, he did so as Los Angeles increasingly entered into dialogue about how the uprising in Watts connected to the Black Freedom movement.[59]

In the years following the Watts Rebellion, Mexican American activists turned to the uprising to participate in national debates about civil rights. Some Mexican Americans argued that the anger at the core of the Watts Rebellion also existed in Mexican American communities. In a 1967 article from the *Atlantic Monthly*, Mexican American interviewees offered their perspectives on the possibility of civil unrest. San Francisco–based activist Herman Gallegos asserted that some Mexican Americans refused to join peaceful demonstrations out of fear that they might become violent. An unnamed interviewee described the state of East Los Angeles: "Man, if East L.A. ever blows, it will really blow," demonstrating how some Mexican Americans drew on the Watts Rebellion to articulate their frustrations.[60] An article in the *Christian Science Monitor* identified the plight of Mexican Americans in Los Angeles as "the best kept American secret." The author argued that inequalities affecting Mexican Americans often remained invisible within broader social justice movements, asserting that continued neglect might lead to "a situation as that which developed in the Watts Negro neighborhood here this past summer."[61] As these articles reveal, Watts ignited a meaningful conversation about race and rights in Los Angeles starting in the summer of 1965. Mexican Americans increasingly cited the Watts Rebellion as an example of what happens when government officials ignore injustices.

The Watts Rebellion's impact reverberated throughout the War on Poverty's longevity in Los Angeles and the United States more broadly. Mexican American and African American youth activists saw power in the Watts Rebellion and the rise of more militant action to address racial and economic inequality. As teenagers and young adults who largely came of age after the *Brown v. Board of Education of Topeka* case in 1954, young people experienced an important transition through the Civil Rights Act and Economic Opportunity Act. Drawing on federal policies, young people challenged their parents' respectability politics by turning to grassroots and community politics to advocate for antipoverty funding.

CHAPTER THREE

The Economic Opportunity Generation

> Today, education is perhaps the most important function of state and local governments. Compulsory school attendance laws and the great expenditures for education both demonstrate our recognition of the importance of education to our democratic society. It is required in the performance of our most basic public responsibilities, even service in the armed forces. It is the very foundation of good citizenship.
> —CHIEF JUSTICE EARL WARREN, *Brown v. Board of Education of Topeka*

> It is, therefore, the policy of the United States to eliminate the paradox of poverty in the midst of plenty in this Nation by opening to everyone the opportunity for education and training, the opportunity to work, and the opportunity to live in decency and dignity. It is the purpose of this Act to strengthen, supplement, and coordinate efforts in furtherance of that policy.
> —Economic Opportunity Act of 1964

On March 5, 1967, President Lyndon Johnson signed Executive Order 11330, establishing the President's Council on Youth Opportunity. Johnson's order reflected the US federal government's intervention in the lives of children and youth since World War II, especially young people of color. Johnson's order declared, "The promise and the future strength of the United States is in our youth," connecting young people to how federal officials envisioned the future of US democracy. Johnson went on to use language about class that became increasingly associated with Black and Brown youth by the late 1960s. "Many youths, particularly those who live in impoverished areas, need special help in improving their lives and finding a place in the mainstream of our society," the executive order stated. "The summer months," Johnson asserted, "provide an exceptional opportunity to enhance the sound growth and guidance of youth through education, employment, recreation, and health services."[1] Chaired by Vice President Hubert Humphrey, the council led a series of youth opportunity campaigns across the United States to call for jobs, education, and recreational resources for young people, with a particular focus on US cities where resistance movements and uprisings took place.

Youth-oriented programming comprised a sizeable number of antipoverty programs created in Los Angeles following the Watts Rebellion. While some War on Poverty–funded programs run by an older guard of activists claimed that youth-centered resources were critical to preventing young people from engaging in criminal or radical activities, youth activists increasingly used antipoverty programs to articulate their specific perspective on racial and economic justice. By the time War on Poverty monies arrived in Los Angeles, the city had already proven to be a place where young Angelenos had the freedom to resist unequal treatment through their civic organizing. As the first generation of young people set to experience high school, college, and adulthood in the post–civil rights United States, Black and Brown youth seized opportunities to participate in antipoverty programs they believed best supported their communities during an exciting next stage in US society. African American and Mexican American youth watched opportunities for social and economic advancement available to Hawkins and Roybal's generation dwindle in the decades immediately following World War II. Youth responded by utilizing Los Angeles's history of civic engagement to develop movements that allowed them to play an active role in shaping the War on Poverty.[2] Organizations, including the Brown Berets and the Organization US sought to create a more just society by ensuring that youth in their communities had access to education, health care, and enrichment programs uniquely tailored to fit their needs. While some officials and older activists celebrated Brown and Black youth movements, these organizations also faced significant surveillance, criticism, and sabotage in response to their grassroots ethos and criticism of the contradictions inherent in US democracy. Officials and older activists attempted to undermine the community work of African American and Mexican American youth by perpetuating claims that young Black and Brown Angelenos were on verge of a race war, and that antipoverty programs could help improve community relations. Such claims sought to weaken the influence youth activists garnered in their communities and further solidified Black-Brown relations as a War on Poverty issue.

Coming of Age in the War on Poverty

The War on Poverty followed a two-decade trend of zeroing in on youth as a specific target demographic. The previous two decades greatly shaped the role of children and youth in the War on Poverty by maintaining a culture of scrutiny about how young people should properly represent the United States. The Economic Opportunity Act of 1964 (EOA) provided a set of policies that specifically targeted children and young adults who resided in low socioeconomic communities, especially African American and Latina/o youth. For example, the EOA emphasized how policy might prepare young people for the responsibilities of citizenship and increase their employability. Youth activist groups in Los Angeles, especially the Brown Berets, the Organization US, and the Black Panther Party for Self-Defense, often grew from programs originally funded through the US federal government's War on Poverty. As founders and members of social justice organizations, these young activists challenged assumptions that the War on Poverty tried to impose upon them by directing their energy to advocating for school resources, ethnic studies programs, community self-determination, and their ability to celebrate Blackness and Brownness.

US federal government policies increasingly targeted young people as a unique urban demographic in the two decades leading up to the War on Poverty. A closer look at Los Angeles reveals a long history of youth-oriented programs that reached back to World War II, when the Zoot Suits Riots of 1943 resulted in increased attention to Black and Brown youth in Los Angeles. Mexican American teens received targeted attention in efforts to set social standards for the city's young patrons. As historian Elizabeth Escobedo examines in her analysis of Mexican American girls and women in World War II Los Angeles, increased anxiety around Pachuca and Pachuco culture coincided with an increase in police surveillance, juvenile incarceration, and media attention to Mexican American children and youth.[3] While historian Elizabeth Hinton's pivotal book about the relationship between the War on Poverty and mass incarceration provides a masterful account of how antipoverty policy came to influence decades of juvenile and adult criminal justice policies, in Los Angeles, this process began to take shape in the 1940s with Mexican Americans.[4] The War on Poverty allowed local officials and community organizers to expand upon a series of youth-oriented reforms that began two decades before the War on Poverty and that targeted Mexican American youth.

Local municipal policies intended for youth became part and parcel of national efforts to police young adults by the 1960s. Under Lyndon Johnson's presidency, the federal government developed a series of policies, councils, commissions, and working groups to research and propose strategies for programs designed to guide children and young adults as they settled into circumscribed roles as contributors to US democracy. Throughout the 1960s and 1970s, teens and young adults faced widespread scrutiny about their personalities, behavior, and bodies. Los Angeles mayor Sam Yorty became a strong advocate for the US federal government's youth-oriented policies and programs.[5] In an October 11, 1961, interview with the *Los Angeles Times*, Mayor Yorty called upon parents, teachers, local officials, and religious leaders to support his efforts to stop alleged youth violence. Under Yorty's leadership, the local municipal government even developed a set of laws to govern its young population as reflected in an informational booklet titled *Los Angeles City Laws for Youth*. The booklet sought to provide parents and children with details about laws pertaining to the use of knives and guns, curfews, fireworks, and most importantly, youth employment.[6] Throughout the United States, and in California more specifically, parents, police officers, and officials reinforced the idea of unruly youth and called for strict regulations in schools and other settings to control young people. Yorty's efforts demonstrate just how much Los Angeles authorities responded to efforts to define the role of youth in society through control and by establishing a narrative that defined young Black and Brown people as violent to themselves and society. This influenced how young activists developed their movements, pushed back against racial stereotypes, created institutions that felt safe for them, and fought to make their own choices.

The United States' increased focus on children and youth also shaped the War on Poverty. The Economic Opportunity Act of 1964, which set legislative priorities for the War on Poverty, began with a clause for "youth programs." Although a myriad of youth-identified resources emerged during early stages of the War on Poverty, the EOA focused its efforts on the alleged crisis of youth unemployment. In outlining the importance of Job Corps and college work-study, the EOA stated, "The purpose of this part is to prepare for the responsibilities of citizenship and to increase the employability of young men and young women aged sixteen through twenty-one."[7] This was not the first time the US federal government identified policies for children and youth as essential to their success as citizens and their ability to contribute to US democracy. When chief justice Earl Warren delivered the Supreme Court's landmark decision in *Brown v. Board of Education of Topeka* in 1954, he characterized laws governing compulsory education as "recognition of the importance of education to our democratic society." Chief Justice Warren went on to identify education as "the very foundation of good citizenship."[8] The *Brown* decision demonstrates national trends stemming back to the 1940s, when policy became a way to contain young people as they actively worked to liberate themselves from the confines of families and respectability politics. The *Brown* decision's focus on creating a blueprint for how child-rearing might help shape US democracy was a common occurrence in how the nation approached young people by the mid-1960s. With many War on Poverty programs focused on youth enrichment, these institutions helped empower young Brown and Black people to promote their own definitions of US progress by bringing awareness to urgent social justice work that remained after passage of the 1964 Civil Rights Act.

Politicization of Black and Brown Youth

The politicization of youth across the United States that culminated in radical movements of the 1960s and 1970s reached back to the Depression and Second World War. Seasoned civil rights warriors, including Ella Baker and Bayard Rustin, cultivated their activist spirits as young people in vibrant US cities. Historian Barbara Ransby writes of the impact that the young Black diasporic population in Harlem had on Ella Baker prior to World War II. "During the late 1920s and the 1930s, Baker came of age politically and began to formulate the worldview and theoretical framework that influenced her organizing work for the next fifty years," Ransby argues.[9] The youth branch of the National Association for the Advancement of Colored People developed an even more radical critique of US society during the Great Depression when they proposed an economic program that considered the dual relationship between race and class.[10] Los Angeles during the Depression also saw the rise of resistance led by young African Americans and Mexican Americans. In the 1930s, *Los Angeles Sentinel* editor Leon Washington Jr. used his African American newspaper to start a "Don't Spend Where You Can't Work" protest campaign that encouraged African Americans across Los Angeles to avoid patronizing businesses that refused to employ them. Founded by Washington in 1933, the *Sentinel*'s slogan, "The People's Paper," further demonstrated some of the leftist influences that came to shape young people's activism starting in the 1930s.[11] In an interview later in life, congressman Augustus Hawkins remembered that Washington decided to establish a newspaper he believed best aligned with African Americans' political transition to the Democratic Party.[12] The *Sentinel* sought to represent voices and perspectives of many young Angelenos who became involved in political activism and who helped usher in a new era for African Americans.

The Second Great Migration of the post–World War II years played a central role in shaping the activism of young Angelenos. Historian Donna

Murch argues in her work on the relationship between higher education and the formation of the Black Panther Party for Self-Defense in Oakland, California, that Black migration to the Golden State starting in World War II led to widespread hostility directed at young African Americans.[13] When the Second World War began in 1939, Black, Brown, and white migrants from across the United States flocked to California as the state became a central location for the war production industry. Los Angeles's total population nearly doubled between 1940 and 1970 as the city grew into one of the most popular destinations for migrants seeking employment. As historian Darlene Clark Hine has argued in her research on Black migration, the act of moving and making choices about one's livelihood has been perhaps one of the boldest acts of resistance for African-descended people in the United States.[14] That increased numbers of Black and Brown residents, especially youth who engaged in new forms of expressive culture, led to heightened scrutiny from politicians, parents, and police, reveals how the Great Migration shaped the lives and experiences of young people of color.[15]

Circumstances surrounding the Zoot Suit Riots of 1943 represent one example of the opportunities for young people of color to resist societal norms and exert their identities in unique ways. Zoot suit culture, derived from the rise of jazz music, often represented experiences from the Black working classes. Historian Eduardo Pagán's analysis of zoot suit culture in Los Angeles argues that although jazz grew out of the migratory experiences of African Americans during the early twentieth century, this music genre became multiracial and multicultural in places like Los Angeles. Mexican American youth became quickly engulfed in jazz music, fashion, and mannerisms, giving rise to their increased wearing of zoot suits. However, because the hairstyles, language, and clothing that made up zoot suit culture directly challenged societal norms, white officials often characterized young zoot-suiters as dangerous and deviant. David Sánchez, founding member of the Brown Berets, reflected on how the Zoot Suit Riots of 1943, where white civilians and servicemen attacked young Mexican American zoot-suiters, impacted his parents. Reflecting on his father's experience as a zoot-suiter, Sánchez stated, "He saw how a lot of the people were being beaten up. A lot of his friends were being beaten up by US Navy sailormen over on Broadway, downtown Broadway. So because of that, my father recognized being a Chicano, and I think a lot of that Chicano mentality came out of the Zoot Suit Riots."[16] As Mexican American youth took part in a cultural movement that allowed them to take control over fashioning their own identities and sense of self, the city of Los Angeles characterized Mexican American youth as dan-

Mexican American students engaged in walkouts in March 1968 to protest educational inequality. Garfield High School, Los Angeles, California, March 6, 1968. *Los Angeles Times* Photographic Archive, UCLA Library Special Collections, uclalat_1429_b611_238809-1.

gerous criminals, increased policing in Mexican American neighborhoods, and expanded programs to address alleged juvenile delinquency. While zoot suit culture simply allowed Mexican American youth to have fun and develop a sense of freedom in how they adorned their bodies, the local government characterized their actions as a challenge to US democracy instead of allowing them to play a role in defining what US society represented for them.[17]

It is no surprise that Los Angeles, and California more broadly, became a center for some of the most successful youth-led movements of the twentieth century. The struggle for ethnic studies on college campuses reflected various youth-centered movements that shaped post–World War II California. Starting with the successful San Francisco State University student strike led by the Third World Liberation Front in 1968, similar advocacy took place on college campuses throughout the greater Los Angeles area at the University of California, Los Angeles, and California State University, Long Beach.[18] As geographer Laura Pulido examines in her work on the rise of radical activism in 1960s Los Angeles, "the Third World Left should be seen as part of

The Economic Opportunity Generation 65

an unfolding political trajectory that dates from at least World War II."[19] Although these movements increasingly meshed with the War on Poverty, they represent several decades of politicization that started with migration, intensified in response to inequality in the justice system, and were further inspired by the national quest for civil rights. As primary targets of the War on Poverty, youth activists drew on thirty years of momentum begun in the 1930s to forge activist movements through antipoverty programs designed to support their unique demographic.

The Economic Opportunity Generation

Youth engagement played a central role in President Lyndon Johnson's administrative goals. Johnson even called upon educated youth to take up the next stage in the fight for civil rights as the nation worked to constrain the radical imaginations of young people of color, demonstrating some of the contradictions between rhetoric and policy during this period. For example, when President Johnson delivered Howard University's commencement speech on June 4, 1965, he announced a new phase in the struggle for equal rights in the United States. Hopeful African American graduates, parents, faculty, and university staff listened intently to Johnson's speech, titled "To Fulfill These Rights." Johnson outlined the limitations of civil rights policy in reaching cities and the role class status played in preventing a significant segment of the African American population from even gaining access to institutions available to them after passage of the 1964 Civil Rights Act. "Men and women of all races are born with the same range of abilities," Johnson stated, "but ability is not just the product of birth. Ability is stretched or stunted by the family that you live with, and the neighborhood you live in— by the school you go to and the poverty or the richness of your surroundings. It is the product of a hundred unseen forces playing upon the little infant, the child, and finally the man."[20] Interestingly, Johnson's speech acknowledged the limitations inherent in policies passed under his administration, but he and other politicians increasingly characterized youth who highlighted these limitations as not advancing the goals of US democracy.

Johnson often cited his background as an educator in Texas as the motivation behind his policies related to K–12 education and youth. During Johnson's Howard University commencement speech, he highlighted his experience working with Mexican American children and youth to further emphasize the role of childhood in shaping one's overall life trajectory. According to Johnson, "There is also the lacerating hurt of early collision with

Graduates, faculty, staff, and families listening as President Lyndon B. Johnson delivers Howard University's commencement address, Washington, DC, June 4, 1965. LBJ Library photo by Yoichi Okamoto, A599-15.

white hatred or prejudice, distaste or condescension. Other groups have felt similar intolerance. But success and achievement could wipe it away. They do not change the color of a man's skin. I have seen this uncomprehending pain in the eyes of the little, young Mexican-American school children that I taught many years ago. But it can be overcome. But, for many, the wounds are always open."[21] As Johnson's speech pointed out, both African American and Mexican American children and youth had suffered unrelenting discrimination that prevented them from experiencing full citizenship rights by the 1960s. As children and young adults were pulled deeper into federal policy and national debates about the proper place of youth in US society, the number of young activists increased to advocate for a voice in how their daily experiences fit into policies like the War on Poverty.

Just as the War on Poverty collided with existing efforts to address post–World War II social, political, and economic inequality, this massive reform program also influenced youth movements across Los Angeles. College campuses became a central location for youth politicization and social justice movements. Historian Donna Murch has found that California's Master Plan for Education, created in the early 1960s, expanded higher education in a way that made college more accessible to underrepresented students. The consolidation of the University of California, California State University, and community colleges to more concretely support transfer to four-year institutions, helped bring students of color together in clubs and campus organizations that led to activist campaigns like the Black Power movement, Chicano movement, Anti-War movement, and protests to establish ethnic studies.[22] President Johnson–era policies meshed with this critical transformation of California's public colleges and as young people of color worked to define their own place within US society.

The federal government's War on Poverty became a connective thread among youth activist organizations across the greater Los Angeles area. The Organization US, a cultural nationalist group, actively participated in Los Angeles's antipoverty programs. Local college student and future Black studies scholar Maulana "Ron" Karenga founded the Organization US shortly after the Watts Rebellion in 1965. Karenga, born Ronald Everett in Parsonsburg, Maryland, migrated west in 1958. He enrolled in Los Angeles Community College, a local hotbed for a new generation of African American and Mexican American student activists. Karenga was elected the first Black student body president of the college in 1961, which contributed to his reputation as an emerging young leader. For many students during this time, California colleges provided a fertile ground for the development of cultural nationalist organizations. Karenga's experience exemplifies the role of colleges in cultivating a new generation of activists, especially those who migrated to California.[23]

Founded in 1965, the Organization US grew from a small reading group that Karenga took part in at Aquarian Bookshop located in Los Angeles, and quickly became a burgeoning organization joined by other young activists critical of the Black Freedom movement's emphasis on liberal democratic policies. For example, the Organization US argued that focusing on political rights was just one avenue to improve the material lives of Black people.[24] The organization's platform identified cultural pride and practices as key to revitalizing African American communities, and members advocated for wearing African garments, learning Black history, and adopting Swahili as the national language of Black people.[25] The rise of cultural nationalism reflects the unique ways that young people contributed to and shaped activist movements that originated in California during a period when the federal government attempted to define how democracy mapped on to age through policy. As Karenga's community work grew, he contributed to several antipoverty organizations, including the Social Action Training Center (SATC). The SATC, funded through the War on Poverty, included a series of youth centers designed to teach African Americans and Mexican Americans about community action and conflict resolution, making the centers an important space for the economic opportunity generation. The Social Action Training Center hired Karenga as a summer employee, and federal officials felt uneasy about Karenga's potential to organize Los Angeles youth. Given Karenga's cultural nationalist activism, officials suspended funding for SATC summer programs while advocating the importance of youth employment during summer breaks. The decision to suspend funding reveals the tensions between how the US federal government envisioned War on Poverty–funded programs for young people and how youth attempted to participate in community institutions that advanced pride and self-determination. While antipoverty programs became spaces through which members of the economic opportunity generation contributed to African American communities in Los Angeles, the local, state, and federal governments' fear of radicalism posed significant challenges for young activists.[26]

Federal officials paid close attention to the rise of militant activism and young people who worked for local antipoverty programs. Watts Rebellion participant Tommy Jacquette raised questions at the federal level when he gained employment with local antipoverty programs. Born and raised in Los Angeles, Jacquette recalled some of the challenges Black youth faced while

Tommy Jacquette (*right*) in Charcoal Alley, a stretch of Watts greatly impacted by the 1965 uprising, Los Angeles, California, July 16, 1967. *Los Angeles Times* Photographic Archive, UCLA Library Special Collections, uclamss_1429_b599 _236839-1. Licensed under CC BY 4.0: https://digital.library.ucla.edu/catalog/ ark:/13030/hb3k4005hh.

growing up after World War II. "Police, community conflict, mainly between the young people, churches and schools and small businesses, that type of thing," Jacquette recalled of his childhood and young adulthood.[27] He went on to state that the Watts Rebellion motivated him to become involved in militant activism, demonstrating the impact that urban uprisings had on a younger generation of Black Angelenos. The Westminster Neighborhood Association (WNA) employed Jacquette as a street aide in Watts, and his responsibilities included going out into the community to recruit for WNA programs. The WNA received funding from both the Department of Labor and the Office of Economic Opportunity (OEO) to expand an outreach program founded and run by the United Presbyterian Church. The program's primary goal included providing resources for youth between the ages of 18 and 21 who stopped attending high school. The WNA hired local teachers to tutor participants, offered job-placement services, and provided college advising. The program contributed to the War on Poverty's emphasis on providing youth with access to resources that improved their educational and employment outcomes. However, the OEO did not anticipate that young activists like Jacquette would bring their vision for social justice and equality into the War on Poverty.[28]

The WNA came under fire for welcoming young activists into their organization and faced criticism from other antipoverty program facilitators. Local community workers saw the WNA as a potential hindrance to organizations that espoused respectability politics. Annabelle Williams of the Catholic Youth Organization feared, for example, that militant activists might use War on Poverty programs to incite a revolution. She stated that by providing opportunities to young people, WNA supported radical philosophies promoted by groups like the Black Panther Party for Self-Defense. According to Williams, "Westminster's approach is to tear down the power structure, to agitate and to build another structure." She added, "You can't arouse people and then leave them with nothing like that."[29] Williams's criticism of the WNA reflected some of the efforts to discredit antipoverty activities carried out by younger activists and the tendency to characterize their community work as a danger to the War on Poverty's longevity.

Members of the National Urban League's local branch differed in their opinions about the WNA. Founded in 1921, the Los Angeles branch of the National Urban League focused primarily on labor and community service. John Crawford, director of the organization's antipoverty-funded program, known as Nickerson Gardens Community Development Project, argued that militant activists encouraged social protest during a period of racial progress in the United States. "We (the Urban League) are free of racism," he stated. "We're not trying to indoctrinate." Crawford went on to assert, "They protest for protest['s] sake and in times like these, with so much social unrest, it can be dangerous." He added, "What people need is guidance and direction."[30] Similar to claims made by Williams, Crawford characterized younger generations as misguided and fighting an unjust cause even though their activism drew directly from daily experiences with inequality. In addition, in contrast to Crawford's assertation that the United States entered a new phase of racial progress, young activists understood that economic justice remained an important battle for Black and Brown people. Williams and Crawford reveal some of the generational differences that influenced how activists conceptualized the post–civil rights decades and the War on Poverty's significance to their movements.

Historically, Black and Brown communities have been galvanized by resistance to respectability politics and repressive authority. In Los Angeles, zoot suits allowed young people, especially Mexican Americans, to engage in expressive culture that challenged norms about dress, dance, and music. African Americans, especially Black women, have tended to join organizations that advance radical visions for Black life and that overtly challenged white supremacy.[31] Local Urban League director Wesley Brazier acknowledged the impact that younger generations had on motivating youth to become active in their communities. Brazier complimented the WNA on the organization's ability to attract participants. "Westminster can talk to the hard-core," he asserted, "while other organizations were not able to connect with youth in the same way."[32] Brazier's complimentary remarks are an example of activists involved in older-guard organizations who saw great success in the work of young poverty rebels. Even though some activists associated with older and more moderate organizations saw the new generation as dangerous, youth were drawn to militant groups because they sought to bring awareness to the structural inequalities that shaped the lives of Los Angeles residents by the 1960s. As Tommy Jacquette described in an interview years later, some children left school at the age of sixteen because the 1960s represented a time when young people could typically find employment without a high school diploma. "The community morality and the morality of the day was to do the right thing," Jacquette described, "get a job or get an education."[33] As youth watched opportunities steadily decline, they took an active role in advocating for themselves and their communities. What emerged from their engagement with the War on Poverty was an opportunity to share a concrete set of experiences as Angelenos and to use antipoverty programs to address gaps in education, employment, and even community pride.

US federal government officials even considered how they might harness the local authority of younger poverty rebels to help make youth programs more effective. For example, when federal officials learned that militant activists played a key role in curtailing an alleged riot in Los Angeles, government representatives organized a meeting with young African American activists and congressman Augustus Hawkins, because of his background working closely with constituents in Los Angeles. Tommy Jacquette even remembered Hawkins as a "key player politically," who took time to actively engage with young activists throughout the city.[34] In March 1966, Hawkins met with members of the Organization US and Self Leadership for All Nationalists Today, a Watts-based organization Jacquette participated in. The organization had successfully received an antipoverty grant to run a job-training program for local youth, further demonstrating how much the War on Poverty shaped the work of young activists. The meeting with Hawkins revealed that federal officials primarily sought to placate young organizers rather than joining forces with them to advance the War on Poverty's goals.[35] An Office of Economic Opportunity memo written to debrief about the meeting drew some sobering conclusions. "We ought to be learning all we can about groups like these and their leaders because it may well be true that Watts and other communities like it will go the direction they go," an official wrote. "The perils of giving them recognition and direction into constructive pursuits must be weighed against the period of ignoring them," the memo stated. "These are not unsophisticated or hardened hoodlums. Their grievances are not imagined."[36] While the meeting held with Congressman Hawkins and local youth-led organizations seemed like an effort on the part of federal officials to recognize strength in community development performed by young people, the meeting also reflected a desire to maintain control of militant activity. Reflecting on his experiences in the War on Poverty decades later, Tommy Jacquette echoed sentiments that antipoverty programs often seemed as if they sought to pacify activists instead of improving the material conditions of the poor.[37]

Elsewhere in the city, especially in East Los Angeles, the War on Poverty contributed to the emergence of a Mexican American economic opportunity generation. The second half of the 1960s saw the rise of the Chicano movement as Mexican American high school and college students rallied for education equality, an end to police brutality, and an acknowledgement of structural racism. In Los Angeles, antipoverty programs and federal funding helped launch the careers of several Chicano movement leaders, including David Sánchez of the Brown Berets. Brown Berets grew directly from an organization funded by the War on Poverty for Mexican American youth, demonstrating the relationship between federal funding and the rise of a new generation of activists in 1960s Los Angeles.[38] Brown Berets began as the Young Citizens for Community Action (YCCA)—a name that reflected the group's connection to the federal War on Poverty—under the leadership of youth activist Vickie Castro. Founded by local Mexican American youth including Castro, Sánchez, and Moctesuma Esparza, YCCA advocated for education reform and rallied for a representative to the Los Angeles Board of Education. As an organization that sought to help young Mexican Americans become involved in their local communities, YCCA received a federal War on Poverty grant to develop a Volunteers in Service to America (VISTA)-affiliated group housed at the Church of the Epiphany in Los Angeles's Lincoln Heights neighborhood.[39] Known as the domestic Peace Corps, VISTA trained and sent young volunteers to impoverished communities in the United States to help with rehabilitative and community revitalization projects, while YCCA President Vickie Castro identified education and political organizing as the cornerstone of YCCA's original mission. Castro remembered YCCA's focus transitioning to police brutality when David Sánchez became president, and the group changed their name to the Brown Berets in 1968.[40]

Under the guidance of Sánchez, the Brown Berets grew from youth meetings held at an SATC program in East Los Angeles. Sánchez, a Los Angeles native, grew up in a primarily African American neighborhood in South Central Los Angeles. When Sánchez was in high school, his family moved to Boyle Heights, an area in transition to a majority Mexican American community in Los Angeles. Like the Sánchez family, long-time Mexican American residents and migrants increasingly moved into East Los Angeles, contributing further to the development of two racially distinct communities for the city's African American and Mexican American populations.[41] Even though these communities became largely associated with one specific racial group, activist movements still reflected a cross-pollination between Black and Brown Angelenos, especially young people. As historian Ernesto Chávez has written in his research about the Chicano movement in Los Angeles, Black militant movements deeply influenced the Brown Beret's founding principles, uniforms, and demands. "Besides the khaki attire," Chávez asserts, "the most revealing feature of their apparel was the beret and the emblem attached to it, depicting a yellow pentagon with two bayoneted rifles behind a cross and the words *La Causa* ("The Cause") above them."[42] David Sánchez reflected on these influences in an interview decades later. "I was always consciously studying civil rights, black Civil Rights Movement," he recalled.[43] Reminiscent of the Black Panther Party for Self-Defense's all-black attire, Sánchez saw Brown Berets as an opportunity to fill a void in militant activism for Mexican Americans.[44]

Young Mexican American activists often participated in programs led by the local government, churches, and schools before their ascension into activism through the War on Poverty. With support from Mexican Americans and African Americans, Sánchez earned a seat on the Los Angeles Youth Council under mayor Sam Yorty. The mayor's office strongly advocated for juvenile delinquency programs and even attempted to organize the War on Poverty around a government agency funded through federal juvenile delinquency policies. Yorty's youth council included Mexican American, African American, and white teenagers responsible for advising the local government on issues related to young adults, further demonstrating the city's long history of youth engagement. Sánchez credits the youth council with bringing him into contact with African American activists who shaped his thinking about race and social justice. According to Sánchez, "They were giving me kind of a lesson as far as what civil rights was about, so I learned a lot from the blacks in the Mayor's Youth Advisory Council, who later became leaders in their communities."[45] Sánchez's involvement in municipal politics demonstrates the ways in which questions about how to address both Black and Brown populations in Los Angeles became central to city-level discussions and how the city's interest in youth shaped their assent into both local and national freedom movements during the 1960s and 1970s.[46]

Young Citizens for Community Action developed a militant stance during the first few years of the organization's existence. When VISTA funding expired, the name of the organization changed to Young Chicanos for Community Action, reflecting an increased identification with the burgeoning Chicano movement. However, with an increase in leftist activism came heightened police harassment for active members of Young Chicanos for Community Action. In response, YCCA once again changed their name and the organization's perspective. Influenced by groups like the Black Panther Party for Self-Defense, YCCA became the Brown Berets in 1968. The new organization not only worked in East Los Angeles communities but also developed a platform to describe their grievances and called for significant revisions to US political priorities.[47] The Brown Berets' ten-point platform suggests that in addition to influences from the Black Panther Party, Brown Berets also advocated for resources that reflected their identity as members of the economic opportunity generation.[48] Some demands that set the Brown Berets apart included the calls for "bilingual education" and "an end to urban renewal programs." These two demands reflected some of the unique experiences of Mexican Americans across Los Angeles. Other demands revealed similar experiences with Black Angelenos, including calls to provide "the true history of the Mexican American," creation of a "civilian police review board," and "that all Mexican Americans be tried by juries consisting of only Mexican Americans."[49] These demands represented a vision for US society espoused by young people who came of age after World War II and who used the War on Poverty to insert their voices into calls for racial and class justice.

Calls for basic resources, including affordable and safe health care, shaped questions about which reforms best supported communities of color during the 1960s. As historian Abigail Rosas describes in her analysis of War on

Poverty programs in South Central Los Angeles, Black and Brown antipoverty activism also included calls for improved and more access to health care. "Community health centers," Rosas argues, "became part of the national landscape in 1965 through the availability of War on Poverty funds. President Johnson's updates to the Social Security Act offered government-sponsored health insurance for the elderly and disabled through Medicare and Medicaid. This legislation expanded the government's role in health care and other social welfare programs."[50] The only woman minister in the Brown Berets, Gloria Arellanes identified the Barrio Free Clinic as an important legacy of Brown Berets in Los Angeles. Like Sánchez's experiences as a teenager, Arellanes credits the development of a Mexican American youth council at her high school as an entry into local activism.[51] Primarily run by women in the organization, including the only woman minister, the Barrio Free Clinic's services included abortion counseling and treatment for sexually transmitted diseases. In addition, the clinic provided a safe environment in comparison to existing health facilities in the area. In an interview decades later, Arellanes asserted that the Barrio Free Clinic offered a comfortable alternative for undocumented patrons, who feared a trip to the hospital might result in unwarranted scrutiny or deportation. As the Barrio Free Clinic shows, Mexican American youth played a vital role in creating a set of resources designed to provide affordable and safe institutions for their communities. The War on Poverty aided in developing these resources and further empowered young activists through their participation in antipoverty programs.[52]

The Economic Opportunity Act meshed with the country's increased interest in defining the role of youth in US society and as representatives of US democracy. The rise of youth activists in Los Angeles can be traced back several decades and represents the unique experiences of Black and Brown Angelenos who came of age after World War II. Young people challenged the authority of government officials, parents, and community workers, who sought to impose respectability politics onto youth movements. However, young activists established programs that had a long-term impact on their communities, and the United States more broadly. Their legacy remains noteworthy in US society and culture today. However, young people have tended to serve as scapegoats in claims that Black-Brown relations are primarily defined by conflict. The War on Poverty became a way for white officials and an older guard of Brown and Black activists to project claims that violent conflict lay at the center of Mexican American and African American relations.

Cultivating a Black-Brown Paradigm

As youth organizations drew inspiration from one another, an older generation of activists increasingly characterized the relationship between young Black and Brown Angelenos as contentious. For example, in March 1966, Ralph Poblano of the Economic and Youth Opportunities Agency of Los Angeles appealed to the local County Human Relations Commission for government support to curb tensions between African Americans and Mexican Americans. Created in the aftermath of the Zoot Suit Riots of 1943, local officials founded the County Human Relations Commission to mediate and improve the relationships between racial groups in Los Angeles.[53] Poblano proposed a series of measures the commission could put into place, stating, "It would be an extremely serious and dreaded occurrence if a flareup started between the Mexican-American and Negro groups, which I am sorry to say would undoubtedly dwarf the Watts Riots." Poblano's recommendations included the development of a "special unit" within the County Human Relations Commission to address Black-Brown relations, a leadership summit, and an official declaration "that a potentially hostile atmosphere exists."[54] While some attendees blamed the "power structure" and the press for creating a racial divide between the city's two largest communities of color, J. Robert López of the Mexican American Political Association argued that the War on Poverty "had done little in the field of inter-minority relations."[55] The County Human Relations Commission concluded by calling for the development of a unity council designed to bring African Americans and Mexican Americans together to address issues that affected both communities.

The March 1966 meeting with the Los Angeles County Human Relations Commission exemplifies the place of the War on Poverty in shaping local debates about Black-Brown relations and how this particular configuration of US race relations entered national visibility during the 1960s. López's assertation that the War on Poverty did not offer much support in building relationships between communities of color demonstrates how federal intervention in Los Angeles after the Watts Rebellion amplified racial differences and neighborhood boundaries. War on Poverty funding required grant proposals to describe how programs supported specific areas and demographics within Los Angeles. Because hypersegregation increasingly separated Mexican Americans and African Americans by the 1960s, antipoverty programs typically served a specific race and space. López's statement highlights the place of the War on Poverty in influencing debates about race in post–civil rights Los Angeles and the need to consider how to define

Black-Brown relations within this new phase of US society shaped by residential segregation.

The War on Poverty did indeed result in conflicts around equal funding and representation. However, tensions that appeared in the news and other reports often included an older guard of local activists and community organizers. For instance, a youth program known as Teen Post gained attention when an older generation of African American and Mexican American activists struggled over how to implement resources for both groups. In describing relationships that Young Chicanos for Community Action developed with Teen Post, Vickie Castro identified these particular antipoverty programs as "youth centers" and "places for young teenagers to hang out, and they were all over the city."[56] Some community members complained that Teen Post locations tended to become monoracial even among outposts in racially mixed locations. In a statement by Lupe Anguiano, a Teen Post coordinator for East Los Angeles, she argued that one main factor in preventing Black-Brown cooperation in Teen Post derived from the lack of Mexican American representation at the administrative level. The desire for greater Mexican American inclusion in decision-making and administration of local antipoverty programs continued to haunt Black-Brown relations.[57] However, conflicts among Teen Post staff, in what appeared to be a workplace struggle around equitable employment and representation, was framed as a hindrance to overall collaboration between African Americans and Mexican Americans. Despite the ways in which organizations like the Brown Berets grew from local youth groups inclusive of Black teenagers, squabbles over leadership roles within antipoverty programs increasingly defined how the broader public viewed Black-Brown relations overall.

The national press even began paying closer attention to debates about the status of Black-Brown relations in Los Angeles. Allegations of a potential race riot between Mexican Americans and African Americans caught the attention of media outlets. The *New York Times*, for example, published an article arguing that federal funding for African Americans in Los Angeles following the Watts Rebellion led to resentment among Mexican Americans. "Mexican-Americans believe their problems have been completely shunted aside as a result of the Watts riots," the article claimed. The story went on to describe Mexican American leaders who decided to call a "Quiet Riot," where they held a conference to discuss ways to prevent violence with Black residents. Like the struggle around Teen Post, claims that young Black and Brown people needed additional programs to prevent them from fighting one another emerged from an older generation of activists and community members. In addition, the use of labels like "Quiet Riot" reinforced respectability politics by further undermining the work of youth activists, who tended to engage in more confrontational demonstrations that highlighted the urgency of their calls for racial and economic justice. At the core of arguments about a looming race riot lay a desire to control a generation of young people who sought to create their own approaches to fighting race and class inequality.[58]

Local-level activists responded to press hysteria by using the War on Poverty to create programs with Black-Brown relations as one of the primary goals. For instance, in March 1966, board members from an antipoverty program known as Joint Ventures held a press conference to address rising concerns and rumors about Black-Brown hostility. Board members who spoke at the press conference included Mexican Americans Miguel Montes and Louis Garcia, along with Dorothy Washington as the African American representative. Conference speakers argued that their work at Joint Ventures represented a positive example of collaboration between Mexican Americans and African Americans that went unnoticed and underreported. Montes pointed to the press, arguing that news sources heightened hysteria about Black-Brown violence. By highlighting the work of Joint Ventures, an antipoverty agency that included both groups, the press conference challenged media portrayals depicting African American and Mexican American relations as volatile. The media's role in projecting an image of Black-Brown relations in Los Angeles as hostile is telling given that white supremacist racial terror that African Americans and Mexican Americans experienced for roughly a century went underreported.[59] Claims that local tensions might lead to a Black and Brown race war seemed more in line with rhetoric used to justify discriminatory juvenile justice laws that characterized African American and Mexican American youth as inherently violent.[60]

The US federal government joined the conversation about Black-Brown conflict. In 1966, Office of Economic Opportunity field reports identified Black-Brown violence in Los Angeles as a major concern after an incident where a Mexican American person shot an African American individual in Watts, exacerbating claims that the shooting reflected an increase in tensions between these two groups rather than describing this as a single incident. Local antipoverty workers argued that media sources magnified this incident, and that irresponsible reporting might actually lead to serious racial violence if the frenzy about conflict continued.[61] Some OEO-funded programs underwent a transition to "improve" the relationship between African Americans and Mexican Americans. One such program known as "Developing Community Relations Through Outdoor Science and Conservation" sought to "combat racial conflicts through outdoor education."⁶² The program's target groups included children from kindergarten through tenth grade and instructed youth in outdoor education on and off their school campuses. Both parents and community organizations were encouraged to actively engage with the program.

Teen Post also developed programming designed to draw parallels between African Americans and Mexican Americans. In 1969, Teen Post proposed a summer program that included a workshop focused on identity and pride for both Mexican American and Black youth. The workshop sought to emphasize "the role of the black and brown individual in the past, present and future community," the proposal stated. Program creators also wrote, "Some emphasis will be placed on the differences in goals and history of the two communities, and on the basis for unity."⁶³ Teen Post's workshop is an example of how antipoverty programs increasingly drew inspiration from youth activist movements. The desire to create a workshop focused on building racial pride and community understanding resembled organizational platforms from the Organization US, the Brown Berets, and the Black Panther Party for Self-Defense. Still, Teen Post identity programs reflected how much the War on Poverty became engulfed in Black-Brown relations and even helped to expand dialogue about the relationship between these two groups.

California officials provided mixed messaging about relationships between African American and Mexican American youth. In a state government memorandum penned in 1968, officials characterized the East Los Angeles "Blowouts" as a "concentrated effort to unify Black Power and Brown Power." While the memorandum identified Brown Berets as the central organizing force behind this vital campaign that advanced the Chicano movement, the state government's memo also characterized Tommy Jacquette as a "behind the scenes instigator" of this regionwide student walkout from East Los Angeles high schools in March 1968.⁶⁴ The memo sought to reveal details they claimed informants and investigators discovered about militant organizations in Los Angeles and to argue that the War on Poverty helped fund social justice campaigns. As this memo demonstrates, officials attempted to curtail youth resistance movements, especially organizations that successfully received antipoverty funding. While conflicts between activists were an inevitable occurrence that took place in most movements, claims that an African American and Mexican American race riot loomed seemed more like an effort to undermine left-leaning youth.

Debating Black-Brown Relations

While the nation focused its attention on Black-white relations in the US South for many decades, Black-Brown relations emerged as a visible and debatable paradigm during the 1960s. The War on Poverty played a central role in projecting this relationship on the nation. However, the United States tended to focus on individual and localized conflicts even though African American and Mexican American movements gained influence from one another. Since the Second World War, Brown and Black youth faced increasing criticism in US society, culture, and politics. In the 1960s, youth once again exerted control over their own lives through activism, resistance, and identity politics. They seized opportunities made available through the War on Poverty to support their community work and in doing so, created long-lasting legacies through their post–civil rights activism. The nation responded by using two decades of rhetoric about unruly Black and Brown youth to characterize young activists as a danger to themselves, and therefore, in need of further control. The legacy of militant activism in Los Angeles includes community institutions, a framework for resistance, and even ethnic studies. One aspect of this legacy that has gone unnoticed is how questions about the nature of Black-Brown relations increased during the second half of the 1960s.

CHAPTER FOUR

Black and Brown at the White House

> We in the Mexican American organizations feel that the fight of Negro Americans for true equality in every sphere of life in our community is our fight as well and every victory and/or defeat that Negro Americans obtain or suffer is ours as well.
> —Letter from Bert Corona, MAPA Director of Alameda County, to Donald McCullom of NAACP-Oakland, 1963

On July 2, 1964, President Lyndon Johnson signed the Civil Rights Act during a televised ceremony at the White House. After a brief address, Johnson signed his civil rights bill into law. Before settling into his chair to sign the bill and gift pens to supporters standing around him, including Rev. Dr. Martin Luther King Jr., Johnson firmly stated the bill's central goals. "Those who are equal before God shall now also be equal in the polling booths, in the classrooms, in the factories, and in hotels, restaurants, movie theaters, and other places that provide service to the public," he stated.[1] Johnson's address confirmed that at the 1964 Civil Rights Act's core lay an effort to outlaw racial segregation in public accommodations, schools, and employment. The civil rights bill synthesized a diversity of struggles for equality that took place in cities and towns throughout the United States down to legal segregation. However, the Watts Rebellion and the growth of youth activist movements reflected the varied and diverse issues that came to shape social justice struggles, especially calls for federal funding. As the Black Freedom and Chicano movements intersected locally and nationally by the mid-1960s, President Johnson's administration promoted a narrow vision for equality they believed might placate middle-class, moderate Black movement leaders.

The Civil Rights Act of 1964 prompted questions about inclusion that brought Mexican Americans and African Americans into closer proximity at the national level, starting with Johnson's presidency. When President Lyndon Johnson announced plans to host a civil rights conference for African Americans to examine the effectiveness of federal protections after signing the 1964 act, Mexican Americans seized this opportunity to call for a meeting to discuss their grievances. President Johnson responded to Mexican Americans by establishing the Inter-Agency Cabinet Committee on Mexican

American Affairs led by Vicente Ximenes of the Equal Employment Opportunity Commission (EEOC). Debates surrounding Johnson's proposed civil rights conference for African Americans, called To Fulfill These Rights, brought further attention to Black-Brown relations during the post–civil rights decades. In the months leading up to the conference, protests by Mexican Americans and Black grassroots activists who also faced exclusion created a moment of possibility to engage in a more expansive assessment of civil rights compared to Johnson's narrow approach. Federal officials failed to create a mutual space for Brown and Black dialogue and instead settled on planning two separate meetings. Just as the funding structure for the War on Poverty reinforced residential segregation, even when doing so did not neatly fit the demographic makeup of Los Angeles, To Fulfill These Rights became another instance where federal officials imposed their narrow understanding of race in the United States onto Black-Brown relations.

Lyndon Johnson and Race in the US West

Lyndon Johnson's professional background and presidency exemplify why he is essential to the history of Black-Brown relations and how the relationship between these groups has developed since the mid-1960s. As a Texas politician, Johnson had a rich history with African Americans and Mexican Americans that ultimately influenced his presidential politics. Born in Stonewall, Texas, on August 27, 1908, Johnson watched his father and grandfather participate in Texas state politics.[2] Growing up in the world of southern politics undoubtedly exposed a young Lyndon Johnson to debates about Jim Crow laws that segregated African Americans and Mexican Americans from their Anglo counterparts throughout the Southwest. Johnson became even more acquainted with the impact of Jim Crow on Mexican Americans during his early career as a teacher and principal. While attending Texas State Teachers College located in San Marcos, Johnson accepted a teaching position at Welhausen Elementary School located in the small town of Cotulla, Texas.[3] Johnson regularly highlighted his time in Cotulla as motivation for his presidential policies on poverty, inequality, and education. Located just sixty miles from the US-Mexico border, Cotulla contained a majority Mexican and Mexican American population.[4] In her comprehensive examination of Johnson's relationship with Mexican Americans, historian Julie Pycior argues that Cotulla helped Johnson better understand the importance of government intervention around issues of race and class inequality in the United States.[5]

The New Deal catapulted Johnson into state politics and allowed him to build further relationships with African Americans and Mexican Americans in Texas. From 1935 to 1937, Johnson directed the National Youth Authority (NYA) for Texas. Approved by President Franklin Delano Roosevelt on June 26, 1935, under Executive Order 7086, the NYA provided resources to advance youth employment. A twenty-seven-year-old Lyndon Johnson became the United States' youngest NYA state director, further demonstrating the Great Depression and New Deal's impact on young people across the United States.[6] The NYA in Johnson's early political career increased his contact with African Americans and Mexican Americans in Texas, which went against the state's southern culture.[7] Scholar Mitchell Lerner cites Johnson's leadership in NYA as "the initial civil rights policies of the future president" because Johnson's approach to NYA offers insight into why he later expanded domestic welfare state programs. For instance, during Johnson's tenure as NYA director, he established a separate board for African American appointees to oversee NYA programs for Black youth. Organized in 1935, Johnson's African American Advisory Board helped high school and college students find employment by partnering with local community institutions and implementing school programs. Texas's African American Advisory Board reflects an early willingness on the part of Johnson to seek out advisors on issues about Black Americans, and Johnson continued this tradition with civil rights advisors during his presidency.[8]

Johnson used his time as NYA director to establish his political career. After serving with Texas's NYA for two years, Johnson campaigned for the state's Tenth District congressional seat in 1937 and won. Johnson's congressional campaign centered on claims that he would fight for more federal funding in Texas if elected. His campaign also differed from that of most white democratic political candidates in the US South because Johnson's supporters included Mexican Americans, African Americans, and working-class white constituents. As a result, Johnson's congressional career reflected an ambiguous stance on civil rights. For instance, he called upon Congress to allot some $500,000 to build a housing project in Austin, Texas, in a neighborhood primarily occupied by African Americans and Mexican Americans, while also voting against anti–poll tax, anti-lynching, and equal employment legislation. This complicated record on racial inequality positioned Johnson as a moderate among staunch conservatives in Texas. Still, Johnson continued to develop relationships with African American and Mexican American organizations, like the League of United Latin Americans Citizens (LULAC), throughout his early career in state politics. Fearful that civil rights might split the Democratic Party, Johnson slowly supported legislation to outlaw racial discrimination, including the Civil Rights Act of 1957, after his election to the Senate in 1948.[9] Passed as mass demonstrations took off across the US South, the 1957 act established a federal Commission on Civil Rights to investigate Fourteenth Amendment violations. With orders to "appraise the laws and policies of the Federal Government with respect to equal protection of laws under the constitution," the Commission on Civil Rights investigated claims of voting and civil rights infringement throughout the United States.[10]

Johnson's relationship and contribution to liberal democratic policies grew during his tenure as vice president under John F. Kennedy from 1961 to 1963. The US federal government's War on Poverty, which Johnson expanded when he assumed the presidency following Kennedy's untimely death, became a cornerstone of Johnson's era in national politics. As scholar Alice O'Connor describes in her analysis of "poverty knowledge" over the twentieth century, social science played a central role in popular and political debates about socioeconomic class in the United States and abroad. In fact, by 1965, the United States federal government invested roughly $3 million in academic and professional research about poverty. Influential studies by scholars and thinkers, including Oscar Lewis, Michael Harrington, Kenneth Clark, E. Franklin Frazier, and Daniel Patrick Moynihan shaped the intellectual foundations of national poverty debates during the 1960s.[11] Harrington's popular book *The Other America* profoundly impacted conversations about economic disparities in the post–World War II United States. Harrington argued that even though many people in the United States had achieved economic mobility, a significant sector of the population experienced widespread poverty, a fact that influenced President John F. Kennedy's decision to establish a federal program to fight poverty in Appalachia.[12] When Kennedy developed his antipoverty agenda in 1962, and like Johnson's later adaptation of the program, Kennedy set out to establish a set of reforms designed to attack the root causes of poverty by developing programs that promoted work ethic and individual improvement. His presidential antipoverty committee believed that creating a program centered on skill development and personal responsibility was more effective than providing monetary assistance. Such comparisons between monetary assistance and employment training reflected deep-rooted stereotypes that identified poor people as lazy. In addition, focusing solely on work ethic detracted from more significant political processes that sustained and increased poverty in the United States.[13] Kennedy's assassination in 1963 prevented his vision for the War on Poverty from reaching fruition.[14]

Johnson expanded upon Kennedy's liberal democratic vision for the United States after assuming the presidency in 1963. Johnson sought to renew Congress's spirit and confidence that as a new president, he would continue programs that began under Kennedy and expand them. Johnson's first presidential address to Congress called upon legislators to support policies envisioned by Kennedy as an opportunity to memorialize his legacy. According to Johnson's address:

> An assassin's bullet has thrust upon me the awesome burden of the Presidency. I am here today to say I need your help; I cannot bear this burden alone. I need the help of all Americans, and all America. This nation has experienced a profound shock, and in this critical moment, it is our duty, yours and mine, as the Government of the United States, to do away with uncertainty and doubt and delay, and to show that we are capable of decisive action; that from the brutal loss of our leader we will derive not weakness, but strength; that we can and will act and act now.[15]

Johnson's address to Congress made his devotion to Kennedy's efforts to pass civil rights legislation clear, asserting, "First, no memorial oration or eulogy could more eloquently honor President Kennedy's memory than the earliest possible passage of the civil rights bill for which he fought so long. We have talked long enough in this country about equal rights. We have talked for one hundred years or more. It is time now to write the next chapter, and to write it in the books of law." He went on to identify a comprehensive civil rights bill as an opportunity to strengthen the United States. "I urge you again, as I did in 1957 and again in 1960," he stated, "to enact a civil rights law so that we can move forward to eliminate from this Nation every trace of discrimination and oppression that is based upon race and color."[16] During his tenure as US president, Johnson passed a series of ambitious reforms, including the Civil Rights Act of 1964, the Voting Rights Act of 1965, and the Economic Opportunity Act (EOA) in 1964. In addition, Johnson-era politics saw passage of reforms for food stamps, K–12 education, urban development, Social Security, Medicare, and Medicaid.[17] As a collective, these policies comprised Johnson's Great Society reforms and helped expand the country's social safety net.

President Lyndon B. Johnson signed the Economic Opportunity Act on August 20, 1964, in the White House Rose Garden. LBJ Library photo by Cecil Stoughton, C661-4-WH64.

The EOA significantly impacted Black-Brown relations in places like Los Angeles. Before formally establishing the War on Poverty, Johnson officially announced the EOA in his 1964 State of the Union address by declaring "an unconditional war on poverty" as one vital cornerstone of his administration.[18] Johnson's address summed up how the War on Poverty and the Great Society might advance his goal to expand economic opportunity throughout the United States: "This budget, and this year's legislative programs are designed to help each and every American citizen fulfill his basic hopes—his hopes for a fair chance to make good; his hopes for fair play from the law; his hopes for a full-time job on full-time pay; his hopes for a decent home

Black and Brown at the White House   87

for his family in a decent community; his hopes for a good school for his children with good teachers; and his hopes for security when faced with sickness or unemployment or old age."[19] Johnson's State of the Union address identified several cabinet measures he thought might provide resources to support the country's most economically vulnerable people. He described employment training and educational programs, minimum wage reform, and improvements to health care. "Our aim is not only to relieve the symptom of poverty," Johnson declared, "but to cure it and, above all, to prevent it. No single legislation, however, is going to suffice." Johnson signed the EOA into law on August 20, 1964.[20]

Black-Brown Relations in the 1960s

African Americans and Mexican Americans played an essential role in Johnson's political career, especially during his 1964 bid for president, when both groups emerged as crucial voting blocs in presidential races. Organizations, including the Mexican American Political Association (MAPA) in California and the Political Association of Spanish-Speaking Organizations in Texas, actively registered Mexican Americans for the vote. "Viva Johnson" campaign groups, following the successful "Viva Kennedy" campaign, emerged throughout the Southwest to rally Mexican American voters behind Johnson. Republican candidate Barry Goldwater even organized an "Amigos de Goldwater" group to counter Johnson's appeal among Mexican Americans. To gain further support from African Americans, Johnson maintained Kennedy's promise to pass a civil rights bill and brought in a cohort of Black activists to consult on issues related to racial discrimination. That both Black and Mexican American constituents rallied behind Johnson is significant because his presidency helped bring their separate civil rights movements into further alignment at the national level.[21]

Still, Johnson and his administration struggled to create an inclusive community for African Americans and Mexican Americans at the White House. In addition, African Americans invited to consult with Johnson often represented an older guard of moderate and middle-class activists who did not represent the intersectional ways that African Americans and Mexican Americans experienced racial discrimination. President Johnson's June 1965 commencement speech at Howard University, where he announced an upcoming civil rights conference in Washington, DC, to assess the status of civil rights for African Americans, exemplified Johnson's tendency to see Black elites as movement leaders. Although Johnson directed his commencement speech at an audience already part of the African American elite or soon to be after graduation, Johnson still spoke about how the civil rights bill might materially impact communities of color. According to Johnson, "This is the next and the more profound stage of the battle for civil rights. We seek not just freedom but opportunity. We seek not just legal equity but human ability, not just equality as a right and a theory but equality as a fact and equality as a result."[22] Johnson understood that the War on Poverty remained one option to address economic challenges that continued to hinder a significant segment of society from fully taking advantage of recent civil rights legislation. While many African Americans showed great excitement about an opportunity to assess the Civil Rights Act's strengths and ways to make the law more effective, Mexican Americans increasingly asked why their communities were excluded from such a significant opportunity to expand the fight for civil rights at the federal level.

Several Mexican American activists from across the United States identified the Equal Employment Opportunity Commission as one institution created by the Civil Rights Act that might address economic justice in their communities. As representatives of the second-largest "minority group" in the United States, Mexican Americans argued that the federal government failed to make strides toward improving employment opportunities for their communities. They claimed that the EEOC's failure to employ more Mexican Americans reflected the US government's pattern of racial discrimination. Alfred Hernández, president of the League of United Latin American Citizens, stated, "Our employment problems are severe and complex, yet we have no one on the commission with any insight into them." Miguel Montes, president of the Latin American Civic Association in San Francisco, highlighted the lack of Mexican American employees at the EEOC as a reflection of discriminatory practices in a federal agency created to uphold equal employment opportunities.[23] While popular culture often characterized Mexican Americans as a "sleeping giant" on issues related to civil rights and politics, Johnson-era policies helped uncover decades of local-level advocacy work underway by Mexican Americans that entered into federal government debates after the 1964 Civil Rights Act.[24]

This was not the first time federal government officials failed to address equal opportunity in employment for Mexican Americans. Two decades earlier, Franklin Roosevelt approved the Fair Employment Practices Committee (FEPC) in 1941, which represented the US federal government's first attempt to put into place a national agency to enforce equal opportunity in the workplace for groups who experienced racial discrimination. Like the Civil

Rights Act of 1964, the FEPC emerged due to protests led by A. Philip Randolph of the Brotherhood of Sleeping Car Porters, who gained a reputation for his courage to criticize US presidents. Randolph argued that presidents who garnered African American support, such as Franklin Roosevelt and Lyndon Johnson, should show public support for civil rights. To protest discrimination in the defense industry during World War II, Randolph planned a march on Washington to urge Roosevelt to pass legislation that outlawed employment discrimination. Even though Roosevelt attempted to curtail Randolph's march by meeting with him, Roosevelt's refusal to pass legislation forced march planners to move forward with proposed protests. Just six days before the scheduled march, Roosevelt signed Executive Order 8802, a policy that called for an end to racial discrimination in the defense industry and established the FEPC to investigate cases of bias in hiring.[25]

Even though Executive Order 8802 outlawed discrimination in the war production industry based on race, color, national origin, and creed, many Mexican Americans argued that FEPC officials prioritized African Americans. When the FEPC held hearings in Los Angeles, for example, grievances from African Americans received the most attention. Mexican American representatives Manuel Ruiz Jr. and Dr. Victor Egas received six minutes each during the hearings to describe Mexican American experiences in the workplace. Both Ruiz and Egas recommended that the federal government establish a regional representative to consult with Mexican Americans on issues regarding fair employment. Even though Mexican Americans made up such a significant portion of California's population, they still faced neglect during FEPC meetings in Los Angeles. This trend continued with the onset of the Equal Employment Opportunity Commission. In time, however, the rise of a sustained Mexican American civil rights movement led to more visible and vocal protests against neglect from federal agencies. For instance, some fifty Mexican Americans participated in an EEOC walkout in March 1966 to advocate for a Mexican American appointee to the national EEOC board of commissioners and to protest their exclusion from To Fulfill These Rights. Several demonstrators held an additional meeting known as the Mexican-American Unity Conference in Los Angeles on April 28–29, 1966, to discuss strategies for garnering greater attention from federal government officials. Some of the middle-class moderate Mexican American activists in attendance included Albert Peña Jr. of the Political Association of Spanish-Speaking Organizations, Eduardo Quevedo of MAPA, Graciela Olivares of the Citizens' Crusade Against Poverty, and Daniel Fernandez of the Council on Mexican-American Affairs in Los Angeles. Mexican American activists gathered together to develop a plan of action to request a meeting with Johnson about inclusion in the upcoming To Fulfill These Rights conference. The unity conference demonstrates how much To Fulfill These Rights galvanized Mexican Americans and how their activism grew in response to Johnson's civil rights–era policy.[26]

In early April 1966, To Fulfill These Rights conference planners crafted a response to inquiries about Mexican American inclusion in the meeting. James Booker, director of information for the conference, distributed a memo with possible answers regarding the inclusion of "other minorities." Booker encouraged conference staff to remind those who requested to include other groups that Johnson's initial proposal for To Fulfill These Rights specifically defined African Americans as the target group. Still, he noted that "decisions and actions will have a decided effect on all minorities in this country."[27] When officials and activists contacted conference planners, special counsel Berl Bernhard echoed Booker's suggested comments. James Farmer and George Wiley from the Congress of Racial Equality also entered conversations about including "a broader spectrum of minority groups" in To Fulfill These Rights. They called for the conference to focus its attention on African Americans even though "the Negro is not alone in facing discrimination and poverty." Farmer and Wiley asserted that Black Americans "faced oppression the longest and [to] the greatest degree," making To Fulfill These Rights essential to their struggle for equality. As Farmer and Wiley's response indicated, African Americans turned to their history of racial exclusion to argue that their civil rights struggles should be prioritized at the upcoming conference. Since Farmer had served as one of Johnson's civil rights advisors, he may have understood To Fulfill These Rights as a vital extension of conversations he and other African American civil rights activists took part in at the White House.[28]

Mexican American activism around To Fulfill These Rights is not simply a reflection of intergroup tension with African Americans. Middle-class Mexican American activists criticized the conference because of their total exclusion, and they advocated for expanding the conference's racial parameters. For example, when delegates at the Mexican American Unity Conference developed a strategy to lead a demonstration during To Fulfill These Rights, they ultimately abandoned this idea out of concern that protests might appear "anti-Negro." Instead, Unity Conference leaders surmised that any opportunity to gain inclusion in To Fulfill These Rights had passed and they settled instead for drafting a letter to Johnson to request a meeting. Although Mexican Americans began a conversation about To Fulfill These Rights that garnered a response from some African Americans, Mexican Americans continued to express their frustrations about Johnson's decision to center one specific group among his supporters. Still, by speaking out against their exclusion from the conference, Mexican Americans brought further attention to their relationship with African Americans. Actions by Mexican American activists regarding the To Fulfill These Rights conference offer another example of how Mexican American advocates attempted to expand the dialogue about race beyond the Black-white paradigm in how Johnson's administration approached civil rights and social justice.

To Fulfill These Rights

Despite Mexican American activists' call for inclusion, To Fulfill These Rights proceeded as planned. Conference organizers developed an agenda designed to create a forum for civil rights leaders, critics, and politicians to discuss the status of recent federal legislation. Many Black leaders hoped To Fulfill These Rights would provide a foundation for leaders to propose recommendations to make civil rights legislation more effective. Planning sessions focused specifically on examining the barriers to equal opportunity for African Americans that remained in 1965. A memo detailing a November 1965 planning session outlined the conference's purpose: "The Conference is a logical continuation of the Administration's complete identification with the civil rights movement and its goals of full equality under law for all citizens."[29] The conference's overall goals reflected influences from African American civil rights movements and shaped the agenda for To Fulfill These Rights meaningfully. What made this conference even more unique was its emphasis on exploring the shortcomings of federal legislation that targeted the country's most economically vulnerable communities and brainstorming solutions to make policy more effective.

President Johnson assembled a team of highly respected civil rights leaders to plan and oversee To Fulfill These Rights, including Dorothy Height of the National Council of Negro Women, Martin Luther King Jr. from the Southern Christian Leadership Conference, Roy Wilkins of the National Association for the Advancement of Colored People, Whitney Young of the National Urban League, and Floyd McKissick of the Congress of Racial Equality. Council members met during March and April 1966 to complete conference planning.[30] The backgrounds of President Johnson's African American advisors are essential for understanding specific regional and political perspectives that contributed to the conference. For example, long-time labor

Black civil rights leaders meet with President Johnson at the White House, April 5, 1968. *Standing from left to right*: Roy Wilkins, Secretary Robert Weaver, unknown, Vice President Hubert Humphrey, Judge Leon Higginbotham, Senator Clarence Mitchell III, Dorothy Height, Mayor Walter Washington, Warren Christopher, Whitney Young, unknown, Bayard Rustin, Rev. Leon Sullivan, unknown, unknown, and unknown. Seated from L–R: Justice Thurgood Marshall, President Lyndon B. Johnson, and Clarence Mitchell Jr. LBJ Library photo by Yoichi Okamoto, A6016-19.

activist A. Philip Randolph served as honorary chairman for To Fulfill These Rights. Randolph held leadership roles in the Brotherhood of Sleeping Car Porters and the American Federation of Labor-Congress of Industrial Organizations (AFL-CIO). Randolph became its only African American representative when the AFL and CIO merged to form one unified organization.[31] That White House staff selected moderate Black activists to lead conference planning demonstrates further the federal government's tendency to appease an older guard of northern and southern leaders who may not have experienced the unique aspects of racial discrimination in places like California.[32]

Conference planners settled on topics that received careful attention, and the group decided on five central focus areas. These included "jobs and economics and welfare," while "education and housing" were the final two.[33] Since planning committee members primarily included middle-class and moderate African American activists, one crucial point of debate that emerged throughout planning sessions was how best to include the voices of people experiencing poverty. At a meeting held in March 1966, Bayard Rustin, who attended on behalf of A. Philip Randolph, asked how to include poor African Americans in planning meetings for To Fulfill These Rights. At the time, Rustin served as cochairman for the A. Philip Randolph Institute and spoke on behalf of To Fulfill These Rights' honorary chairman. As a young organizer in 1941, Rustin worked to recruit youth to join Randolph's march on Washington and showed great concern when Randolph decided to call off his unprecedented march. However, both men worked together again when they organized the March on Washington in 1963 and brought their history of collaboration into To Fulfill These Rights.[34] At the March 5 meeting, Rustin asked planners to consider inviting poor representatives to participate in conference organizing, arguing that poor people deserved a voice in the conference planning process. Rustin echoed sentiments from the federal government's War on Poverty, which stipulated that poor people best understood their daily experiences better than professionals and politicians. However, the conference fell short of upholding this central tenet of antipoverty policy. Roy Wilkins responded to Rustin, asserting that poor representatives might lead to more complaints rather than developing concrete solutions during planning sessions. Whitney Young suggested consulting the Office of Economic Opportunity, stating that its staff might be a great resource for advice about how best to include the perspective of poor African Americans in To Fulfill These Rights. Some committee members even suggested that representatives from poor Black communities might find a subsequent conference more effective.[35]

A. Philip Randolph shared Rustin's sentiments. At the first planning session on November 17, 1966, Randolph used the Watts Uprising to call upon the US federal government to establish a "Freedom Budget." He stated that the War on Poverty offered an opportunity to broaden the civil rights movement to ensure that low-economic Black urbanites also experienced the fruits of the Black Freedom movement. Allocating a federal "Freedom Budget," Randolph argued, might serve as an essential tool toward abolishing urban poverty. "A nationwide plan for the abolition of the ghetto jungles in every city, even at the cost of a hundred billion dollars," Randolph stated, would be "a cost which may be vastly less than chance of another unhappy Watts of Los Angeles, especially as a legacy of racial hate. Nothing less than such a 'Freedom Budget' will suffice."[36] Randolph's early calls to center poor urban residents demonstrated the growing awareness of class limitations inherent in civil rights legislation and how class needed to serve a vital role in the country's next stage in the struggle for civil rights.

Class differences shaped debates beyond conference planning sessions. The failure to include representatives of the poor and grassroots activists meant To Fulfill These Rights did not receive unanimous support. Grassroots activists and their supporters rightly argued that planning sessions and conference invitations favored moderate organizations. In April 1966, grassroots activists interviewed with *Jet Magazine*, where they described plans to lead a "Black March on Washington" in response to the failure to recognize militant and "ghetto" representatives. March planners included Fannie Lou Hamer, Jesse Gray, and Ernest Thomas. Their proposed march sought to rally 1,000 participants to protest To Fulfill These Rights and to dissuade some 2,000 conferees from attending sessions.[37] Some activists even declined their invitation to participate in the To Fulfill These Rights meeting.[38] The exclusion of grassroots activists from conference planning sessions may have reflected Johnson's tendency to deemphasize their perspectives on issues of racial inequality and his interest in ending mass demonstrations. Conference protestor Fannie Lou Hamer experienced Johnson's attempt to repress grassroots activists during her testimony for the Democratic National Convention on behalf of the Mississippi Freedom Democratic Party in 1964 when Johnson interrupted Hamer's televised testimony for the Democratic Credentials Committee to give an alleged emergency speech to the nation. Resistance from African American grassroots activists during preparations for To Fulfill These Rights demonstrates President Johnson's tendency to welcome moderate and middle-class activists into discussions about civil rights while suppressing the perspective of organizers who placed economic justice at the core of their activism.[39]

Amid criticism from grassroots activists and Mexican Americans, To Fulfill These Rights took place June 1–2, 1966, in Washington, DC, with roughly 2,500 participants in attendance. Even though the conference brought together an old guard of moderate African American activists, in many ways, they attempted to set an agenda for a "new phase" in movements for equal rights. One of the conference's central themes included developing an agenda to address the unique experiences of urban residents, a topic representative of the belief that civil rights legislation fell short in US cities.[40] Conference session summaries described conversations that took place during the two-day meeting. Legislation such as the Civil Rights Act of 1964 and the Economic Opportunity Act occupied many discussions. For instance, in a session on employment and economics, many participants argued in favor of skill training and public works programs to improve the economic plight of African Americans. Through these programs, federal funding could help provide jobs in local and state agencies for African Americans. The group also argued that government funding could offer grants to private companies to support hiring African Americans.[41] Conference discussions linked Watts to the need for greater access to employment opportunities for youth. The development of more youth programs might, conference participants argued, "reduce the dangerously high rate of joblessness among Negro youth—both male and female—and . . . bring them into the mainstream of the nation's economic life." Furthermore, they claimed that such programs targeted efforts to "reduce the social tensions and symptoms of disorganization evidenced in such areas as Watts."[42] Sessions that referenced Watts in the final conference recommendations reveal the uprising's impact on making African Americans in Los Angeles, and urban residents in general, more visible in national civil rights and social justice discussions.

Some participants asked why sessions focused specifically on African Americans rather than organizing a conversation about how patterns of racial discrimination in the economy affected "minorities" in general. Conferees passed resolutions for greater support and inclusion of other groups and called for interracial collaboration. "It is resolved," one such resolution noted, "that the emphasis in this conference has been to transform opportunity into achievement for Negro Americans but we also proclaim that we seek this end and goal for all disadvantaged minorities, whatever their ethnic groups or national origin, and invite them to make common cause with us 'to fulfill these rights.'" Conferees went on to state, "We express our concern over setting the limits of this conference to include only Negro Americans. We stress our commitment and promise all minority citizens of this nation to pledge ourselves to strike down discrimination and prejudice against all men." The To Fulfill These Rights conference took place during a period when other groups, especially Mexican Americans, articulated national civil rights agendas, and this resolution reveals an effort on the part of African Americans to place their struggle into context with other racially marginalized groups. The final resolution, which called for expanding the national civil rights agenda, reflected a central tenet of the Mexican American civil rights movement. "We urge the administration to broaden its focus and to reaffirm its concern for the problems of all our citizens," the resolution stated.[43]

To Fulfill These Rights, especially the final resolutions, revealed that an African American–centered conversation facilitated by an older guard of Black men would no longer suffice. Mexican American protests surrounding To Fulfill These Rights were rooted in a desire to expand how the US federal government understood civil rights. While Mexican American–African American relations during the 1960s included challenges and difficulties, To Fulfill These Rights uncovers the broader project of Black-Brown relations, which sought to expand the national government's approach to civil rights. African Americans and Mexican Americans continued to consider how federal protections might focus attention on both groups as the 1960s progressed. When the Inter-Agency Cabinet Committee on Mexican American Affairs hearings took place in 1967, organizers invited prominent African American leaders such as Augustus Hawkins, Dorothy Height, Roy Wilkins, and Whitney Young. Whether they attended is unclear, but Mexican Americans still allotted time at the hearings to examine their relationship with African Americans.[44]

The Inter-Agency Cabinet Committee on Mexican American Affairs

In response to growing frustration from Mexican Americans, Johnson's administration began organizing a civil rights conference explicitly focused on Latinas/os. In May 1966, Joseph Califano, special assistant to President Johnson, invited representatives from "Spanish-speaking" communities to a White House dinner meeting. Well-known activists, including Bert Corona (Los Angeles) of MAPA, Augustine Flores (Riverside, California) of the American GI Forum, and Alfred Hernández (Houston, Texas) of LULAC, received invitations to "discuss and obtain your views on the problems of the Mexican-American and the other Spanish-speaking peoples in our country."[45] The meeting marked the early planning stages for a White House conference with Mexican Americans as the target group. By August 1966, White House officials developed plans for a conference to bring Mexican Americans, Puerto Ricans, and federal officials together. The conference, initially called Equality of Opportunity, a Conference on the Civil Rights of the Spanish Surname Communities, was tentatively scheduled for December 1966 in Austin, Texas. Officials listed employment as the primary focus of early conference planning meetings organized by the Department of Labor. Other topics included the Bracero Program (a twenty-year-long contract labor system between the United States and Mexico terminated by Congress in 1964), government funding, and immigration policy.[46]

Bert Corona contributed to conference discussions from the beginning. An El Paso, Texas, transplant, Corona moved to Los Angeles in 1936 to play basketball at the University of Southern California. Corona shaped and contributed to a wide array of social justice issues, including labor, undocumented workers, civil rights, politics, "Viva Kennedy," and "Viva Johnson." The *Los Angeles Times* characterized Corona as the "urban counterpart to César Chávez" because of Corona's work with Mexican Americans in California cities and his role in founding MAPA in 1959.[47] Corona offered his reflections on the initial meeting with Johnson to discuss a Mexican American civil rights conference in an interview that followed the cabinet committee hearings on Mexican American Affairs two years later. Corona argued that White House officials gave Mexican American leaders the impression that they would play a crucial role in planning a conference that explored the status of Mexican Americans in the United States. In reflecting on the cabinet committee hearings, Corona stated, "Instead all we got was this phony conference."[48] Corona's comments reflected the tenuous history behind bringing a White House conference for Mexican Americans to fruition.

Conference planning took on various guises throughout the fall of 1966 as President Johnson's special assistant Joseph Califano and David North of the Department of Labor began laying the blueprint for a convention. The emphasis on "Spanish-speaking" communities meant that government officials initially planned to invite Mexican Americans and Puerto Ricans. Conference planning included four specific areas, with sessions dedicated to education, employment, farm labor, and immigration. The White House reserved these four sessions for Mexican Americans, whom federal officials often identified as a rural population. Officials designated a fifth session on "urban problems" for Puerto Ricans. Some Mexican American leaders from California who received invitations included Dr. Ernesto Galarza, a dentist, and activist Miguel Montes, Audrey Kaslow of the Los Angeles County Probation Department, Bert Corona of MAPA, and Eduardo Quevedo of War on Poverty Incorporated. Other well-known Mexican American invitees included Corky Gonzales of the Crusade for Justice in Denver and César Chávez of the United Farm Workers in California.[49]

Planning for the conference moved slowly, and Mexican American activists became frustrated with the federal government's pace. In September 1966, Vice President Hubert Humphrey wrote Califano asking for an update on the conference for Mexican Americans, noting that concerned constituents eagerly awaited more concrete details from Johnson's administration to finalize a convention. Humphrey said, "As you know, there is considerable unrest among the Spanish-speaking Americans relating to the Administration's failure to give them enough attention." He urged Califano to complete plans for the conference, especially with elections fast approach-

President Lyndon Johnson met with several leaders from Mexican American organizations on May 26, 1966. Attendees included Alfred J. Hernández, Augustine Flores, Dr. Hector Garcia, Bert Corona, Roy Elizondo, and Robert Orneles. LBJ Library photo by Yoichi Okamoto, A2518-25

ing. Because Mexican Americans supported Johnson's political career, Humphrey feared the detrimental impact Johnson's slow pace with conference planning might have on this critical voting bloc.[50]

A civil rights conference for Mexican Americans still failed to materialize by the fall of 1967. The California delegation, which included Mexican Americans who attended conference planning sessions, demanded answers. Delegates Ralph Guzmán, Audrey Kaslow, Miguel Montes, Lupe Anguiano, Bert Corona, and Eduardo Quevedo sent a telegram to Johnson with their list of demands. Their telegram called for a conference organized and attended by Mexican Americans, stating that "the conference focus and participation be restricted to the Mexican-American." The telegram went on to state, "And [with] the problems which this ethnic group of six million now faces in our society, that such conference be named The White House Conference on the Problems of the Mexican American." They also called for regular updates, asserting "that those who participated in the planning sessions be informed on the progress if any, of the conference planning," adding, "we urgently await your reply."[51] In contrast to original plans for the conference, Mexican Americans called for sessions dedicated to their unique history and

Black and Brown at the White House 99

experiences, reflecting the growing significance of identity politics in their approach to civil rights. While California's delegation did not offer an explanation about why they no longer wanted to share a conference with Puerto Ricans, their call for a Mexican American–specific conference may have stemmed from some old guard members who still emphasized claims of whiteness as a civil rights strategy. In addition, because African Americans experienced a dedicated conference, Mexican Americans may have resisted any requests for a multigroup gathering.

Mexican American leaders also reached out to congressman George E. Brown Jr. to request answers regarding the status of their conference. Brown represented Los Angeles's Forty-Second Congressional District, which included San Bernardino and portions of East Los Angeles. He also joined congressman Augustus Hawkins in developing the Community War on Poverty Committee to pressure local government officials to include poor African American and Mexican American residents in administering local antipoverty programs in 1964. In a January 1967 letter to President Johnson, Congressman Brown stated that he received numerous inquiries from Mexican American leaders in California asking him to support their demands for further information about the proposed White House Conference. As a congressman for a region of Los Angeles that included a significant contingent of Mexican Americans, Brown backed the conference, stating, "I, being the representative voice of the Congressional District having the largest concentration of persons of Mexican descent in California, cannot stress too strongly the need, justification, and importance for having such a conference." He went on to assert, "I urge you to re-assure all parties concerned" and encouraged Johnson to finalize a date for the conference.[52] Brown's appeal to Johnson clearly showed that Mexican American activists placed pressure on local officials in their efforts to secure a civil rights conference.

Planning for a White House Conference on Mexican Americans gained greater clarity in June 1967, when Johnson established the Inter-Agency Cabinet Committee on Mexican American Affairs (I-AC). Johnson appointed Vicente Ximenes of the Equal Employment Opportunity Commission as I-AC chairman. His career in national politics began when John F. Kennedy selected Ximenes to serve as a program officer and economist for the US Agency for International Development in 1961. Ximenes then moved to Panama City, Panama, where he served as the agency's deputy director. In 1967, President Johnson selected Ximenes as the first Mexican American commissioner to the EEOC. That same year, Johnson appointed him to head the Inter-Agency Cabinet Committee on Mexican American Affairs.[53]

Federal officials saw mixed reactions to the Inter-Agency Cabinet Committee on Mexican American Affairs. The White House recorded reactions from Mexican American leaders and shared them in an internal memo. "Dr. Hector Garcia, founder of the GI Forum, said he has been working in this field for twenty years and this is certainly the best thing that has happened," White House correspondence revealed. The memo stated, "Louis Téllez, current president of the Forum, echoed Garcia's feelings." The memo cited judge Alfred J. Hernández of LULAC's Houston chapter as identifying I-AC as the "best news received; a great step forward and something that is needed and sure to be helpful." Bert Corona responded, "A great step in the right direction." The overall reaction of Mexican American activists whom Johnson consulted showed that they viewed the I-AC as a positive development in their fight for inclusion in national debates and policy considerations about racial inequality.[54]

The I-AC hearings finally offered an opportunity for a Mexican American civil rights conference. In addition, the I-AC provided Mexican Americans a forum to give testimony about their experiences, unlike FEPC hearings in 1941. The I-AC hearings took place October 26–28, 1967, in El Paso, Texas, and sessions focused on economic and social development, labor, education, welfare, housing, and the War on Poverty. Some fifty-one Mexican American representatives presented testimony at the hearings, including educator and activist Dr. Ernesto Galarza, Dr. Miguel Montes of the California State Board of Education, and Dr. Ralph Guzmán of the Department of Government at California State University, Los Angeles. Several presenters, including Guzmán and Montes, urged President Johnson to follow through with plans to organize a conference to address their unique and shared views on civil rights. The hearings finally allowed Mexican Americans to speak on behalf of their communities in the presence of federal officials.[55]

Some important themes emerged during I-AC hearings, especially conversations that acknowledged Mexican Americans' diverse experiences, such as the differences between rural and urban communities. I-AC sessions offered an opportunity to learn about the need for civil rights legislation that reached central city neighborhoods. Augustine Flores, former national chairman of the American GI Forum, presented at a session on housing chaired by the only African American cabinet secretary, Robert C. Weaver of the Department of Housing and Urban Development. Flores discussed programs, such as those administered by Housing and Urban Development, to argue that officials failed to address the housing needs of Mexican Americans. He described in detail urban renewal projects, which Flores characterized as "the most objectionable of all Federal Housing Programs to the Mexican American." Flores argued that municipal governments often made decisions about urban renewal projects without community input and tended to cause resident displacement. Some of the policy recommendations Flores suggested included having "knowledgeable Mexican Americans" in decision-making positions regarding renewal projects, that residents be allowed to submit surveys about renewal proposals, and that any plans to restructure neighborhoods focus on improving the plight of residents in affected areas. Just as To Fulfill These Rights allowed African Americans to make recommendations to improve current policy, Flores used the I-AC hearings to propose ways to make legislation more effective in Mexican American communities.[56]

As expected, the War on Poverty entered discussions at the Inter-Agency Cabinet Committee Hearings. In one session, Daniel Lopez of the East Los Angeles Service Center offered insight into his experience working in antipoverty programs. He also shared recommendations for improving the War on Poverty at the federal level. Lopez stated that programs including Head Start, Job Corps, and Neighborhood Youth Corps saw great success in communities and advocated for sustained funding. He asserted that much of the poverty war to date emphasized African Americans' history of discrimination and that the War on Poverty programs offered an opportunity to improve the plight of Mexican Americans as well. Lopez recommended that Congress allocate the total amount of antipoverty funding proposed by President Johnson, allow the Office of Economic Opportunity to remain open, and offer antipoverty programs an opportunity for "experimentation and failure which is an important component of the learning process."[57] The War on Poverty emerged as an essential point of analysis throughout the Inter-Agency Cabinet Committee on Mexican American Affairs hearings and To Fulfill These Rights, demonstrating the centrality of the Economic Opportunity Act in Black and Brown activism during the 1960s. As Lopez's testimony argues, the War on Poverty offered a series of programs that positively impacted Mexican Americans and, if continued, might lead to larger-scale change.

Throughout the hearings, the trope of Mexican Americans as a forgotten and invisible population emerged when speakers described conditions that plagued their communities. In his discussion of Mexican Americans and employment, George Roybal, executive director of a federal employment program known as Operation SER, argued that the US federal government failed to provide support to Mexican Americans. Roybal lamented and posed critical questions: "Why has government failed so miserably with the Mexican

American, admittedly, the second largest minority group in the country, and certainly the largest minority group in the Southwest?" He went on to argue that the federal government's failure to prioritize their movement created tension among Mexican Americans. "Although it has been made clear that both socially and economically, Mexican Americans are worse off than non-whites as a group; and although it has been made clear that this nation's second largest minority group is largely misunderstood and ignored, it will remain a mystery to many," he asserted, "how this country has remained relatively unscathed by violence from elements within this group."[58] Roybal's critical testimony reflected frustration that had developed among Mexican Americans as a result of their neglect by federal policymakers. In addition, Roybal used the rhetorical strategy of describing Mexican Americans as the most oppressed racial group to stress the urgency of his demands. Unfortunately, these claims during the 1960s contributed to assumptions that conflict defined Black-Brown relations. He even invoked a critical rhetorical strategy among Mexican Americans during this time to suggest the possibility of an uprising if government officials did not take their demands seriously. "One can now observe, however, increasing signs of new and dangerous mood of desperation, cynicism, and extremism," Roybal stated. "Coalition of these addicted elements within the Mexican American community and the new, violent, far left is now being tried," he declared. Roybal went on to argue that "the future course of events in intergroup relations with respect to Mexican Americans, may well be affected, if not determined by what decisions are made here today—by what follow-up and follow-through is generated from the President's statement that the time has come for action, not words."[59] Roybal's testimony reflected how Mexican Americans became restless with Johnson's failed promises and called upon federal officials to consider I-AC recommendations seriously.

Just as intergroup relations emerged in conversations at To Fulfill These Rights, this topic also entered testimony at the Inter-Agency Cabinet Committee on Mexican American Affairs hearings. Carlos Truan's presentation on community action programs compared Mexican Americans to other groups. "In the past, the Indian, the Negro, the Filipino, the Puerto Rican, and all other peoples in a situation similar to that of the Mexican American have been the object of moral responsibility," Truan stated. "Not so [for] the Mexican American," he described. "He has been, and he continues to be, the most neglected, the least sponsored, the most orphaned minority group in the United States."[60] Like George Roybal, Truan reinforced claims that when compared to other racial groups, Mexican American civil rights received the least support and recognition. Leonel J. Castillo of the Neighborhood Centers Association in Houston, Texas, encouraged cross-racial collaboration at a session titled "Inter-Minority Relations." Castillo characterized the relationship between Mexican Americans and African Americans as "probably one of the least discussed problems of poverty in the Southwest."[61] He cited demographic shifts in US cities to highlight the need for African American and Mexican American collaboration. According to Castillo, white flight left Mexican Americans and Black Americans behind in central cities, making it even more important that both groups worked together. He stated that in addition to joining forces with African American civil rights groups, the Model Cities program offered an opportunity for Black and Brown movements to unite and take control over rebuilding central city neighborhoods. Castillo's and Truan's testimonies revealed the impact that federal civil rights and antipoverty legislation had on bringing the experiences of Mexican Americans and African Americans into conversation. Both presenters demonstrate the diverse ways Mexican Americans described their experiences vis-á-vis African Americans. The broader US society was more likely to react to Truan's comparative perspective than Castillo's call for collaboration.

Like To Fulfill These Rights, the I-AC hearings did not receive unanimous support from Mexican Americans. As the hearings began, a La Raza Unida Conference occurred at Sacred Heart Catholic Church in El Paso, Texas. Many college activists, including José Angel Gutiérrez of the Mexican American Youth Organization, attended the La Raza Unida conference and criticized older activists for participating in the hearings. A younger generation of Mexican Americans argued that protests and demands for equal rights as US citizens served as the most effective way to gain attention from policymakers. The La Raza Unida conference revealed the growth of grassroots movements among younger Mexican American activists who went on to bring the Chicano movement to fruition by the end of the decade.[62] Some long-time activists refused to support the hearings as well. Limited audience participation, a lack of economic class representation, and limited inclusion of youth made many critical of the hearings. The Mexican American Political Association's executive board voted overwhelmingly to boycott the hearings. Ralph Guzmán described frustrations surrounding the event: "This was a sad conference in many ways. First, it was clearly Lyndon Johnson's happening and not that of the Mexican-American people," he stated. "Second, it was poorly organized. Third, a tight security set up involving secret-service types and FBI personnel kept many delegates on edge," Guzmán asserted. "Fourth, the hearings themselves featured every conceivable old-time hack imaginable, but almost no young people."[63] While the hearings finally allowed Mexican Americans to share their experiences with federal officials, the meeting still fell short of including a diversity of Mexican American voices.

Following the hearings, President Johnson announced the next steps that federal government offices planned to take to expand support for Mexican Americans. "The aim of the 3-day conference," Johnson asserted, "was to assure that America's second largest minority was receiving its fair and just share of Federal programs in these areas."[64] Johnson described some of the concrete measures that emerged from the hearings. For instance, Johnson stated that his administration would support federal laws for bilingual education and modify applications for federal programs. Johnson also declared that the national government would support Model Cities programs throughout the Southwest to help reform Mexican American communities. As Johnson's post-conference agenda suggested, Mexican Americans gained greater federal recognition on civil rights and social justice issues. However, the struggle for federal protections still required further work, especially with the rise of a new generation of activists aptly reflected by the La Raza Unida conference in El Paso.

The West and the White House

Lyndon Johnson's unexpected ascension to the presidency in 1963 resulted in the US West gaining greater attention in national politics. As a Texas politician, Johnson was indebted to African Americans and Mexican Americans, who emerged as avid supporters throughout his political career. In return, Mexican American and African American constituents demanded that Johnson refine and pass federal legislation to provide their communities with full citizenship rights and federal resources. Johnson responded by proposing equal opportunity policies, including civil rights, economic opportunity, and voting rights. For the first time in US history, Mexican American and African American advocacy for equality converged nationally as both groups pushed to define the next steps in the struggle for racial equality.

The intertwined history between To Fulfill These Rights and the Inter-Agency Cabinet Committee on Mexican American Affairs offers insight into how the struggle for equal rights brought African Americans and Mexican Americans into conversation within the context of civil rights policy. Widespread resistance among Mexican Americans made clear that the Black-white paradigm in US racial politics was outdated and required revision. As the I-AC's history shows, activists wrote letters, held meetings, boycotted, and demanded access to decision-making opportunities. These efforts forced African American activists to consider how their experiences converged with other "minority groups" during To Fulfill These Rights. Similarly, the "Inter-Minority Relations" session at the Inter-Agency Cabinet Committee on Mexican American Affairs hearings reveal that some Mexican Americans sought opportunities to work more cooperatively with their African American counterparts. Black Americans and Mexican Americans continued to struggle over equal representation and recognition at the national level as the 1960s ended. The multiracial Poor People's Campaign of 1968 allowed both groups to build a mass coalition to pressure the US federal government to expand the War on Poverty, a goal expressed during their separate civil rights conferences. While Johnson hoped that passing the Civil Rights Act of 1964 would end mass demonstrations, the Poor People's Campaign revealed the role of federal policy in galvanizing a multiracial coalition of activists who helped define social justice in the post–civil rights United States.

CHAPTER FIVE

Su Lucha Es Mi Lucha (Your Battle Is My Battle)

> I'm here because at bottom we are brothers and sisters and whatever pains you pains me. When you suffer I suffer. When you're happy I'm happy. We all go up together or we all go down together. We are not free in the South and you are not free in the cities of the North.
> —REVEREND DR. MARTIN LUTHER KING JR., *Los Angeles Times*, August 1965

In May 1969, roughly one year after the Southern Christian Leadership Conference (SCLC) launched the Poor People's Campaign (PPC) in Washington, DC, SCLC President Ralph Abernathy journeyed to California to participate in a labor demonstration organized by the United Farm Workers.[1] Abernathy's trip marked an opportunity to continue multiracial activism that made the PPC one of the most significant economic justice movements of its time. Under the leadership of labor organizer César Chávez, the United Farm Workers gained national attention after successful protests against California grape growers in 1966 and 1967, which helped place the plight of Mexican American farm workers and civil rights advocates on the radar of prominent Black activists across the United States. Even though the SCLC, an African American organization, was apprehensive about joining with Mexican Americans earlier in the decade, Abernathy sought to forge relationships across racial and regional lines.[2] During his May 1969 visit to California, Abernathy led a march that included 500 Mexican and Mexican American laborers from California agricultural towns in Brawley and El Centro (located in the state's southernmost region). Abernathy stopped along the trek to deliver bilingual speeches, drawing connections between the experiences and goals of African American and Mexican American civil rights movements. He told the marchers in Spanish, "Yo tambien soy Mexicano" (I too am Mexican), identifying himself and the work of the SCLC as an ally to Mexican Americans. Abernathy's speech asserted, "Su lucha es mi lucha" (your battle is my battle), further identifying the Black Freedom and Chicano movements as linked to the same social justice goals. As a national figure within the Black Freedom movement, especially in efforts to overturn Jim Crow in the US

South, Abernathy's speeches sought to assure Mexican Americans that he understood their plight and that his social justice commitments extended outside southern states.[3]

While middle-class African American activists, professionals, and politicians failed to adequately include Mexican American representatives in the To Fulfill These Rights conference, the Chicano movement's growth between 1967 and 1969 garnered attention from the Southern Christian Leadership Conference. Abernathy's visit to California represented a continuation of multiracial work that started in 1967 when the SCLC increasingly tried to consolidate social justice movements by collaborating with Mexican Americans and other groups impacted by economic inequality. Harnessing multiracial discontent with US society into one mass movement became essential to the SCLC's desire to push for large-scale political change following the passage of the 1964 Civil Rights Act and 1965 Voting Rights Act. While civil rights and social justice scholars have established the Black Freedom movement's impact on Chicana/o and Latina/o movements for racial equality, the PPC reveals how these movements came to shape calls for multiracial economic justice during the post–civil rights decades. The SCLC redirected their attention to the dual relationship between race and class after the passage of the Voting Rights Act in 1965 and, in doing so, helped advance a second phase in the fight for civil rights. While an older guard of African American activists, including A. Philip Randolph, Dorothy Height, and Bayard Rustin, played significant roles in helping Lyndon Johnson's administration pass groundbreaking civil rights policies, Black Freedom movement leaders did not have authority in other racial or economic justice movements. By the time the SCLC began their second-phase campaigns, the Chicano movement had started to make national headlines as Mexican Americans who resided in metropolitan areas around Los Angeles, Denver, San Antonio, and Chicago mounted protests against the unique forms of discrimination they faced as urbanites.[4] As Mexican Americans waged mass demonstrations throughout the United States to fight discrimination in education, employment, and the justice system, influential Black activists in the US South began to identify similarities between both groups more closely.

When leaders of the Southern Christian Leadership Conference began planning a Poor People's Campaign in 1967, they saw Chicano activism throughout the Southwest as an excellent opportunity to build a truly national movement by joining other racial groups. When the PPC began in 1968, this mass movement for economic justice brought together African Americans, Mexican Americans, Indigenous groups, Puerto Ricans, and poor white people to illustrate the deep institutional and structural roots of poverty in the United States. However, media coverage placed Black and Mexican American participants at the center of debates about the PPC's effectiveness and, in doing so, overshadowed this movement's diversity and impact.[5] The fact that African American and Mexican American relations stood out among this multiracial coalition indicated just how significant these groups were in national debates about poverty starting in 1964. As the country's two largest communities of color, African Americans, Mexican Americans, and their leaders in the PPC struggled over how to build a movement that included grievances from both groups. Conflicts between Brown and Black factions in the PPC made national headlines throughout their six-week occupancy of Washington, DC, reflecting how conflict emerged as a dominant paradigm in how the nation conceptualized Black-Brown relations throughout the remainder of the twentieth century. Like To Fulfill These Rights, media portrayals failed to understand that tensions around federal policy during this period derived from a more significant history of ignoring Mexican Americans as a group that faced racial inequality in the United States.[6]

Planning a Multiracial Movement

The Southern Christian Leadership Conference first introduced the Poor People's Campaign as part of its 1967 platform under Martin Luther King Jr.'s leadership. SCLC activist work in the 1950s and early 1960s focused on dismantling Jim Crow laws throughout the US South that supported voting restrictions, segregation in public accommodations, and white supremacist violence. Mid-1960s urban uprisings led the SCLC to redirect their attention to the plight of Black city residents who often faced de facto discrimination, which created segregation in US cities. The Watts Rebellion occurred just five days after Martin Luther King Jr. stood with President Johnson at the signing of the Voting Rights Act. The SCLC's leadership increasingly identified Watts as an example of why the US needed economic reform. In an effort to bring cities outside the US South into their activist priorities, the SCLC launched the Chicago Freedom movement in 1966. King and his family even relocated to Chicago to join residents and organizations with whom he sought to mount a fight for economic justice.[7] The PPC grew out of this transition for the SCLC, which began developing mass movements for African Americans who remained constrained by inequality in schools, housing, and employment during the post–civil rights decades.

In stark contrast to previous mass movements organized by the SCLC, the Poor People's Campaign included Mexican Americans, Indigenous peoples, Puerto Ricans, poor white Americans, welfare rights activists, and many others. Although economic inequality disproportionately affected communities of color, over 40 million people in the US lived in poverty by 1960. African Americans made up one-third of citizens who lived below the poverty line, while Mexican Americans made up one-fourth.[8] As a result, class status and poverty were ripe with possibility for multiracial activism. Drawing on common experiences with economic inequality shared by African Americans and other groups, especially Mexican Americans, the SCLC developed one of the largest multiracial campaigns in US history. The Reverend Andrew Young, executive director of the SCLC, highlighted the role of class in unifying groups represented in the PPC during a speech delivered for the American Jewish Congress in May of 1968.

> We are poor black Americans, poor white Americans, poor Mexican Americans, poor Indian Americans and poor Puerto Rican Americans. We are from the rural south and urban ghettoes. We are from the mountains of Appallachia [sic] and the Great Western plains. We are young and old, male and female, parents and children. We have labored to make America great. We have done all of the dirty chores. We have picked the cotton and the tomatoes, cut the wood and mined the coal. We have fought the wars but never have we known peace for America is not America for us. We are aliens in our own land.[9]

The PPC represented the culmination of cross-racial organizing in local communities and, through the SCLC's desire to mobilize seemingly disparate movements, reached the national stage by 1968. Young's speech reflected the urgency around economic justice that emerged during the post–civil rights decades and the need for federal policy that recognized class as a central aspect of racial inequality in the United States.

The PPC represented the galvanizing power that emerged from the War on Poverty, which allowed the SCLC to harness the Chicano movement's momentum. By 1968, the Chicano movement was well underway throughout the United States, with Los Angeles as a central location for Mexican American activism.[10] While efforts to build national multiracial campaigns took place on a smaller scale before the late 1960s, momentum from the Chicano movement and Black Freedom movement created an opportunity to organize on a national level.[11] As demonstrated by To Fulfill These Rights in 1966, well-known southern and northern civil rights activists who advised President

Johnson often directed their energy to Jim Crow laws—however, labor leader A. Philip Randolph increasingly influenced the SCLC and President Johnson. For example, Randolph spoke of a "Freedom Budget" during To Fulfill These Rights. Joining forces with King after the passage of the Voting Rights Act, Randolph and King called for an "Economic Bill of Rights for All Americans" to secure funding to address poverty in communities across the United States. Plans for a "Freedom Budget" called upon the US federal government to allocate $100 billion to address poverty over ten years.[12] The effects of urban inequality, hypersegregation, underfunded public schools, and neglectful municipal governments galvanized Black and Brown activists to call upon President Johnson's administration to take economic justice more seriously.

By the time PPC planning began in 1967, the Black Freedom movement had gained global support, and the SCLC played an essential role in nonviolent activist campaigns throughout the Deep South.[13] Founded in 1957, the SCLC's primary aim included training local citizens in nonviolent protest strategies and organizing mass demonstrations against Jim Crow in southern states. Martin Luther King Jr., who led the SCLC until his death, first emerged as a leader during the Montgomery Improvement Association's bus boycott in 1955. Members of the Montgomery Improvement Association organized the Montgomery Bus Boycott following Rosa Parks's historic arrest in December 1955 for violating segregation laws in the local bus system.[14] After a year of organizing, protests, and boycotts, the Montgomery Improvement Association succeeded in outlawing segregation on city buses. The SCLC offered King a vehicle to continue his activism against racial segregation in the South.[15] The Poor People's Campaign provided an opportunity to spread the SCLC's work into new regions and to connect with movements that took place outside the US South.

As urban uprisings defined struggles for social justice in US cities and inspired younger generations to push for community self-determination, the SCLC expanded its nonviolent campaigns to northern cities. King described this new phase in the SCLC's community work: "The best remedy we had to offer for riots was to press our nonviolent program even more vigorously." He went on to state, "We stepped up our plans for nonviolent direct actions to make Chicago an open and just city."[16] The call for "Black Power" by Stokely Carmichael of the Student Nonviolent Coordinating Committee in 1966 also influenced the SCLC's decision to develop a national campaign for economic justice. King argued that one limitation of "Black Power" as a protest philosophy was its emphasis on confrontational tactics. He argued that "Black Power"

Su Lucha Es Mi Lucha (Your Battle Is My Battle)

lacked focus and discipline, while these attributes led to the SCLC's successful southern campaigns.[17] "Only through our adherence to nonviolence—which also means love in its strong and commanding sense—will the fear in the white community be mitigated," King stated.[18] However, at the same time that the SCLC sought to expand its work to other US regions, its approach to activism increasingly adapted protest strategies espoused by power movements. For instance, in a 1967 address to the Nation Institute in Los Angeles, King characterized the Vietnam War as "a new form of colonialism," citing the United States' involvement in Vietnam as a reflection of imperial aggression. King argued that the war in Southeast Asia redirected resources and attention away from domestic policies like the War on Poverty. "A third casualty of the war in Vietnam is the Great Society," King asserted. "The pursuit of this widened war has narrowed domestic welfare programs, making the poor, white and Negro, bear the heaviest burdens both at the front and at home," he stated.[19] While the SCLC attempted to consolidate economic justice under their leadership, the organization increasingly incorporated philosophies promoted by leftist activists, demonstrating the impact a diversity of movements and protest strategies had on shaping economic justice campaigns.[20]

The impact of "Black Power" on the SCLC became apparent during planning for the PPC in the fall of 1967. The PPC proposed a new protest strategy termed "militant nonviolence" in preparation for their mass antipoverty campaign in Washington, DC. "Militant nonviolence" tried to encompass the PPC's decision to occupy Washington, DC, to allow participants to engage in both organized and spontaneous protests at various federal government offices.[21] "This will be no mere one-day march in Washington," King asserted in a 1967 statement, "but a trek to the nation's capitol [sic] by suffering and outraged citizens who will go to stay until some definite and positive action is taken to provide jobs and income for the poor." He went on to say, "What we now need is a new kind of Selma or Birmingham to dramatize the economic plight of the Negro, and compel the government to act."[22] For King, establishing an encampment in Washington, DC, would bring federal officials into direct contact with the country's poor residents, and he hoped to gain the type of national publicity the SCLC had received during their southern campaigns against Jim Crow. The SCLC entered new organizing territory by attempting to consolidate such diverse movements under "militant nonviolence" as a new protest strategy. Still, the Poor People's Campaign reveals how activism in Los Angeles, including the Watts

Rebellion and Chicano movement, helped expand the SCLC's regionally specific campaigns.

In early 1968, the SCLC began recruiting activists to join its National Poor People's Steering Committee, which met to prepare for the PPC and participate in initial protests. On March 14, 1968, African American, Indigenous, Puerto Rican, white, and Mexican American representatives who accepted invitations to join the PPC's steering committee attended a Minority Group Conference in Atlanta, Georgia, to plan the PPC. Characterized as a "historic group meeting of American minority group leaders" by the *Chicago Defender*, conference discussions highlighted common ways poverty and economic inequality impacted groups invited to participate in the PPC. King offered his perspective on this cross-racial meeting to the press, stating, "This is a highly significant event, the beginning of a new co-operation, understanding, and a determination by poor people of all colors and backgrounds to assert and win their right to a decent life and respect for their culture and dignity."[23] King's response reflected how the PPC envisioned their work during a period when antiracist activism took place across the country, with poverty as a central organizing point for almost every movement. King's interview suggests that he understood the power of joining forces with other racial justice movements, especially as the struggle for civil rights increasingly took shape in regions outside the US South.

Class emerged as the most powerful strategy in bringing diverse groups and activists together. During the National Poor People's Steering Committee meeting in 1968, representatives drew connections between their labor histories. The *Chicago Defender* offered insight into the experiential connections participants expressed during the meeting. An article stated, for example, "There were songs and stories of the poor white miner, the Mexican-American migrant worker, the Negro slave, the Puerto Rican worker, the proud original American-the Indian."[24] Conference discussions helped reveal how poverty and economic status served as a strong connecting thread to build a multiracial movement for greater governmental protections and resources. Historian Gordon Mantler argues in his research on Black-Brown relations and the Poor People's Campaign that economic justice was an essential connecting thread for multiracial activism. Although the mid-1960s marked a period when African Americans and Mexican Americans increasingly articulated their uniqueness as a form of racial self-determination, economic inequality connected their struggles for a more just US democracy. As a result, the PPC emerged as an opportunity to demonstrate how US policies fell short of improving the plight of communities of color in every region of the country.[25]

The Poor People's Campaign allowed the SCLC to expand its outreach programs to new cities. SCLC representatives visited Baltimore, Philadelphia, Chicago, and Detroit, among other cities, to train participants in nonviolent protest strategies and to garner national participation. Workshops played a vital role in the SCLC's work since the organization's founding in 1957. Recruiting and training a multiregional, multiracial, and multigenerational group of protestors became critical to staging "a dramatic confrontation with the government until our nation responds to the terrible conditions of poverty and racism in America," King argued.[26] In Los Angeles, for example, the city's SCLC branch worked to recruit Angelenos to participate in the PPC and held fundraising events. Founded in 1964 under the guidance of pastor Thomas Kilgore Jr., the SCLC established a Los Angeles branch to gain outside support for southern nonviolent campaigns against Jim Crow. Other church officials, including Rev. A. A. Peters and Rev. James Hargett, served as local organizers for the PPC. As demonstrated by the place of Los Angeles in the PPC, organizing around economic justice helped consolidate movements for social justice across the country. What made the PPC unique was the campaign's focus on an issue at the core of each movement for racial justice and their use of economic inequality to create one of the biggest multiracial activist campaigns of the twentieth century.[27]

Officers from the SCLC's national headquarters also visited Los Angeles as part of their outreach efforts and met with California residents and activists. Hosea Williams, a field organizer for the SCLC who trained volunteers in nonviolent protest strategies, visited Los Angeles in May 1968 to participate in a donation drive for the Poor People's Campaign. Williams spoke at the University of California, Los Angeles, during an event organized by Black students at colleges and universities throughout the city. Williams also attended an event organized by the Black Congress, an umbrella organization that brought Black activists in Los Angeles together. By 1968, Black and Brown students in Los Angeles and California more broadly played a central role in critiquing institutional and structural forces that shaped racial inequality in the United States and beyond. Because the SCLC wanted to bring together movements from throughout the United States, especially with groups that took a more militant stance on racial justice, building relationships with student activists was necessary for the PPC's success as a mass movement.[28]

The *Los Angeles Sentinel* polled residents to capture their perspective on the Poor People's Campaign's feasibility and effectiveness. "The march will definitely put some pressure on Congress," interviewee Harriet Beasley asserted. "It is so integrated. It is composed of an array of races with a common bond. I am sure that some good will come out of it," Beasley stated. Frances Robinson, another resident, pointed to the importance of class as a central organizing strategy. "It depends on how much impact that such a huge group of people can exert. Since this march is composed of so many diverse races it will change the emphasis from race to class and thus it will be very effective," Robinson asserted.[29] For Los Angeles residents like Beasley and Robinson, the PPC's strength rested in bringing diverse groups together to protest economic inequality. Both Angelenos characterized multiracial participation as the campaign's most powerful component, which speaks to Los Angeles's longer history of cross-racial activism and institution-building. The PPC provided an opportunity to bring a familiar version of activism for Angelenos to the national stage. In addition, their emphasis on economic inequality while delivering remarks to media outlets further demonstrates how post-1964 activism emphasized class limitations in civil rights legislation.[30]

Once activists throughout the United States committed to participating in the Poor People's Campaign alongside the SCLC, the movement's first phase commenced in April and May 1968, when the Committee of 100 traveled to Washington, DC, to testify at hearings with government agencies. The Committee of 100 met with federal officials to warn them of the potential for mass demonstrations if they did not make immediate strides toward crafting policies and programs for economic justice. Some organizations represented on the Committee of 100 included the National Welfare Rights Organization (NWRO), Operation Breadbasket, and Women Strike for Peace. Jesse Jackson of Operation Breadbasket in Chicago and Corky Gonzales of Crusade for Justice in Denver participated on behalf of their cities. Bert Corona of the Mexican American Political Association in California, who actively advocated for a Mexican American civil rights conference during debates over To Fulfill These Rights, also received an invitation to join initial protests. Committee members attended hearings held at the Departments of Agriculture; Justice; Labor; Housing and Urban Development; Health, Education, and Welfare; and the Office of Economic Opportunity (OEO) to present their grievances and recommendations. The Committee of 100 demonstrates the growth of multiracial activism from local civil rights movements to the national stage through War on Poverty initiatives. That the

PPC garnered support from such a prominent group of activists who founded organizations across the country speaks to the strength and urgency of multiracial activism by the late 1960s.[31]

The Committee of 100 hoped that participating in hearings with federal government officials might offer a preview of the multiracial coalition assembled by the SCLC before participants traveled to Washington, DC, for mass protests. During the hearings, the SCLC presented each government agency with a list of demands that reflected the Poor People's Campaign's goals. Some demands included, among other requests, "a meaningful job at a living wage for every employable citizen" and "access to land as a means to income and livelihood." Furthermore, committee members asked for "recognition by law of the right of people affected by government programs to play a truly significant role in determining how they are designed and carried out."[32] The call for access to a living wage and for citizens to play a role in administering programs designed for their communities reveals how language from the Economic Opportunity Act provided legislative justification for those impacted by economic inequality to advocate for rights and recognition. Deciding to begin the PPC by meeting with federal legislators demonstrates how post-1964 activist movements were critical in facilitating political change. The Civil Rights Act of 1964, and especially the Voting Rights Act of 1965, motivated Black and Brown people to advocate for policies designed to improve their daily lives at unprecedented levels in US history.

Perceived interconnections between the Economic Opportunity Act and civil rights legislation came to the fore when committee members visited the Department of Justice. Ralph Abernathy provided testimony to substantiate growing awareness of how race and class shaped poverty in the United States. "Despite the Civil Rights Acts of 1957, 1960 and 1964 and the Voting Rights Act of 1965, justice is not a reality for the black, Mexican-American, Indian and Puerto Rican poor," he declared.[33] Committee members pointed to the long history of discrimination in education and housing as examples of how inequality continued to shape communities of color after recent civil rights victories. Abernathy's speech argued that economic justice helped to make civil rights legislation more effective. The Committee of 100 reveals how antipoverty legislation helped galvanize African American and Mexican American people after 1964 to advocate for resources they believed might help civil rights policies make a more concrete impact on the masses. As Abernathy's testimony described, a lack of economic resources meant that poor African Americans and Mexican Americans had fewer education and housing options. As a collective, the Committee of 100 helped demonstrate how the

Civil Rights Act of 1964 required additional programs and legislation to become a truly effective policy to eradicate total inequality in the United States. Combined, the Economic Opportunity Act and the Civil Rights Act, passed in 1964, provided a blueprint to help address the racialized history of economic inequality in the United States. The Poor People's Campaign sought to make the vital connections between these two policies more apparent to the people who drafted them.

When the Committee of 100 testified at the Office of Economic Opportunity, committee members argued that the OEO had also fallen short in their plans to defeat poverty. "You have failed us," the committee lamented. "You were to be our spokesman within the federal government, but our needs have gone unspoken."[34] Meetings with OEO staff offered the Committee of 100 an opportunity to state their concerns about the status of the War on Poverty in communities throughout the United States. They went on to demand "citizen participation from poverty communities," which was an integral requirement of the original Economic Opportunity Act. The Committee of 100 also used their meeting with OEO officials to request more support from the federal office when local authorities blocked antipoverty funding. According to committee members, the national OEO needed to do a better job of holding "local politicians responsible for respecting the civil and human rights of the poor" and that if local authorities failed to address basic human needs, "poor people must be able to operate their own programs."[35] By calling upon the national OEO to reevaluate community participation in local antipoverty programs, the Committee of 100 demonstrates how antipoverty policy galvanized a multiracial coalition of people impacted by economic inequality. When committee members returned to Washington, DC, in May 1968 with protestors, they revealed how War on Poverty policies ignited a multiracial fight for economic justice.

The Poor People's Campaign

Martin Luther King Jr. was murdered on April 4, 1968, before the PPC's mass protest phase took place. King's death led to uprisings across the United States and motivated even more people to support the PPC. Albert Barnes, director of the Pasadena branch of the National Urban League (located within the greater Los Angeles area), extended his support for the SCLC and sought to join the organization's mass campaigns in the South. In a letter to Andrew Young, Barnes stated, "I certainly feel renewed and strengthened convictions to act in a direct and meaningful way to enhance the great work of Dr. King."

Barnes continued, "I am not sure of the areas in which my background, training, and experience could be most effectively utilized, but I want to become directly involved with the action!"[36] For Barnes and countless others, King's death brought further urgency to the Southern Christian Leadership Conference's work and vision for a more just society. Government officials responded by arguing that the PPC might bring uprisings to Washington, DC, and introduced over seventy-five bills to prevent protestors from occupying the capital. However, President Johnson approved a thirty-seven-day renewable permit to allow the SCLC to proceed with demonstrations, reflecting Johnson's long-term relationship with King and the SCLC.[37]

Poor People's Campaign organizers kicked off protests with a rally at the Lorraine Hotel in Memphis, Tennessee, on May 2, 1968, the location of King's murder. Ralph Abernathy, the SCLC's new president, Coretta Scott King (Martin Luther King Jr.'s widow), and Reies López Tijerina participated in the rally. Scott King delivered an address that tied her husband's legacy to the fight against poverty. "On this spot where my husband gave his life, I pledge eternal loyalty to the work which he so nobly began," she stated. Scott King added, "His legacy will lead us to the point where all of God's children have shoes."[38] Tijerina addressed the crowd of about 1,000 who traveled to the Lorraine Hotel to participate in the PPC's kickoff rally. Tijerina encouraged Mexican Americans and African Americans to join forces and pressure the US federal government to pass additional civil rights reforms. He stated that Mexican Americans "have been kept away from you and turned against you for the last 120 years by white people. If our government is more intelligent than the old pharaohs of Egypt, then something will come from this campaign."[39] In weeks following the Lorraine Hotel rally, caravans filled with activists and poor residents from throughout US cities and towns descended on Washington, DC, in honor of King's final planned mass demonstration. Driven by the War on Poverty, the SCLC sought to challenge discrimination by weaving together various movements for social justice that included welfare rights, disability rights, children's rights, and middle-class allies.[40]

Regional caravans brought protestors from all over the United States to Washington, DC. Los Angeles residents boarded buses destined for DC on May 15, 1968, as part of the western caravan. Following a sunrise rally and welcome from Rev. Jesse Jackson and Tijerina, white and Mexican American participants boarded buses primarily made up of local African American residents. The bus took them on a journey to pick up demonstrators in other major cities, including Arizona, Colorado, and Missouri.[41] Many participants traveled with their families. For instance, Emilio Domínguez brought his family because he saw the PPC as an opportunity to challenge assertions that Mexican Americans were passive in efforts to advocate for equal rights. In an interview with the *Los Angeles Sentinel*, Domínguez stated, "Perhaps by this sacrifice, our dream may come true. . . . There is not any other way left but to demonstrate." Another local resident interviewed by the *Los Angeles Sentinel* was an African American woman who boarded the bus with her seven children. When reporters asked why she decided to participate in the PPC, the woman stated that she simply desired to take part in "something historical."[42] For Domínguez, the unnamed African American woman, and thousands of others who boarded caravans in May 1968, the PPC offered an opportunity to join a national mass demonstration with SCLC officers that for the first time in US history included large numbers of residents from outside the US South.

Participating in the Poor People's Campaign allowed youth activists to engage with diverse poverty rebels from across the United States. Some young activists, like Walter Bremond of Black Congress, helped with local organizing in Los Angeles, while others boarded buses to participate in PPC demonstrations directly. Former Brown Beret minister Gloria Arellanes recounted her trek to Washington, DC, in an interview years later. Arellanes remembered meeting many young Chicana/o activists from other cities, and she even had an opportunity to join Corky Gonzales's bus once western caravanners stopped in Denver to pick up participants. However, while Arellanes's experience growing up in Los Angeles shielded her from southern Jim Crow policies and practices, her caravan's journey through Texas exposed Arellanes to southern-style law enforcement firsthand. "I had never seen anything like this. I had never left El Monte in my life," she described. "There was [were] these uniformed officers."[43] Arellanes's culture shock when her caravan arrived in Texas exposed her and other young activists who came of age in California to southern racial regimes that sat at the core of the SCLC's work before building their national movement to fight poverty.

Western caravanners arrived in Washington, DC, on May 23, eight roughly ten days after initial occupancy by other protesters began. For many, a fifteen-acre shantytown known as Resurrection City became home during their time with the Poor People's Campaign. Located near the Lincoln Memorial, Resurrection City included a series of triangular plywood dwellings that participants resided in during their time in Washington, DC. To make their stay comfortable, especially since many participants brought their families, protestors attempted to transform their temporary plywood bungalows into homes. Images of Resurrection City show that campaigners

Su Lucha Es Mi Lucha (Your Battle Is My Battle) 119

hung photos on their walls, brought toys for children, and watched television during downtime.[44] Resurrection City planners even established many bureaucratic agencies in US cities, such as City Hall and the Coretta Scott King Day Care Center. Participants sometimes brought their children to protests, including Crusade for Justice leader Corky Gonzales, who marched to the Department of Justice holding his young son's hand. Resurrection City's Welfare Department provided clothing and donations for demonstrators, while health care resources included physical exams, chest X-rays, dental treatment, and a pharmacy.[45] These community institutions in Resurrection City demonstrate how movements for economic justice led by welfare mothers, youth activists, central city residents, and others influenced the SCLC's vision for the PPC.

Some challenges that might arise in multiracial coalitions appeared almost immediately when Reies López Tijerina and other Mexican American participants decided not to reside in Resurrection City and found lodging at a local school. With demonstrators already residing in Resurrection City for about a week, western caravanners received word of rain, unsanitary conditions, and slow construction, making living conditions difficult for many participants.[46] In addition, one difficulty in cross-racial organizing between African Americans and Mexican Americans on the local level was residential segregation, which, in cities like Los Angeles, became hypersegregated after World War II. Tijerina and others carried hypersegregation into Resurrection City by attempting to consolidate Mexican American participants into the basement of the Hawthorne School. Segregation within the Poor People's Campaign reflected challenges with building cross-racial coalitions that sought to highlight both commonality and differences between African Americans and Mexican Americans. As historian Neil Foley argues in his analysis of debates about Black-Brown solidarity, residential segregation is fundamental to understanding relationships between African Americans and Mexican Americans in the United States.[47] While Mexican Americans showed great optimism about joining Black activists, their actions at Resurrection City revealed that coalition-building requires learning to navigate a history of group isolation while also attempting to establish interconnections.[48]

While some Mexican Americans refused to move into Resurrection City, SCLC President Ralph Abernathy argued that occupying the nation's capital was the best course of action to gain more attention from liberal democratic politicians. Abernathy recounted some of the challenges that arose when working with liberal politicians compared to the predictability of staunch segregationists in a June 14, 1968, address: "You know—the demonstrations that SCLC led in the past—ones like Birmingham in 1963 and Selma in 1965—they were easy. And the reason was: you knew who the enemy was, or you thought you did. You didn't have to do much like Bull Connor or a man like Jim Clark. But–as you well know–Washington is a lot more sophisticated than Birmingham or Selma. Bull Connor and Jim Clark did-in a way-spoil us. We knew where they stood."[49] Abernathy and other civil rights organizations who participated in the PPC understood that gaining support from politicians who identified with liberal democratic policy agendas, including President Johnson, required new demonstration and negotiation tactics to counteract color-blind arguments that racial conditions were better in post–civil rights America. Abernathy highlighted how some liberal democratic politicians believed the Civil Rights Act of 1964 and Voting Rights Act of 1965 completed their racial justice work. His speech acknowledged the hard work that lay ahead for multiracial activism as PPC demonstrations sought to confront politicians with the urgency of economic justice.

Poor People's Campaign demonstrators participated in mass protests throughout their entire occupation of Washington, DC. The campaign's multiracial and multi-issue focus included antidraft advocates, National Welfare Rights Organization members, and land rights activists. Reports from Solidarity Day (June 19, 1968), a moment within the PPC organized to further highlight the campaign's demands, suggest that some 50,000 to 100,000 people attended Solidarity Day events. Thousands of protestors holding signs that stated "End Hunger in America" gathered at the Lincoln Memorial to hear Solidarity Day speakers. Ralph Abernathy, Coretta Scott King, Reies López Tijerina, and Walter Reuther of United Auto Workers addressed the crowd. While Tijerina lamented that Mexican Americans faced cultural genocide under the US government, Roy Wilkins of the National Association for the Advancement of Colored People reminded protestors why the PPC represented their experiences.[50] "The Poor People's Campaign does not see profit or preference," Wilkins stated. "It seeks food, shelter, jobs, health, and welfare and good schools for the children."[51] Solidarity Day events helped bring further attention to the PPC's racial diversity and broader social justice goals. Looking out on the crowd, organizers saw a visible representation of how the War on Poverty provided a platform for cross-racial collaborations between communities of color determined to advance economic justice.

Women played a central role in efforts to expand federal antipoverty resources, and the PPC offered a forum to bring awareness to how economic inequality disproportionally affected women. At the Solidarity Day March, Coretta Scott King and Dorothy Height spoke about the status of African

American women in the United States. While Scott King asked women to speak out about their experiences with poverty and to put themselves on the front lines of protests, Height, one of President Johnson's civil rights advisors, highlighted the fact that Black women suffered from high rates of poverty. Height went on to describe some differences between African American and white women's struggles for equality, asserting that while white women fought for independence from white men, Black women fought for both race and gender liberation. Groundbreaking activist work facilitated by women was often overshadowed by men who were President Johnson's civil rights advisors. By focusing on diverse social justice movements, the PPC offered a platform for women of color to articulate how poverty significantly impacted their daily lives and communities.[52]

The National Welfare Rights Organization fought for women to play a vital role in Poor People's Campaign protests. George Wiley, NWRO's executive director, contacted Andrew Young in 1968 to demand that the NWRO participate in negotiations with federal officials about policies and programs to reduce poverty. "NWRO have prime responsibility for policy, negotiation, and public statements on welfare issues," Wiley stated. To maintain some of the NWRO's grassroots activism within the PPC, Wiley called for "separate welfare rights workshops and opportunities for welfare rights presentations in general workshops and general meetings."[53] As Wiley's correspondence reveals, economic justice shaped movements before the SCLC's transition from desegregation to structural inequality, especially for women. Authorizing the NWRO to play a prominent role in advocacy around welfare rights reflects some of the challenges that emerged from developing a mass movement that included diverse activists and issues. NWRO members traveled to Resurrection City and actively participated in mass demonstrations to highlight how much class hindered recent civil rights legislation.

While the PPC was a multiracial campaign designed to unify a diversity of groups and movements around structural inequality, the campaign provided an opportunity to protest discrimination unique to Mexican Americans. When Denver-based Chicano movement activist Corky Gonzales led a march of some 350 participants to the Department of Justice, Hosea Williams of the SCLC joined the marchers. Gonzales's march served as a protest against a recent indictment of thirteen Mexican Americans who faced charges for participating in the East Los Angeles "Blowouts" in 1968.[54] Mexican American protestors called for a meeting with attorney general Ramsey Clark and demanded seventy-two-hour immunity for the defendants. Gonzales and others used the PPC to advocate for their independent groups, while also calling for reforms that served each demographic represented in the PPC. Chicana/o activists also held protests at the Office of Education to call for culturally relevant teaching materials in schools with significant Mexican American enrollment, a central goal of the Chicano movement. Protestors called upon government officials to withdraw funding from schools that failed to teach Mexican American experiences, and they advocated for bilingual education.[55] Although conflict and difficulties emerged throughout the PPC, the ability to engage in collective and group-specific protests made this campaign unique, especially as an SCLC movement. Discrimination faced by African Americans and Mexican Americans was intertwined and similar but also included essential differences.[56] For instance, Tijerina held mass protests at the Department of State to bring awareness to the Land Grant movement. He provided a list of demands to pressure the US federal government to acknowledge the Treaty of Guadalupe Hidalgo, and he demanded that lands confiscated in the nineteenth century be returned to original owners along with compensation. The ability to bring an amalgam of civil rights violations to Washington, DC, made the PPC stand out as an essential representation of Black-Brown relations during the late 1960s.[57]

The Spector of Black-Brown Relations

While the Poor People's Campaign offered an arena for African Americans and Mexican Americans to advocate for their shared experiences with racial inequality in the United States through a series of protests, debates about Black visibility and Brown invisibility posed challenges for the PPC. Even though PPC planners designed the movement as a multiracial effort to pressure federal policymakers, the relationship between African Americans and Mexican Americans consumed media reports about the PPC's effectiveness. The status of African Americans and Mexican Americans as the nation's two largest underserved populations came to the fore during the PPC and dominated public opinion about this multiracial coalition. Mexican American and African American relations emerged as one of the most examined aspects of the PPC. They took center stage in reports about whether the SCLC succeeded in its quest for a multiracial economic justice campaign. For instance, an article published in the *Chicago Defender* just one day before Washington, DC, authorities shut down Resurrection City revealed that reporters pressed Ralph Abernathy to discuss rumors that a conflict between the SCLC's leadership and Mexican American activists surfaced early in the

PPC. Abernathy avoided directly answering these questions, stating that any movement challenges are "not [R]esurrection City, but poverty."[58] That Black-Brown relations became the main public focus demonstrates how relationships between African Americans and Mexican Americans increasingly faced scrutiny and interest by the end of the 1960s.

The press played a pivotal role in disseminating stories about Black-Brown tension throughout the Poor People's Campaign. National news sources zeroed in on claims made by Tijerina that the SCLC ignored demands compiled by Mexican American activists. The *Washington Post* closely followed the PPC and published articles as protests developed. One such article ran a story where Tijerina argued that Black leaders failed to adequately include Mexican American land rights in their demands to the federal government even though the Committee of 100 made land rights a priority before occupying Washington, DC. As historian Lorena Oropeza argues in her comprehensive analysis of Reies López Tijerina's life, several activists, reporters, and writers tended to characterize Tijerina as a fraud who attempted to deceive Mexican Americans through his land grant activism.[59] However, reporters who covered the PPC tended to ignore existing criticism about Tijerina as irrational and deceptive in their reporting about Black-Brown relations in Resurrection City. The *Washington Post* even published an article titled "Tijerina Charges Poor Were Betrayed: Mexican-American Assails SCLC Leaders" that portrayed Tijerina's perspective. While tensions between activists in any movement are inevitable, especially in such a racially, regionally, and philosophically diverse mass campaign like the PPC, the media's use of Tijerina to write provocative articles is an example of how Black-Brown relations increasingly gripped public attention in post–civil rights America.[60]

Abernathy responded to Tijerina's claims by meeting with him and Corky Gonzales to discuss their grievances. Even though Abernathy avoided questions about Black-Brown relations during some media interviews about the PPC, he attempted to make amends with Tijerina. After Gonzales, Abernathy, and Tijerina's meeting, Abernathy arrived at a press conference with his arms around both men, stating, "Things are well in hand here for my Mexican-American brothers." Tijerina corroborated Abernathy's claims, asserting, "We are having minor problems, but the next steering committee meeting will iron out the important issues relating and uniting black people, red people and brown people."[61] That the press awaited Abernathy's, Tijerina's, and Gonzales's comments about their meeting is an example of how US society began to consume details about interactions between African Americans and Mexican Americans at higher rates.

Poor People's Campaign mass demonstrations continued until June 23, 1968, when President Johnson's permit for Resurrection City expired, and he did not approve a renewal. The following morning, law enforcement officers arrived in Resurrection City near the Lincoln Memorial and cleared occupants from the shantytown they had transformed into temporary homes. As PPC planners scrambled to organize travel arrangements for participants to return home, some Resurrection City residents moved into the Hawthorne School where many Mexican Americans found shelter. Other participants remained in Washington, DC, along with the SCLC's leadership, to continue demonstrating, which shows the urgency and momentum behind these protests. As police moved forward with bulldozing Resurrection City, they arrested Abernathy along with approximately 200 protestors for refusing to leave. Resurrection City's destruction reflected the tendency to appease activists around calls for economic justice by allowing them limited authority in conversations with officials. Federal policymakers tolerated Resurrection City for several weeks but quickly instituted an aggressive demise of the encampment to force demonstrators out of Washington, DC. Abernathy remained committed and shared his perspective with reporters aboard a bus headed for a local Washington jail on charges of camping without a permit. Abernathy told reporters that his arrest, along with other demonstrators, offered a lens into how the PPC would continue until officials met their demands.[62]

Following the PPC, national media outlets proceeded to report on Tijerina. For instance, a *Washington Post* article claimed that Tijerina continued publicly expressing his frustration toward the SCLC's leadership. The article described allegations that the SCLC frivolously spent campaign money and failed to advocate for land rights. The article stated that PPC leadership fell short of working effectively as a coalition because the SCLC failed to communicate significant changes to the movement's itinerary. Still, amid articles claiming to reflect Tijerina's perspective, he continued forging a multiracial army of the poor.[63] To meet this goal, Tijerina joined with representatives from across the United States to develop a permanent coalition after the PPC ended. The new organization, the Poor People's Coalition, included representatives from racial groups who participated in the Poor People's Campaign. Tijerina served as the spokesperson for Mexican Americans, while others represented poor white Americans, Puerto Ricans, African Americans, and Indigenous groups.[64]

In addition to activism that continued once the Poor People's Campaign ended, federal government agencies approved some of the PPC's initial demands. First, policymakers approved a $100 million program to provide free and reduced-priced lunches for children in low-income families. Second, calls to distribute food to the most impoverished areas in the United States led government officials to approve sending surplus food items to some of the country's poorest counties. Finally, even though the Office of Economic Opportunity increasingly faced attacks from conservatives, the agency still responded to demands made by protestors by budgeting an additional $25 million for Head Start programs in Alabama and Mississippi. In addition, the OEO adopted a plan to open 1,300 positions for low-income people to work in various OEO agencies. While federal offices did not meet most of the demands made through the PPC, these small victories reflected how much power existed within multiracial coalitions by the late 1960s, especially around federal policy to address poverty.[65]

Economic Justice as a Multiracial Fight

The Poor People's Campaign directly reflected how activism around economic justice encouraged communities of color to consider their shared experiences as working people in the United States. More specifically, the PPC offered an opportunity to build a movement that highlighted the 1964 Civil Rights Act's limitations for poor communities. While this monumental piece of legislation lifted barriers to education, housing, and employment, the Civil Rights Act included class biases that made the legislation most effective for middle-class people of color and white women. While the PPC's leadership primarily included activists who could take advantage of opportunities made available by the Civil Rights Act, they used their power and authority to advocate for economically vulnerable people. As President Johnson's civil rights advisors, leadership in the SCLC received an official permit that allowed a multiracial set of activists to occupy Washington, DC, for roughly a month to confront policymakers. In doing so, they made a significant imprint on post–civil rights activism and a national quest to bring awareness to the deep roots of class inequality in every corner of the United States.

Internal fractures around race and class came to the fore when some Mexican Americans decided to reside away from Resurrection City, and media coverage emphasized claims of interracial strife centered on Tijerina. The media's deep interest in Tijerina and claims that he clashed with Black leaders in the SCLC demonstrates how this particular movement designed to fight for economic justice further contributed to a national interest in Black-

Brown relations. While Los Angeles had a long history of Black-Brown community building, coalitions, and, at times, conflict, the PPC helped move interactions between these groups to the national stage. News articles primarily focused on conflict when describing the relationship between groups, even though mass protests took place all over Washington, DC. The tendency to zero in on conflict as the dominant trope of Black-Brown relations remained a constant throughout the second half of the twentieth century.

CHAPTER SIX

The Magna Carta to Liberate Our Cities
African Americans, Mexican Americans, and the Model Cities Program in Los Angeles

> The Congress hereby finds and declares that improving the quality of urban life is the most critical domestic problem facing the United States. The persistence of widespread urban slums and blight, the concentration of persons of low income in older urban areas, and the unmet needs for additional housing and community facilities and services arising from rapid expansion of our urban population have resulted in a marked deterioration in the quality of the environment and the lives of large numbers of our people while the Nation as a whole prospers.
>
> —Demonstration Cities and Metropolitan Development Act, 1966

Conservatives began challenging mid-1960s antipoverty reforms shortly after each legislation's inception, especially as the 1960s ended. However, the US federal government continued with antipoverty programs outside the Office of Economic Opportunity. For example, in a November 1967 press conference, Robert C. Weaver, cabinet secretary for the Department of Housing and Urban Development (HUD), announced grant recipients under a federally funded initiative called Model Cities. After reviewing 193 applications from small and large cities across the United States that sought to receive a percentage of the $11 million allocated by Congress to draft community revitalization plans, Angelenos eagerly awaited Weaver's announcement. Although Los Angeles, the community of Watts more specifically, played a foundational role in 1960s popular and political debates about the urgent need to improve inner-city neighborhoods, Weaver did not announce Los Angeles among the sixty-three cities slated to receive planning grants for Model Cities programs. However, Weaver did name other California cities, including Oakland, Richmond, and Fresno, as planning grant recipients, creating a local and national scramble to bring Los Angeles into Model Cities. As a federal initiative led by the first African American HUD secretary, Model Cities reflected deep ties among civil rights, economic justice, and political engagement during the 1960s. City residents in northern and western cities leaped at an opportunity to secure additional federal funding for community revitalization projects and, in doing so, extended struggles for economic justice through policy into the 1970s amid aggressive challenges from conservative politicians and constituents.

As an extension of the War on Poverty, Model Cities continued to shape Black-Brown relations as the US federal government entered Richard Nixon's presidency. Like the original War on Poverty, officials characterized Model Cities as a "total attack" on the social and physical problems in slum and blighted neighborhoods. The concept of maximum feasible participation also appeared in guidelines for Model Cities and required that "planning must be carried out with as well as for the people living in the affected areas."[1] One crucial difference between the War on Poverty and Model Cities was the place of racial, identity, and community pride in programs proposed during the early 1970s. At the core of many Model Cities community programs lay a desire to promote racial pride, address gaps in education, improve medical care, and expand the creative arts for Brown and Black people. The Watts Rebellion and Chicano moratorium helped add these priorities to Model Cities in ways unavailable when Lyndon Johnson first approved the Economic Opportunity Act in 1964. Furthermore, Model Cities took place mainly as a national Chicano movement became more pronounced in Los Angeles and around the country.[2] Model Cities reconceptualizes the War on Poverty's longevity in Los Angeles and demonstrates how the Chicano movement more closely engaged with the next stage in antipoverty funding through Model Cities. The Chicano moratorium protests in particular offer an important example of how the legacy of civil unrest is so profoundly intertwined in Black and Brown post–civil rights histories.

Model Cities' Origins

Labor organizer Walter Reuther proposed Model Cities while serving as a member of President Lyndon Johnson's Task Force on Urban Problems. Reuther's original blueprint for a federally funded urban revitalization program, Demonstration Cities, identified comprehensive programs to improve infrastructure and social services as the next step toward improving material conditions for poor African Americans in major US cities. While the 1964 Civil Rights Act lifted exclusions in education, housing, employment, and other institutions vital to upward mobility for marginalized groups in the United States, middle-class and wealthy African Americans most often benefited from this significant civil rights victory because they had financial resources required to take advantage of US institutions fully. Before being elected president of the United Auto Workers in 1946, Reuther developed a reputation as a strident advocate for labor rights, unions, and economic justice.[3] His engagement with federal officials reveals how activists with institutional power spoke on behalf of impoverished communities. Reuther's vision for Model Cities sought to address the role of poverty in stymieing Black upward mobility during a period when civil rights laws lifted barriers to racial inequality. In response to resistant legislators weary about using the term "demonstration" in the title of a government program during the height of social justice movements throughout the United States, modifications to Reuther's proposal resulted in a new antipoverty initiative known as Model Cities.[4]

Uprisings in Black city neighborhoods across the United States changed the tenor of Reuther's proposed program and provided the impetus to earn legislative approval for Model Cities. When uprisings devastated several Black urban neighborhoods between 1964 and 1968, these explosive moments laid bare the impact of economic inequality on central city life—including underfunded schools, poor infrastructure, unemployment, and neglect from government officials.[5] For example, looting of grocery, clothing, furniture, and electronics stores during the Watts Rebellion reflected how urban uprisings as a protest strategy are deeply rooted in economic justice. As historian Michael Katz argued in his research on poverty and social welfare policy in the United States, the 1960s ushered in a period when "intellectuals and politicians rediscovered poverty."[6] Model Cities is an example of how uprisings played an essential part in this so-called rediscovery that helped Black and Brown communities in US cities articulate their specific frustration with the relationship between race and class. Because many local, state, and federal policymakers were eager to stop further uprisings, a riot prevention clause helped Model Cities gain support from skeptical legislators. For instance, Los Angeles congressman Augustus F. Hawkins responded to Model Cities with ambivalence after experiencing a yearlong stalemate with the mayor's office over War on Poverty programs in 1964.[7]

US federal government officials approved Model Cities as a response to post–World War II demographic shifts as the country transitioned from a rural to an urban society, including suburban growth. The post–World War II decades exacerbated divisions between city and suburb. Between 1940 and 1950, Los Angeles's total population increased by just over 400,000, and the city's African American population more than doubled from 67,000 to just over 171,000 (see table 1). Although the city's Mexican-origin population experienced a slight increase during and immediately following the Second World War, this population nearly doubled between 1950 and 1960 (see table 2). The significant growth of urban populations during the second half of the twentieth century forced the US federal government to develop policies aligned with these critical demographic changes. As a popular location for newcomers, partially due to the defense industry, Los Angeles represented an ideal location for migrants who descended on California from all over the United States.

Once the Demonstration Cities and Metropolitan Development Bill passed in 1966, Model Cities emerged as the second phase in the US federal government's War on Poverty program.[8] The Demonstration Cities and Metropolitan Development Act mimicked some of the arguments used in the Economic Opportunity Act to articulate how Model Cities would help economically depressed urban areas throughout the United States. For instance, the act identified blighted areas and inadequate housing as an example: "Cities, of all sizes, do not have adequate resources to deal effectively with the critical problems facing them."[9] The act described the types of programs legislators believed might accommodate the number of people relocating to cities, and these closely aligned with the original goals of the War on Poverty. According to the Demonstration Cities and Metropolitan Development Act, "population density, poverty levels, unemployment rate, public welfare participation, educational levels, health and disease characteristics, crime and delinquency rate, and degree of substandard and dilapidated housing" reflected some pressing issues behind Model Cities.[10] An informational packet compiled by the assistant secretary for demonstrations and intergovernmental relations in 1966 further summed up the goal for Model Cities as an urban reform. "Title I of the Demonstration Cities and Metropolitan Development Act of 1966 provides for a new program to substantially improve the living environment and the general welfare of people living in slum and blighted neighborhoods in the selected cities of all sizes and all parts of the country. It calls for a coordinated attack, bringing to bear the resources of Federal, State, and local government, as well as private efforts, to develop 'model' neighborhoods."[11] Having learned lessons from the War on Poverty, Model Cities included more concrete goals around improving city infrastructure and community resources to advance residents' physical, social, and economic well-being.

Demographic transitions ushered in what politicians, intellectuals, and critics termed the nation's "urban crisis" during the 1960s. "Urban crisis" referred to decades following World War II, when the United States experienced an economic boom that further solidified racial divisions in US city neighborhoods. While white city residents gained access to middle-class jobs, suburban homes, and consumer culture, inner-city residents of color sank deeper into economic despair. This growing economic division between central cities and suburbs contributed to African American urban uprisings during the second half of the 1960s.[12] Arguments about the "urban crisis" justified President Johnson's push for the first Housing and Urban Development Act through Congress in 1965. Johnson's predecessor, President John F. Kennedy, attempted to establish a Department of Urban Affairs to address demographic changes. Still, the United States had not yet realized how much migration into cities had transformed the country. By 1965, Lyndon Johnson's administration established the Department of Housing and Urban Development to meet demands associated with the country's transition from a rural to an urban society. African American economist Robert C. Weaver became the first Black cabinet member when President Johnson selected him as secretary of the newly established HUD. Weaver held a strong record of intellectual research and professional experience in urban development that reached back to his appointment in the Public Housing Administration under President Franklin Roosevelt, further demonstrating the deep connections between the New Deal and antipoverty policy.[13] Weaver's experience as an urban reformer made him a staunch advocate for federal resources in US cities and placed him in a leadership role over Model Cities. Like his other underrepresented colleagues in the political sphere, Weaver used his power as a member of President Johnson's cabinet to shape a policy and program that originated through Black urban resistance. Weaver demonstrates how national politics became even more critical during the second half of the 1960s.[14]

In Johnson's remarks upon signing the Housing and Urban Development Act in 1968, he declared this legislation "the Magna Carta to liberate our cities." Johnson described the road to establishing HUD as an extension of the New Deal, the ambitious social reform program passed under Johnson's presidential role model, Franklin Roosevelt, in response to the Great Depression.[15] According to Johnson, "The journey began more than three decades ago—with President Franklin D. Roosevelt's conviction that a compassionate and far-sighted government cannot ignore the plight of the ill-housed or ill-fed or the ill-clothed." For Johnson, the Department of Housing and Urban Development offered city residents "a voice at the Cabinet table" for the first time in US history. Through Model Cities and other urban initiatives, HUD became connected to broader economic and racial justice debates about

US cities. In doing so, HUD joined the broader war against poverty as a plausible solution to economic inequality in cities. Exploring Model Cities as an extension of federal antipoverty initiatives reveals the vast impact of the War on Poverty beyond the Economic Opportunity Act. In addition, Model Cities demonstrates the central role mid-1960s policy played in shaping Brown and Black protest movements after the 1964 Civil Rights Act.[16]

Los Angeles, a Model City

Both small and large cities responded to the Model Cities Program with a great sense of urgency, further demonstrating the broad reach of antipoverty initiatives during this period. Because Model Cities emphasized riot prevention, neighborhoods where uprisings took place received priority during the pilot year two-step process for Model Cities in 1967. First, several cities received planning grants to develop city demonstration agencies to draft comprehensive programs for youth, housing development, unemployment, and other critical community resources. Inspired by Reuther's original Demonstration Cities plan, HUD stipulated that adequate funding requests emphasize infrastructure and resident rehabilitation through proposed programs. Second, city demonstration agencies that submitted plans deemed feasible by HUD received operating funds to implement programs at the local level. The emphasis on infrastructure-building set Model Cities apart from its precursor by prioritizing urban renewal projects in plans to revitalize central city neighborhoods.[17] While urban renewal was a unique aspect of Model Cities, similar programs had an unequal history characterized by displacement and destruction of Black and Brown communities. Scholar Mike Davis identified Los Angeles as a city with a long history of redevelopment projects that reached back to the late nineteenth century, when people flocked to Los Angeles to purchase affordable land for development. Furthermore, historian Gerald Horne shows that between the Watts Rebellion of 1965 and the Rodney King uprising in 1992, predominately African American neighborhoods saw a decline in infrastructure building as other areas in Los Angeles experienced investment and revitalization. These historical factors made Mexican Americans, who experienced displacement earlier in the twentieth century, anxious about Model Cities.[18]

Although Los Angeles played a vital role in the legislative struggle to bring Model Cities to fruition and was, therefore, slated to receive priority as a city where an uprising occurred, local officials failed to comply with HUD regulations during the application process. Secretary Weaver broke the news to mayor Sam Yorty in a telegram. "It is with regret," the telegram stated, "that I inform you that Los Angeles was not selected to receive a planning grant out of the first year's Model Cities Appropriation."[19] When Secretary Weaver announced the first set of Model Cities grants in 1967, he stunned Angelenos when their city did not receive a planning grant. Further investigation into Secretary Weaver's decision revealed that Los Angeles officials submitted a planning grant application for a neighborhood known as Green Meadows even though they should have created a plan for Watts, which qualified for Model Cities as a site where one of the country's most significant mid-1960s urban uprisings took place. Furthermore, guidelines for Model Cities applications distributed to state and local governments in 1966 required that proposed neighborhoods "should contain such problems as serious housing and environment deficiencies, and high concentrations of poverty, unemployment, ill health, and educational deficiencies."[20] Just outside of Watts, Los Angeles officials decided to draft a proposal for Green Meadows South, an area bordering South Central Los Angeles, because Green Meadows "represented 'neither the best nor worst of the blight picture' in Los Angeles."[21] Some of the main improvements proposed for Green Meadows included a community center and plans to upgrade five homes. Unfortunately, Los Angeles's proposal seemed to align more with city revitalization than social services. In addition, the controversy surrounding Green Meadows harkened back to some of the initial struggles over the Economic Opportunity Act, when mayor Sam Yorty attempted to merge the War on Poverty with existing municipal government youth programs.[22]

As Los Angeles struggled to develop a new Model Cities proposal in preparation for the next round of applications, questions surfaced about the need to create a program that served both African Americans and Mexican Americans equally. During the early stages of the federal War on Poverty in 1964, Mexican Americans were still in the process of building and defining a vocal mass movement for social justice. By the time HUD announced Model Cities, the Chicano movement had grown in Los Angeles, Denver, Houston, and Chicago, among other cities. Southwestern states saw the emergence of a vibrant Chicano movement, with 1968 as the focal year for increased national coverage of large-scale Mexican American demonstrations. A younger generation of Mexican American activists, like their African American neighbors, came of age in hypersegregated communities characterized by police harassment, a lack of educational institutions to meet their needs, and limited community resources. The Chicano movement reflected a direct confrontation with the everyday ills of urban life from the perspective of Mexican American youth, demonstrating the movement's deep ties with issues that surfaced in public debates after the 1965 uprising in Watts. Younger Mexican Americans took activism into educational institutions and local communities, reinforcing grassroots engagement as part of the Chicano movement.[23]

The Chicano movement had an important impact on the call for Model Cities funding. For instance, Los Angeles mayor Sam Yorty advocated for Mexican Americans following Los Angeles's initial denial of a Model Cities planning grant. Yorty appealed directly to the city council to include East Los Angeles, which housed a significant Mexican American population, in forthcoming Model Cities applications. Yorty followed up by writing to HUD's regional office in San Francisco to ask permission to amend Los Angeles's recent proposal to ensure Mexican American inclusion. Yorty wrote, "I hoped the Council would consider including a major portion of the Mexican-American and Spanish surname population in the application. It is my hope that the planning process and the subsequent period of implementation of programs will provide this ethnic group an opportunity to participate more fully in the life of the city."[24] As Yorty's letter demonstrates, further consolidation of the Chicano movement by 1968 encouraged Mexican Americans to apply pressure on the most reluctant government officials. Yorty's actions may have also been tied to his interest in gaining Mexican American voters in an upcoming mayoral election for Los Angeles because Brown and Black constituents had become important voting blocs throughout Yorty's time in politics. African American councilman Thomas Bradley, Yorty's strongest opponent, assembled a powerful voting coalition comprising Black and Jewish Angelenos and actively worked to bring Mexican Americans into this historic coalition. As historian Raphael Sonenshein describes in his analysis of Los Angeles's mayoral politics, many Mexican American voters had doubts about both candidates. Yorty seized this opportunity to present himself as a friend to Mexican Americans by arguing that a Black mayor would not take their needs seriously. Yorty's efforts around Model Cities may have reflected his campaign strategy to divide African Americans and Mexican Americans to secure office.[25] Because multiracial democratic coalitions had a successful past in Los Angeles politics, it is no surprise that Yorty attempted to discredit a Black candidate and identify himself as a better representative for a group he held in little regard.

Vicente T. Ximenes, head of President Lyndon Johnson's Inter-Agency Cabinet Committee on Mexican American Affairs and the first Mexican American Equal Employment Opportunity commissioner, entered conversations over Los Angeles's Model Cities plans in 1968. Just one year prior, Ximenes held a series of hearings in El Paso, Texas, to discuss civil rights for Mexican Americans, where some speakers identified Model Cities as an important next step for Mexican Americans and their relationship to African Americans. As the highest federal authority on the status of civil rights in Mexican American communities, Ximenes argued in a letter to Yorty that he felt "anxious to recommend to Secretary [Robert] Weaver that he approve the program." Commissioner Ximenes critiqued the lack of Mexican American participation in Model Cities. He suggested that Mayor Yorty "inquire into the program with a view towards a wider voice for the Mexican American community."[26] Commissioner Ximenes's letter to Mayor Yorty points to how Johnson's presidency created a line of communication between local Mexican American communities and the US federal government. While some Mexican Americans criticized the Inter-Agency Cabinet Committee on Mexican American Affairs hearings held in El Paso, Ximenes, like Weaver, reflects how educated Black and Brown people were brought into the federal government to facilitate communication between local communities and the president. Even though some African American and Mexican American federal officials chose not to participate in public protests, many served as a conduit for local people who sought federal intervention in municipal government decisions about communities of color.[27]

Some Mexican American activists and community organizers reached out to federal government officials, like Ximenes, because they saw Model Cities as an important initiative for East Los Angeles and wanted to ensure they were included. The Community Service Organization (CSO) also rallied behind the call for an East Los Angeles Model Cities plan. As a Mexican American civil rights group derived from Edward Roybal's 1947 bid for city council, the CSO maintained a strong history of activism around anti-police violence, voting, and labor unions. In an interview with the *Los Angeles Times*, Anthony Ríos of the CSO stated that Boyle Heights, an East Los Angeles area where the Mexican American population grew throughout the twentieth century, might benefit from community development funds. Ríos, who had been part of the CSO since its founding after Edward Roybal's first city council campaign, demonstrated how an older generation of Los Angeles activists who started their careers around the New Deal participated in debates about federal programs during the 1960s.[28] For a neighborhood facing significant change, Ríos argued, Model Cities funds supported future redevelopment plans. In addition, he asserted that Model Cities offered opportunities to "upgrade the neighborhood physically, socially, and economically."[29] For

Ríos, Model Cities held the potential to directly address inequality left behind by white exodus from cities and government neglect in East Los Angeles neighborhoods. In addition, he also cited economic change, further revealing the significance of class in shaping activist movements during this time.[30]

In some cases, Mexican American activists pointed directly to resources created by African Americans through Model Cities to advocate for the program's significance. For example, Dionicio Morales from the Mexican American Opportunity Foundation (MAOF) presented his organization to Mayor Yorty as a potential East Los Angeles subcontractor for Model Cities. Founded by Morales in 1963 after a meeting with then Vice President Lyndon Johnson, MAOF began community work in Los Angeles with funding from the Department of Labor. The Mexican American Opportunity Foundation provided childcare, job training, and social events for Mexican Americans in Los Angeles.[31] Writing to Mayor Yorty in May 1968, Morales described a local African American community organization recently accepted as a Model Cities affiliate. The letter demanded, "We hereby request that we be given equal consideration and be designated by you as a major subcontractor to perform like services to the East Los Angeles Model Neighborhood area." He argued that MAOF "successfully demonstrated its capabilities as a prime source of leadership in the Mexican American community," as Morales advocated for his organization to play a leadership role in Model Cities.[32] Morales's letter to Yorty is an example of how some Mexican Americans characterized resources extended to African Americans as a reflection of how the country neglected Brown urban communities. Instances like these illuminate how antipoverty policies prompted important questions about the limitations of understanding inequality as Black and white and how Mexican Americans might help make federal policy more inclusive. On the surface, some might conceptualize Morales's letter to Yorty as an example of competition and hostility against African Americans. However, this letter reflects a more complicated story of an influential Mexican American community advocate highlighting how unequal distribution of funding restricted opportunities rather than lifting barriers.

In other cases, the history of coalition-building among earlier generations of African Americans and Mexican Americans influenced debates about Model Cities.[33] For example, assemblyman Mervyn Dymally aligned himself with well-known Chicano activists to build a coalition around advocacy for African Americans and Mexican Americans.[34] Dymally had served in California's State Assembly since 1962, succeeding Augustus Hawkins. Although Dymally immigrated to the United States from Trinidad, he became deeply invested in Black American political engagement and representing African American Angelenos.[35] Like his state assembly predecessor who sought to bring Black and Brown Los Angeles together, Dymally stepped in to support Morales's interest in gaining approval for MAOF to subcontract for Model Cities. In a letter to Mayor Yorty in 1968, Dymally urged the city government to support the Mexican American Opportunity Foundation's appeal. "I feel this group would speak for the Mexican-American community, a segment of our population that needs representation," Dymally wrote. He described why MAOF seemed suitable for the task, asserting, "I have been impressed with the concern and experience of MAOF in the areas of housing, economic and general social problems of that community."[36] Dymally's letter to Yorty reflected an effort to build Black-Brown solidarity around Model Cities and articulated the lack of Mexican American representation in federal programs to promote equal opportunity. By highlighting that Mexican Americans experienced neglect, Dymally provides an important example of how some politicians working on behalf of African Americans also understood the potential impact of a more inclusive approach to social justice. Dymally's interest in Black-Brown relations built on decades of work that Hawkins and Roybal brought to the US federal government upon their election to Congress.

Still, Model Cities recalled a history of displacement for some Mexican Americans. The US federal government's emphasis on infrastructure and human rehabilitation in Model Cities planning grants made some Angelenos fearful that this new phase in antipoverty funding might cause community destruction and displacement. Urban renewal is also foundational to Mexican American history in Los Angeles, including demolishing a neighborhood known as Chavez Ravine to construct the Dodgers baseball stadium in the 1950s.[37] Locals, including Arthur Montoya of the Maravilla and Belvedere Property Owners Association, argued that Model Cities might allow local officials to implement slum clearance under the guise of community reform. Others, including *Eastside Sun* publisher Joseph Kovner, recounted earlier stories of displacement among Mexican Americans, stating, "It will be another Bunker Hill. Another Chavez Ravine."[38] While some East Los Angeles residents and activists, especially Mexican Americans, characterized Model Cities as an ideal opportunity for community revitalization, others like Kovner saw the program as a recipe for community destruction.

Starting with planning grant applications in 1967, Los Angeles continued to debate how to implement Model Cities programs, especially as a city where African Americans and Mexican Americans resided. In contrast to the War on Poverty, the municipal and county governments primarily administered

Model Cities to placate officials who had become highly resistant to the role of community participants in previous antipoverty programs. However, some of the imbalances in funding remained as Mexican Americans struggled to make Model Cities more inclusive like they had done with the War on Poverty. When Model Cities finally arrived in Los Angeles in 1969, it clashed with the Chicano movement.

Los Angeles received Model Cities funding during the 1969 application cycle. Over the next several years, Los Angeles joined New York and Chicago as the highest-funded Model Cities regions in the United States. The US federal government projected California to receive the most funding over the first five years of Model Cities. San Francisco, Fresno, Compton, and other cities were slated to receive grants.[39] What made Los Angeles unique compared to other Model Cities grants was that city and county governments received funding to develop demonstration programs. While the county government implemented programs in African American areas of Willowbrook and Florence-Firestone, city officials oversaw the Greater Watts Model Neighborhood to serve primarily Black residents and the East/Northeast Model Neighborhood, a grant that served predominantly Mexican Americans.[40] Los Angeles officials proposed to direct first-year funding to education and job development, demonstrating the impact of these programs on fundamental rights defined by rhetoric about US democracy. The emphasis on creating two distinct model neighborhood programs also reveals how post–World War II hypersegregation mapped onto federal policy and attempted to confine Mexican Americans and African Americans to different streams of Model Cities funding. Shared neighborhoods and community institutions before World War II had largely influenced the development of multiracial coalitions. However, federal policies increasingly emphasized defining the racial makeup of specific neighborhoods by the 1960s, creating a barrier to the cross-racial organizing that played a vital role in pre–World War II Black and Brown Los Angeles.[41]

As Model Cities programming grew between 1969 and 1974, the Greater Watts Model Neighborhood tended to develop more projects when compared to resources provided to the East/North East Model Neighborhood. For instance, the Los Angeles Unified School District administered nine education programs in Watts under Model Cities, including early childhood education, literacy training, and recruitment for aides and counselors. In the East/North East area, the school district established two programs, which included learning centers at local high schools and literacy programs. Two critical factors might account for the attention given to Black Los Angeles. First, the

Department of Housing and Urban Development earmarked Model Cities funding for neighborhoods where uprisings occurred. The Watts Rebellion of 1965 meant that Los Angeles received priority in application processes for Model Cities. For instance, Los Angeles's city government submitted a $26.3 million Model Cities Proposal in 1971 and asked that funds be "equally divided between the two model neighborhoods with special emphasis going to areas of education, job training, housing rehabilitation, business development and additional health services." However, officials did not distribute this way.[42] Second, Los Angeles had the support of local and national Black politicians, including Augustus Hawkins in Congress and Thomas Bradley in city council, who advocated for resources in their districts. The presence of Black politicians placed African American neighborhoods in a strong place politically by the second half of the 1960s. In contrast to other localities where uprisings took place, like Detroit and Newark, the focus on uprisings created a power imbalance in a city like Los Angeles, where both African Americans and Mexican Americans advocated for federal funding. While Mexican Americans were often characterized as "quiet" during debates about how to implement antipoverty programs after the Watts Rebellion, the Chicano moratorium folded them into conversations about civil unrest as Los Angeles entered the 1970s.

"The Worst Mexican American Riot Ever Recorded"

African American communities in South Central Los Angeles continued to receive priority for funding due to its designation as a "riot area." The Chicano moratorium catapulted Mexican Americans into discourse about civil disorders. As one of the largest student-led demonstrations by Mexican Americans in Los Angeles, the four moratoriums that took place in Los Angeles between 1969 and 1971 focused specifically on police brutality and the war in Southeast Asia. Although movement activists initially proposed the Chicano moratorium, anti–Vietnam War activist Rosalio Muñoz pushed these demonstrations onto the national scene. Muñoz first gained local popularity when he organized Mexican American youth in Chale con el Draft (To Hell with the Draft), where he worked to bring awareness to the disproportionate number of Mexican American casualties in the Vietnam War and to educate draftees about their civil and human rights.[43] When approached with an opportunity to organize mass antiwar demonstrations as part of the Chicano moratorium, Muñoz enthusiastically accepted.[44]

Moratorium demonstrations quickly grew larger as the Chicano movement gained momentum. By the third moratorium on August 29, 1970, an estimated 20,000 participants descended on Los Angeles to join mass protests designed to bring awareness to disproportionate death rates among Mexican Americans sent to Vietnam. The contentious relationship between Mexican Americans and the Los Angeles Police Department (LAPD) led moratorium protests to turn violent in August. Protestors marched down Whittier Boulevard, the main business district in East Los Angeles, before settling into Laguna Park for a rally. An alleged incident at a nearby liquor store where participants walked to purchase soft drinks changed the Chicano moratorium's tone, resulting in what the *Los Angeles Times* later described as "the worst Mexican-American riot ever recorded."[45] LAPD officers descended on demonstrators, beating protestors, shooting tear gas, and arresting participants as demonstrators scattered in all directions. Even though some demonstrators responded by throwing rocks and bottles, police perpetuated violence during this event. When this police-initiated disturbance concluded later that evening, what started as a peaceful demonstration to bring awareness to Mexican American deaths in Vietnam became known as the "Chicano moratorium riot" by officials.[46]

Following the August 1970 moratorium, Los Angeles officials and residents debated who carried the blame for events on August 29. Some participants and residents argued that LAPD officers arrived intending to harass and brutalize protestors. An East Los Angeles woman interviewed by the *Los Angeles Times* joined local people who questioned police presence at the August moratorium. "About 1,000 cops in battle gear just to direct traffic? What a bunch of bull. They were just waiting for a little something so they could move in," she stated. Other interviewees also identified the amount of police during protests as suspicious. One resident asserted, "But here at a peaceful rally, they're waiting around the corner with more cops and paddy wagons. I wasn't there but I talked to a lot of people who were. They aren't liars."[47] As East Los Angeles residents described, police aggression emerged as a critical post-Chicano moratorium debate. As historian Edward Escobar argues in his research on policing in East Los Angeles, the city's police department, like other post–World War II forces, justified racially motivated aggression by characterizing Black and Brown people as a danger to white neighborhoods.[48] Police responses during the August 29, 1970, Chicano moratorium represents an important example of how local authorities met Mexican American protests with aggression.

Aerial view image of East Los Angeles buildings on fire during the August 1970 Chicano moratorium. *Los Angeles Times* Photographic Archive, UCLA Library Special Collections, uclamss_1429_b662_265105-6. Licensed under CC BY 4.0.

The August 1970 disturbance between Mexican Americans and LAPD officers resulted in property damage, 400 arrests, numerous injuries, and three deaths. Notable *Los Angeles Times* reporter Rubén Salazar was one of three individuals killed during the August 29 protests. Salazar developed a strong local reputation for reporting on important issues in Mexican American communities, including the group's relationship with African Americans. From the early 1960s, when federally funded youth programs started to gain further attention, to when the Chicano movement increased momentum in 1968, Salazar identified Black-Brown relations as an integral part of local politics. The police brutality that resulted in Salazar's death and the unjust dispersal of a peaceful protest further motivated the Chicano Moratorium Committee to bring awareness to unequal treatment in the criminal justice system and to organize future demonstrations around calls for equality within the justice system.[49]

The police-instigated Chicano moratorium riot created widespread hysteria about the potential for an uprising like the one in Watts years earlier. While the August 29 disturbance grew from police harassment, officials placed blame on demonstrators. They responded by assembling the Ad Hoc Committee for Better Community Understanding to strategize about how to "maintain the peace" at future mass protests. The ad hoc committee's primary task included urging moratorium organizers to postpone future demonstrations for several months until the city clarified how to prevent unrest. The Chicano moratorium proceeded with their next demonstration, scheduled for January 31, 1971. Leading up to the subsequent moratorium, the ad hoc committee met and organized a public forum for concerned residents fearful of the prospect of violence. Unfortunately, the ad hoc committee still focused on demonstrators instead of the police. Some 200 Angelenos attended, and judge Leopold Sánchez, an East Los Angeles municipal judge, proposed a resolution to postpone future demonstrations. Sánchez argued that postponement allowed the community more time to reach a compromise with activists about how to stage mass protests.[50] While this community meeting reinforced assumptions that Mexican Americans, especially youth, were inclined to violence, such discussions placed the Chicano movement into context with urban uprisings. Because Model Cities funding named "riot prevention" as a priority, the Chicano moratorium facilitated opportunities for Mexican Americans to claim further access to federal antipoverty funding.

Despite local fears that another mass demonstration might end in police violence, Chicano activists designed the subsequent moratorium to advocate

Demonstrators gather in East Los Angeles for the Chicano moratorium on January 31, 1971. *Los Angeles Times* Photographic Archive, UCLA Library Special Collections, uclamss_1429_b672_266695-2. Licensed under CC BY 4.0.

for equality within the justice system and to call for an end to police brutality. On January 31, 1971, approximately 400 demonstrators from across Southern California joined "Marcha por Justicia" (March for Justice) at Belvedere Park to protest police misconduct. At the moratorium's conclusion, Rosalio Muñoz asked participants to disperse peacefully to avoid another police raid. Despite Muñoz's request, municipal government reports claimed several moratorium participants relocated to the Los Angeles County Sheriff's substation in East Los Angeles and continued their protests. Several demonstrators turned to destroying squad cars and property surrounding the police station. Sheriffs responded by opening fire on the crowd, further demonstrating the importance of "Marcha por Justicia" to address how police interacted with Mexican Americans. Local government representatives once again labeled this incident a riot, which ended with the destruction of some eighty stores, ninety arrests, numerous injuries, and one death. While this incident devastated many Mexican Americans, especially those who participated in moratorium protests, the riot label provided a basis for officials to request Model Cities funding to support Mexican American–centered programming. The Chicano moratorium is one of the most significant protest campaigns in Mexican American social justice history. A closer look at the moratorium's history reveals connections to debates about civil disorders and antipoverty programs, further demonstrating the centrality of policy in shaping post–civil rights activism.[51]

The Chicano moratorium protests reflect how Mexican American activism grew substantially by the end of the 1960s, especially in response to unequal treatment from police and the criminal justice system. Whereas many Mexican Americans attempted to maintain "respectable" protest strategies, including marches, sit-ins, and rallies, the Chicano moratorium demonstrated that Mexican Americans would still be met with police violence. Legal scholar Ian Haney López identifies police brutality and inequality within the criminal justice system as the reason why Mexican Americans transitioned from defining their identity and movement around whiteness to an emphasis on Brownness during the late 1960s. As Mexican American activists defined Brown as a racial and political identity, they articulated a social justice agenda that emphasized the United States' disregard for their culture, heritage, and language. The call to construct the Plaza de la Raza community center in East Los Angeles through Model Cities illuminates this vital transition.

Plaza de la Raza included a fifty-acre multipurpose community center for Mexican Americans to house a performing arts center, library, and museum. This ambitious community center sought to provide a full-service recreational facility for the East Los Angeles area that paid homage to Mexican American heritage, fostered a sense of pride among residents, and offered community services. Plaza de la Raza proposal writers argued that police violence during the Chicano moratorium represented years of neglect, drawing on national discourse used to describe reasons behind African American civil disorders. A 1972 proposal for Plaza de la Raza argued that developing a community center supported a group held in "poor regard—or no regard at all." The proposal stated that the US federal government's neglect of Mexican American communities "resulted in violent confrontations in East Los Angeles in the summer of 1970."[52] Los Angeles's City Demonstration Agency responded by allocating $147,000 to Plaza de la Raza in 1970. A list of executed contracts indicates that administrators ultimately approved a grant to establish a cultural center at Lincoln Park in East Los Angeles. The focus on culture and community pride demonstrates how imagery around civil disorders shaped Model Cities in essential ways.[53]

The Chicano moratorium linked Mexican Americans to the history of grassroots resistance in Los Angeles. As planning for Plaza de la Raza began, project director Frank López called for African Americans to join efforts to bring the community center to fruition. In an interview with the *Los Angeles Sentinel*, López invited African Americans to visit Latin Nites at the Los Angeles Sports Arena to help raise operating funds for the center. "We want to stress that we hope the black community will join us for these evenings of fun," he stated, "and also help us in the Chicano Community to realize our dream of the Plaza de la Raza."[54] In a city where both African Americans and Mexican Americans made up sizeable segments of the poor, the federal government's decision to prioritize "riot prevention" limited East Los Angeles's ability to gain full access to Model Cities early on. The Chicano moratorium helped Mexican Americans further articulate their position as a racially marginalized population in US cities, as demonstrated by efforts to establish Plaza de la Raza. Just as the War on Poverty and Model Cities entered Los Angeles through the Watts Rebellion of 1965, these programs began to wind down as both Mexican Americans and African Americans further established programs that centered on racial pride and radical resistance.

Community Pride and Model Cities' Decline

Millions of dollars flowed into Los Angeles from HUD between 1969 and 1974, leading to several programs organized by activists, teachers, and community organizations. Throughout Watts, residents saw the development of community enrichment, arts, early childhood education, substance abuse programs, and numerous other resources under Model Cities. Like the Chicano moratorium, Model Cities mapped onto local efforts to build cultural and community pride. For instance, Sons of Watts, a local African American organization, received Model Cities funding to establish a program known as Own Recognizance Assistance and Rehabilitation Project for residents recently released from prison. This program offered counseling resources, employment and job-training referrals, and court appearance reminders. The prison rehabilitation project reflected the unique guidelines for Model Cities, which defined juvenile delinquency as a central goal. Sons of Watts capitalized on this priority to create a program that aligned with Model Cities priorities and supported their community in the face of a highly discriminatory criminal justice system. The ability to use Model Cities' priorities, although rooted in white supremacist criminal justice practices, to develop community programs is why 1960s and 1970s antipoverty policies are essential to Los Angeles's social justice history. In communities trying to combat unfair treatment due to economic deprivation, Model Cities provided financial support for some of the most pressing issues that plagued Black Los Angeles in the 1960s and 1970s.[55]

Local and federal officials remained extremely critical of grassroots activists who used antipoverty funds to advance movements for social justice while mimicking some of their programs. For example, in Oakland, California, the Black Panther Party for Self-Defense (BPP) used Model Cities funding to maintain their groundbreaking survival programs during the late 1960s and early 1970s.[56] However, a brutal LAPD raid on Southern California's BPP headquarters in 1969 decimated Southern California Panthers and weakened survival programs throughout the area. Model Cities approved several programs for Los Angeles that closely resembled efforts by the BPP and other grassroots organizations determined to bring vital resources to poor Black residents. For example, the city approved a program known as the Sickle Cell Anemia Education and Detection Program at a local medical center serving South Central Los Angeles. As an illness that impacts people of African descent at higher rates, sickle cell anemia and its testing gained national prominence when BPP chapters established screenings in Black communities across the United States. As sociologist Alondra Nelson argues in her research on the Black Panther Party's medical advocacy, access to adequate health care became a vital aspect of post–civil rights activism that sought to highlight the limitations of the 1964 Civil Rights Act. Nelson points out that while the act expanded political citizenship for African Americans, it did not guarantee "social and economic citizenship," which had a profound impact on the availability of health care.[57] The Model Cities funding of the Sickle Cell Anemia Education and Detection Program maintained a critical resource rooted in the work of the BPP and their commitment to tackling injustice faced by African Americans through medicine. However, local, state, and federal officials remained strident in their efforts to undermine the BPP, its platform, and its members.[58]

Artistic expression also emerged as a strongly supported resource through Model Cities. One community-sponsored event to celebrate Black culture included the Watts Summer Festival starting in 1966. This communitywide event included booths, food, performances, and speeches from Black activists. Because of the festival's ties to antipoverty policy, Office of Economic Opportunity director Sargent Shriver served as the festival's first grand marshal to preside over the event.[59] Another important institution supported by Model Cities, the Watts Towers Art Center, received funding to "provide apprentice experience for 20 Model Neighborhood Residents in the performing, producing, and graphic arts."[60] Art programs offered an opportunity to harness expression and cultivate skills in a community with limited access to these resources. Watts continued to build cultural programming through the Watts Writers Workshop. With funding from Model Cities, the Watts Writers Workshop grew into a well-known organization that sought to support up to 300 local people interested in creative writing and performance.[61] In addition to offering community events, the writer's workshop supported creative pursuits that celebrated Black life, and participants even went on to write for television and other national platforms. The depth of creative and community programs developed for Watts as part of Model Cities allowed programs that typically faced widespread criticism for promoting racial pride to thrive during the War on Poverty's second phase.

The Chicano movement profoundly impacted programs established in the East/North East Model Cities area. East Los Angeles saw community health, college readiness, tutoring, and legal programs for Mexican American residents. For example, in 1971, "Blowout" schools were part of a Model Cities program based at California State University, Los Angeles, a branch of the state's public university system located in the heart of East Los Angeles, to provide students in surrounding communities with college scholarships. Mexican American high school and college students emerged as important leaders in the Chicano movement, especially during the East Los Angeles "Blowouts" in March 1968, when thousands of Mexican American students walked out of East Los Angeles high schools to protest discrimination. First, Mexican American students walked out of local schools in their community over the local, state, and national governments' failures to reform central city education. Second, East Los Angeles "Blowouts" demonstrated the Chicano movement's growth and momentum in Los Angeles by 1968.[62] Colleges throughout California became a vital meeting ground for young activists by the late 1960s, when state government officials revamped higher education to make it more accessible.[63] The connection between Model Cities and East Los Angeles "Blowout" schools demonstrates the impact of local movements led by young activists on implementing federal policy during the 1970s.[64]

East Los Angeles welcomed several education programs to support children and youth. A desire to train local residents in medical fields to help combat discrimination Mexican American patients experienced at the hands of white doctors, Model Cities helped fund a program known as Medical Scholarships for Minority Students. The program awarded scholarships to students of color to attend medical school at the University of Southern California. Another program, the Area Program for Enrichment Exchange, received funding to establish tutoring centers at several East Los Angeles High Schools to "provide the opportunity for students to meet and study with other students having different socio-economic and ethnic backgrounds."[65] These programs represent some of the antipoverty resources established in East Los Angeles to support Mexican American residents during the early 1970s. While funding remained disproportionate, Model Cities offered an opportunity to create programs more concretely aligned with Chicano movement goals.

Mexican American activists played a critical role in bringing awareness to discrimination in the criminal justice system throughout the twentieth century, especially around police brutality. In the 1950s, with the support of then city councilman Edward Roybal and the Community Service Organization, Mexican American civil rights activists fought to reform the LAPD and to highlight misconduct in Brown and Black neighborhoods.[66] Model Cities–funded programs allowed Mexican Americans to continue this work in the post–civil rights United States. In 1971, the Mexican-American Lawyers Club earned approval from Los Angeles's City Demonstration Agency to open a Model Neighborhood Legal Center. The center expanded work begun two decades earlier by the CSO to educate poor Los Angeles residents about their fundamental civil liberties. Such resources became even more critical as anti-immigrant and xenophobic sentiment against Mexican Americans and Latinas/os increased by the end of the twentieth century. Like their African American neighbors, Mexican Americans turned to Model Cities to expand existing initiatives and to build new programs that strengthened movements for social justice. Because the timeline for Model Cities took place as the Chicano movement grew throughout the United States, Mexican Americans used the momentum from their national social justice movement to position their communities for Model Cities funding.[67]

Although the War on Poverty and Model Cities programs faced attacks almost immediately, Richard Nixon's presidency began a process of restructuring Johnson's antipoverty policy. When Nixon entered the White House in 1969, he capitalized on racial and class divisions in US cities and suburbs after World War II by rallying on the side of white suburban residents. White suburbanites across the United States increasingly identified liberal democratic policies, such as forced busing to desegregate schools, as an impingement on their freedoms as US citizens. Nixon's anti–strong central government rhetoric emboldened white suburbanites who built organizations to protest desegregation, giving rise to the silent majority.[68] The myth of meritocracy sat at the core of the silent majority rhetoric, which identified hard work as the reason for homeownership and economic stability among white suburban residents. The silent majority failed to acknowledge the three decades of social reforms, including the New Deal, GI Bill, and federal home subsidies, that helped fund suburban dreams for numerous white families.[69] For Brown and Black people, a strong central government had created opportunities for political engagement unprecedented in US history. Still, African Americans and Mexican Americans faced increased criticism from conservative politicians and their supporters around social reform during Nixon's presidency.

While Nixon held a complicated position as a moderate conservative because he decided to nearly triple social welfare funding during the early years of his presidency, he quickly moved to decentralize several antipoverty programs put in place by Lyndon Johnson. For years, local and state officials strongly resisted direct lines of communication between constituents and officials through the War on Poverty. President Nixon restructured federal funding to allow local and state officials to decide how to best utilize funds. In addition, revenue sharing, a process where federal officials disbursed a lump sum of money to states and cities directly, replaced the individual grant system that allowed a variety of entities to apply for antipoverty funding early on. While uprisings played an essential role in previous funding streams, Nixon argued that uprisings should be met with greater law enforcement measures rather than funding to support creating programs to address economic equality.[70] Nixon's resistance to federal engagement with local programs challenged decades of work from African Americans and Mexican Americans who stood behind a strong central government. For Brown and Black Angelenos, decades of liberal democratic politics had played an essential role in their ability to run for office, create community programs, and advocate for economic justice. When President Nixon entered the White House as a representative of the so-called silent majority and a proponent of state's rights, Mexican Americans and African Americans saw increased attacks on decades of hard work.

When President Nixon began decentralizing the Model Cities and War on Poverty programs in 1973, Los Angeles officials emerged as some of the president's most fearless adversaries.[71] For example, when Nixon omitted the Office of Economic Opportunity from his fiscal year budget for 1974, congressman Augustus Hawkins helped lead advocacy to maintain programs. With support from his congressional allies, Hawkins cosponsored a bill in 1973 to secure congressional oversight in approving changes to the Office of Economic Opportunity. The bill became a strategic measure to "insure [sic] the opportunity for congress to re-examine and re-evaluate OEO," allowing Congress to block attempts to eliminate the War on Poverty by White House officials. For Hawkins and his allies, Congress played an integral role in federal decision-making, and they sought to continue dialogue about the future of antipoverty legislation in the United States.[72] Legislative struggles to save the Office of Economic Opportunity further demonstrate why Los Angeles is critical to the national story of mid-1960s antipoverty policies. Congressman Hawkins used his authority in national politics to fight for resources he understood as essential to a broader struggle for racial justice. Challenging President Nixon impacted Los Angeles and supported neighborhoods that faced consistent divestment during the 1970s.

Unfortunately, Angelenos fell short of preventing President Nixon's proposed cuts. Nixon instituted revenue sharing to decentralize programs and place decision-making power in the hands of local governments. When President Nixon handed down his 1974 fiscal year budget, he omitted funding for Model Cities. His administration wrote Los Angeles in 1973 with guidelines about preparing for the transition from Model Cities to Community Development Revenue Sharing as of fiscal year 1974. In a letter to Mayor Yorty, federal officials sent notice to cease funding for any new projects in the pipeline and to create a plan for the highest priority programs for transfer to a revenue sharing plan. Model Cities joined other federal programs that experienced restructuring by the mid-1970s. The final financial challenge to antipoverty initiatives occurred when President Ronald Reagan dissolved the Office of Economic Opportunity in 1981.[73] However, Model Cities, like other Johnson-era antipoverty measures, lives on through the story of the Chicano moratorium, Watts Rebellion, Augustus Hawkins, and other vital figures in Los Angeles's Mexican American and African American history.

The War on Poverty in Historical Perspective

When labor union activist Walter Reuther first proposed Demonstration Cities in 1965, he envisioned a program to revitalize African American communities in the country's largest cities. For Reuther, an ideal social program for cities required focusing on human services and infrastructure rehabilitation. However, like earlier antipoverty initiatives, Mexican Americans and African Americans in Los Angeles used Model Cities in creative and unimaginable ways to improve their daily lives. While some critics have identified 1960s and 1970s antipoverty measures as a failure, looking closely at local

Model Cities programs that helped send students to college, fund public school programs, and even revitalize parks reveals the historical significance of federal antipoverty programs beyond the original War on Poverty.

Examining Model Cities from the vantage point of Los Angeles brings the intertwined history between Mexican American and African American movements for social justice into sharper view. The Chicano moratorium remains one of the most foundational campaigns in Mexican American civil rights history over fifty years since the first protest occurred in Los Angeles. The Chicano moratorium was significant for many reasons, including bringing awareness to the disproportionate number of Mexican Americans who died in the Vietnam War; police brutality; and criminal justice reform. In addition, the moratoriums brought greater awareness to Mexican American city residents. Through the lens of Model Cities, the Chicano moratorium emerges as a central moment in post-1964 Mexican American social justice history and as part of a broader struggle for equality alongside other racial advocacy campaigns like the Black Freedom movement. More than fifty-five years since the War on Poverty and Model Cities program first came to Los Angeles, Black-Brown relations continue to influence ongoing themes in the history of race and ethnicity in the United States, including criminal justice reform, xenophobia, unemployment, grassroots organizing, and access to government resources. As poverty rebels, Mexican American and African American Angelenos helped set the stage for economic justice programs and reforms for decades.

Epilogue
The War on Poverty's Legacy in Black and Brown America

> Like other urban conflagrations—from Watts to Miami—the 1992 Los Angeles Crisis was sparked by a single incident, yet rooted in grievances and tensions which had accumulated for years.
> —Special Committee on the Los Angeles Crisis, *To Rebuild Is Not Enough*, 1992

Although popular and political culture tend to characterize Lyndon Johnson's War on Poverty as a failure, Black and Brown Angelenos reveal that antipoverty policy was met with excitement, successes, and admiration. For roughly ten years between 1964 and 1974, federal antipoverty dollars galvanized African Americans and Mexican Americans into poverty rebels and allowed them to address deep-rooted economic barriers to racial equality. As Los Angeles became one of the highest funded cities for federal antipoverty dollars, Brown and Black Angelenos developed community enrichment programs for all ages, expanded existing social justice movements, and advocated for political change. Mexican Americans and African Americans from a diversity of backgrounds, including Augustus Hawkins, Edward Roybal, Tommy Jacquette, Gloria Arellanes, and numerous others, sought to create a more inclusive US democracy through the War on Poverty.

National and local efforts to address poverty through the Economic Opportunity Act faced attacks since the program's inception in 1964, forcing Mexican Americans and African Americans to fight for leadership roles in antipoverty programs as they did with Los Angeles mayor Sam Yorty. From the vantage point of Black and Mexican American social justice history, support for antipoverty programs led to a decline in overall poverty rates. However, after decades of economic justice activism rooted in the New Deal and expanded by the War on Poverty, the number of people living below the poverty line, especially women and children, increased by the time Ronald Reagan dissolved the Office of Economic Opportunity in 1981. Poverty and homelessness grew as federal officials slashed antipoverty and social welfare budgets. In addition, political and public attacks on programs that provided cash benefits to low-income families, including Aid to Families with Dependent Children, intensified after 1980 as conservatives and liberals alike increasingly defined welfare recipients as lazy, unmotivated, pathological Black mothers. At the same time, federal, state, and local officials diverted funds to criminal justice in central city neighborhoods where African Americans and Latinas/os resided. After several decades of victories that outlawed racial discrimination and segregation and reduced poverty, the final decades of the twentieth century emerged as some of the most devastating years for low-income central city residents.[1]

Mexican Americans and African Americans in Los Angeles, especially those residing in poor neighborhoods, continued to face neglect, police harassment, and character attacks in popular and political culture in the final decades of the twentieth century. As mistrust against local, state, and federal officials grew, Angelenos once again responded in rebellion following Rodney King's trial against Los Angeles police officers in 1992. Like the Watts Rebellion and Chicano moratorium, the 1992 uprising provided local people, activists, and officials with an opportunity to reflect on the status of economic justice since the War on Poverty.

1992: A Moment of Reflection

On March 3, 1991, Los Angeles resident George Holliday videotaped motorist Rodney King's encounter with officers from the Los Angeles Police Department (LAPD) and California Highway Patrol. Holliday captured officers brutality beating King upon apprehending him following a high-speed chase. Holliday's video recording provided concrete and admissible evidence to charge officers with excessive force in what became a historic trial.[2] Angelenos of color understood Holliday's vivid evidence of police misconduct against King as a snapshot into decades of police violence that impacted their daily lives. Still, jurors acquitted officers of misconduct charges and concluded that Holliday's video footage only reflected King's portrayal of events.[3] Angelenos of color wondered how King's beating by officers, confirmed by video evidence, yielded a not guilty verdict.[4]

The jury's verdict amplified the city, state, and federal governments' failure to acknowledge the intertwined relationship between cuts to antipoverty resources, investment in policing communities of color, and racism since 1980. The verdict in King's trial caused roughly ten years of frustration and injustice to result in rebellion. Starting in the afternoon on April 29, 1992, Angelenos of all racial backgrounds took to the streets of Los Angeles to set buildings on fire, throw bottles at motorists, and loot businesses. Like the Chicano moratorium, they even protested at LAPD headquarters. California officials declared a state of emergency for the greater Los Angeles area and called some 10,000 California National Guard to back up LAPD officers. After roughly five days of resistance that expanded into other areas of Los Angeles County, including Hollywood, Long Beach, and Pomona, the final estimate of damages and loss of life was staggering: fifty deaths, $750 million in property damage, 16,291 arrests, and an overwhelming number of injuries.[5] Residents across Los Angeles County looted and destroyed businesses, demonstrating the economic underpinnings of the 1992 uprising. The centrality of looting in 1992 helped local, state, and federal officials reopen conversations about the relationship between race and class in African American and Latina/o Los Angeles.

Following the 1992 uprising, local officials, activists, and journalists identified many of the same issues that plagued Black Los Angeles in 1965 as causes behind community responses to King's trial. A special committee called by California assemblyman Willie Brown identified a lack of community resources and employment opportunities, and police misconduct as some of the most significant issues impacting Black Angelenos. Assemblyman Curtis Tucker Jr., representing the city of Inglewood, was appointed to lead an Assembly Special Committee on the Los Angeles Crisis. Established in May 1992, just one month after the uprising, California's special committee assembled seventeen officials to investigate ways to reduce poverty and improve race relations in Los Angeles. As part of their investigation, the committee convened eight hearings, where Los Angeles residents shared their recommendations and grievances about life in the City of Angels. The assembly special committee released their final thoughts and recommendations in a fifty-four-page report titled *To Rebuild Is Not Enough* and an accompanying video titled *Welcome to Los Angeles: April 29, 1992*. The report centered on the impact of economic inequality in depriving Black and Brown Angelenos from living full lives. For instance, recommendations highlighted the history of credit discrimination and redlining in preventing African Americans and Mexican Americans from owning homes and businesses in their neighborhoods.[6] The same set of issues that impacted Brown and Black communities in the 1960s remained a continued struggle over twenty-five years after Lyndon Johnson signed the Economic Opportunity Act and Civil Rights Act. The assembly special committee concluded that the uprising following King's trial reflected the long-term struggle for economic justice in Los Angeles and its deep roots in federal policy.

To Rebuild Is Not Enough reflected the long history of critiquing reform programs that did not center institutional and structural inequalities, specifically mayor Thomas Bradley's Rebuild L.A. project.[7] The assembly special committee further emphasized their critique by making connections between Los Angeles in the 1960s and 1990s. "The Committee finds that the causes of the 1992 unrest were the same as the cause of the unrest of the 1960's," the report stated, "aggravated by a highly visible increasing concentration of wealth at the top of the income scale and a decreasing Federal and State commitment to urban programs serving those at the bottom of the income scale."[8] The Assembly Special Committee on the Los Angeles Crisis found that poverty continued to affect neighborhoods throughout Los Angeles. They cited districts with high concentrations of Latina/o, African American, and Asian American residents as having some of the lowest annual income rates across Los Angeles. Findings reflected how poverty remained a central barrier for Angelenos of color just one decade after the US federal government repealed the Office of Economic Opportunity. The committee's research found that roughly 19 percent of Angelenos lived below the poverty line. Of this overall amount, some 33 percent of South Central and 28 percent of East Los Angeles, along with other Mexican American majority areas, earned incomes below the poverty line. The special committee argued that poverty increased over time due to the state and federal governments' failure to provide resources to low-income communities, once again harkening back to the vital historical role policy has played in shaping US society.[9] The committee made salient points about how the local, state, and federal governments increasingly redirected funding away from social programs. They cited Mayor Bradley's Rebuild L.A. campaign, which focused on a plan for business and economic development instead of antipoverty resources, as an example of how politicians increasingly became disconnected from their constituent's material needs.[10]

The 1992 assembly special committee highlighted demographic changes that heightened financial insecurity in Los Angeles and that made social and political reform even more critical. By 1980, Los Angeles County's total population was 7,477,503. African Americans made up 943,968 (12 percent) residents, while the Hispanic-Origin population grew to 2,066,103 (27 percent).[11] By 1992, Los Angeles County's Latina/o population saw a 10 percent increase, while the county's Black population experienced very little growth.[12] As African American migration into Los Angeles slowed, Latina/o immigration ushered a new wave of mass movement into Los Angeles throughout the 1980s. While Black Americans and Mexican Americans stood at almost equal numbers earlier in the twentieth century, by 1980, a diverse array of Latinas/os had grown far larger than their African American counterparts. Census records listed the city's total population in 1980 at 2,966,850. Among the total number of residents, African Americans made up 505,210 (17 percent) and the Hispanic-Origin population stood at 816,076 (27 percent). The percentage of African Americans in the city of Los Angeles began to decline over the next decade, while the Hispanic-Origin population increased by 12 percent. These important demographic shifts and the visible presence of Latinas/os in the 1992 uprising made it difficult for the assembly special committee to use the framework of Black noise, Brown invisibility. In fact, the committee even created a set of recommendations designed to improve and harness collective support.

Multiracial Los Angeles since 1965

The assembly special committee's focus on how a diversity of neighborhoods was affected by the 1992 uprising, including Pico-Union (Latina/o), South Central (Black), and Korea Town (Korean and Latina/o), allowed for a serious analysis of Los Angeles's multiracial residents. The report's opening statement illuminates their interest in multiracialism, stating, "The city that prided itself on its diversity had become the site of the worst multiethnic urban conflict in United States history."[13] The committee's report reflected on how the 1992 uprising required Los Angeles to pay closer attention to relationships between communities of color.[14] *To Rebuild Is Not Enough* went on to further critique racial frameworks used to assess urban uprisings during the 1960s, namely the Kerner Commission Report. According to the Assembly Special Committee on the Los Angeles Crisis, "In 1967, the Kerner Commission issued the famous warning that America was 'moving toward two societies, one black, one white, separate and unequal.' In 1992, Los Angeles is also moving toward a society divided by race—yet the fault lines here will be drawn in black, brown, yellow, and white. No American city has ever faced the task of providing economic opportunity and a climate of mutual tolerance for so many different ethnic groups."[15] The committee's report reflected the ways in which Los Angeles, and California more broadly, shaped new ways of conceptualizing race relations over the course of the twentieth century that included African Americans, Latinas/os, and Asian Americans. In addition, the committee attempted to make sense of tensions brought to the fore through the 1992 uprising, such as conflicts between Black residents and Asian American business owners.[16] As the assembly special committee pointed out, addressing racial injustice in Los Angeles required paying close attention to relationships between communities of color, in addition to how white supremacy shaped their group-specific experiences. In doing so, the committee reinforced a long-term struggle to make debates and policy related to racial inequality more inclusive.

Black-Brown Relations in Twenty-First Century Los Angeles

Since the 1980s, rapid demographic shifts in Los Angeles have made national headlines as African Americans and Latinas/os continue to grapple with how to share space and resources. While identity politics have remained central to debates about race and representation, interracial conflict has also endured as a popular symbol of Black-Brown relations in Los Angeles. For example, during an April 2005 interview with former Los Angeles mayor Antonio Villaraigosa conducted by the *Los Angeles Sentinel*, reporters asked Mayor Villaraigosa about his approach to intergroup relations as a twenty-first century politician. Villaraigosa highlighted his efforts to prevent and reduce rivalries between African Americans and Latinas/os in local schools, which received widespread attention by national news outlets throughout the 1990s and early 2000s, as an example of how a Mexican American mayor might support both groups. While Villaraigosa's election in 2005 reflected Los Angeles's changing demographic profile, questions about his investment in both African American and Latina/o Los Angeles demonstrates that long-standing efforts to define Black-Brown relations continued into the new millennium.[17]

Rodney King's trial and subsequent protests represented the state of race relations and economic justice in Los Angeles on the cusp of the Economic Opportunity Act and Civil Rights Act of 1964's thirty-year anniversary. To understand why Angelenos responded to King's trial against police officers in rebellion, the Assembly Special Committee on the Los Angeles Crisis revisited uprisings that took place in the 1960s and reevaluated the McCone and Kerner Commission reports. They identified a lack of financial investment in communities of color, hypersegregation, and overpolicing as the three most pressing issues, just as poverty rebels argued in the mid-1960s. At the core of Black-Brown relations in Los Angeles since the New Deal was a long-term struggle for equality rooted in a desire to create a more inclusive approach to economic justice. *To Rebuild Is Not Enough* finally considered both groups equally almost thirty years after Lyndon Johnson signed the Economic Opportunity Act.

Notes

Abbreviations Used in the Notes

Federal Acts

CRA	Civil Rights Act
DCMD	The Demonstration Cities and Metropolitan Development Act
EOA	Economic Opportunity Act

Government Agencies and Reports

I-AC	Inter-Agency Cabinet Committee on Mexican American Affairs
TFTRS	Report of the White House Conference "To Fulfill These Rights"

Archives

CSA	California State Archives, Sacramento
Green	Cecil H. Green Library, Stanford
Huntington	Henry E. Huntington Library, San Marino
LACA	Los Angeles City Archives, Los Angeles
LBJL	Lyndon Baines Johnson Presidential Library and Museum, Austin
NACP	United States National Archives, College Park
UCLA-YRL	Charles E. Young Research Library, University of California, Los Angeles

Manuscript Collections

Bradley Papers	Thomas Bradley Administrative Papers
Corona Papers	Papers of Bert Corona
Hahn Papers	Papers of Kenneth Hahn
Hawkins Papers	Papers of Augustus F. Hawkins
REOLS	Records of Agencies for Economic Opportunity and Legal Services
RSCLC	Records of the Southern Christian Leadership Conference, Atlanta
Ruiz Papers	Papers of Manuel Ruiz Jr.
Snyder Papers	Papers of Councilman Arthur Snyder
SOEO	Inventory of the State Office of Economic Opportunity
TFTRS	Report of the White House Conference "To Fulfill These Rights"
WHCF	White House Central Files
Yorty Papers	Papers of Mayor Samuel Yorty

Newspapers

AW Atlanta Daily World
BA Baltimore Afro-American
CD Chicago Daily Defender
LAT Los Angeles Times
LAS Los Angeles Sentinel
NYT New York Times
WP Washington Post

Introduction

1. The Depression and New Deal had a profound impact on mid-1960s struggles for equality. See Vargas, *Labor Rights*, 5–6; Flamming, *Bound for Freedom*, 336–42.

2. Over 40 million people across the United States lived below the poverty line when the War on Poverty was approved. See Orleck, "Introduction: The War on Poverty," 5.

3. CRA, 1964.

4. Scholar Gaye Theresa Johnson uses the framework of "constellation" to examine the mutual benefit of simultaneous activism by Latinas/os and African Americans during World War II. See Johnson, "Constellations of Struggle," 156–57.

5. For scholars who have critically examined the question of whether conflict or cooperation has shaped Black-Brown relations, see Vaca, *Presumed Alliance*; Kun and Pulido, *Black and Brown*.

6. Several scholars have examined the impact of residential segregation on cultivating Black-Brown relations in early twentieth-century Los Angeles. See Wild, *Street Meeting*; Varzally, *Making a Non-White America*.

7. Several scholars have explored the impact of multiracial civil rights in Los Angeles and California more broadly. See Bernstein, *Bridges of Reform*; Kurashige, *Shifting Grounds of Race*; Brilliant, *Color of America*; Johnson, "Constellations of Struggle"; Araiza, *To March for Others*; Pulido, *Black, Brown, Yellow, and Left*.

8. Behnken, *Fighting Their Own Battles*; Mantler, *Power to the Poor*.

9. Recent research has explored Black-Brown histories in southern states. See Krochmal, *Blue Texas*; Márquez, *Black-Brown Solidarity*.

10. See Rosas, *South Central Is Home*; Bauman, *Race and the War*.

11. For a recent analysis of voting rights history, see Jones, *Vanguard*. For an overview of civil rights history, see Holt, *Movement*.

12. Several scholars have critically examined the role of race, class, and politics in shaping experiences and protests in African American history. For an earlier scholarly analysis, see Robinson, *Black Marxism*. For a recent analysis, see Taylor, *Race for Profit*.

13. For an analysis of Los Angeles, see Bauman, *Race and the War*, 21; Rosas, *South Central Is Home*, 44. For an analysis of California more broadly, see Self, *American Babylon*, 179–80.

14. Several scholars have examined the War on Poverty's impact on activism across the United States. See Clayson, *Freedom Is Not Enough*; Orleck, *Storming Caesars Pal-*

ace; Ashmore, *Carry It On*; Phelps, *People's War on Poverty*; Germany, *New Orleans*; Kiffmeyer, *Reformers to Radicals*.

15. Historian Gerald Horne argues that Los Angeles was home to "rainbow racism," where African Americans shared the burden of white aggression and repression with other racially marginalized groups. See Horne, *Fire This Time*, 25. Historian Albert Camarillo has proposed the framework of "crow cousins" as a historical framework for considering interrelated experiences between African Americans and Mexican Americans. See Camarillo, "Navigating Segregated Life," 645-62. Historian and American studies scholar George Lipsitz argues that relational research helps to step back from privileging whiteness as the primary framework for analyzing communities of color. See Lipsitz, et al., "Race as a Relational Theory," 23. Scholars Josh Kun and Laura Pulido have argued that historically, intellectual and community discussions about Black-Brown relations have been bogged down in debates about racial strife. See Kun and Pulido, *Black and Brown*, 2-4.

16. Several scholars have closely examined the unique nature of Black and Brown life in the West as a region rooted in US colonization. See Hernández, *City of Inmates*; Sánchez, *Becoming Mexican American*; Campbell, *Making Black Los Angeles*, 29-30.

17. Economic justice became an important common thread between a diversity of movements during the 1960s and 1970s. For an analysis of the National Welfare Rights movement, see Nadasen, *Welfare Warriors*; Orleck, *Storming Caesars Palace*. For an analysis of the Chicano movement, see Chávez, *My People First! "¡Mi Raza Primero!"*; Garcia, *Chicano Generation*; Oropeza, *¡Raza Sí! ¡Guerra No!*. For analysis of Black nationalism, see Horne, *Fire This Time*; Brown, *Fighting for US*.

18. During the 1960s, a series of urban studies was published that examined "the urban crisis." These studies expertly examined the growth of widespread segregation in US cities since World War II, when African Americans became the most isolated group in US cities. See Hirsch, *Making the Second Ghetto*; Sugrue, *Origins of the Urban Crisis*.

19. For an analysis about the relationship among protest, policy, and criminal justice, see, for example, Hinton, *War on Poverty*, 13; Escobar, "Dialectics of Repression," 1485-88.

20. Several scholars have explored how city residents, especially women, have utilized reforms in inventive ways to fight economic inequality. See Williams, *Politics of Public Housing*; Levenstein, *Movement Without Marches*.

21. The Watts Rebellion helped reveal many of the difficulties African Americans faced in Los Angeles. See Horne, *Fire This Time*; Sides, *L.A. City Limits*.

22. Honey, *To the Promised Land*, 110.

23. Curtis J. Sitomer, "Mexican-Americans, A Minority's Plight," *Christian Science Monitor*, November 5, 1965.

24. Haney López, *Racism on Trial*, 1-2.

Chapter One

1. African American migrants to Los Angeles arrived in a US-Mexico borderland city. The relationships between African Americans and Mexican Americans, in addition to both groups' relationship with Mexican immigrants, is vital to understanding

race relations in Los Angeles since the late nineteenth century. For further reading on US immigration history, see Gutiérrez, *Walls and Mirrors*; Ngai, *Impossible Subjects*. For an analysis of racial formation and immigration, see Molina, *How Race Is Made*. For research about Black migration into Los Angeles as a former Mexican city, see Campbell, *Making Black Los Angeles*.

2. Deverell, *Whitewashed Adobe*, 16.

3. Legal scholar Ian Haney López describes the important transition many Mexican American civil rights groups made from centering their activism around whiteness to constructing a racial identity as Brown. See Haney López, *Racism on Trial*, 9-10.

4. Deverell, *Whitewashed Adobe*, 12-14; Treaty of Guadalupe Hidalgo.

5. Hernández, *City of Inmates*, 35.

6. For an analysis of the experiences of Mexicans and Mexican Americans when the Southwest transitioned from Mexico to the United States, see Camarillo, *Chicanos in a Changing Society*; Carrigan and Webb, "Lynching of Persons," 411-38; Gómez, *Manifest Destinies*; Martinez, *Injustice Never Leaves You*; Villanueva, *Lynching of Mexicans*.

7. Part of what makes Los Angeles's history of race relations unique is the city's multiple transitions over time starting with Indigenous peoples, Spanish conquistadors, Mexico, and the United States. Practices of identity formation and othering took place in each of these transitions and continued to shape how communities of color experienced Los Angeles. See Hernández, *City of Inmates*, 8-15.

8. Campbell, *Making Black Los Angeles*, 15-18.

9. Flamming, *Bound for Freedom*, 2.

10. Gómez, *Manifest Destinies*, 62.

11. Flamming, *Bound for Freedom*, 60-61.

12. Hämäläinen and Truett, "On Borderlands," 346.

13. Bernstein, *Bridges of Reform*, 4.

14. Pagán, *Murder at the Sleepy Lagoon*, 44-46, 87-88.

15. Black activists of the late nineteenth and early twentieth centuries were often described as "race women" and "race men." For an analysis of some of these activists and civil rights organizations in California, see Hudson, *West of Jim Crow*, 59-70.

16. For background on early Mexican American activism, see García, *Memories of Chicano History*; García, *Mexican Americans*.

17. For an analysis of how race mapped onto neighborhoods, see Wild, *Street Meeting*, 21-31; Sides, *L.A. City Limits*, 96-97.

18. See Self, *American Babylon*; Fernández, *Young Lords*.

19. Flamming, *Bound for Freedom*, 17-18, 24, 41-44; Sánchez, *Becoming Mexican American*, 65.

20. Wilkerson, *Warmth of Other Suns*, 15.

21. Camarillo, *Chicanos in California*, 76-78; Sánchez, *Becoming Mexican American*, 51-54, 67.

22. Hernández, *City of Inmates*, 34.

23. See Bunch, "Greatest State," 129-31.

24. For further insight into how Mexican Americans in Los Angeles have experienced urban displacement, see Avila, *Popular Culture*.

25. See Taylor, *Race for Profit*; Rothstein, *Color of Law*.

26. Flamming, *Bound for Freedom*, 93–97, 99–100; Sides, *L.A. City Limits*, 23.

27. Du Bois, "Colored California," 193–94; Bunch, "Greatest State," 129. For additional reading about the history and legacy of Black towns, see Slocum, *Black Towns, Black Futures*.

28. Scholars have argued that, by design, racial terror has historically undermined African American efforts to gain upward mobility, claim bodily autonomy, and live freely. See Mitchell, *From Slave Cabins*, 1–3; Anderson, *White Rage*, 1–2; Higginbotham, *Righteous Discontent*.

29. See Flamming, *Bound for Freedom*, 2.

30. Molina, *How Race Is Made*, 4.

31. Hawkins interview, audio recording, tape no. 1, side A, transcript 1–27; Flamming, "Becoming Democrats," 285.

32. Deverell, *Whitewashed Adobe*, 46.

33. Sánchez, *Becoming Mexican American*, 69–72.

34. Gregory, *Southern Diaspora*, 13–16.

35. Sánchez, "'Good for Boyle Heights,'" 634; Sánchez, "Edward R. Roybal," 57.

36. White, *Railroaded*, 37–38.

37. See Kelley, *Hammer and Hoe*; Hunter, *To 'Joy My Freedom*.

38. Flamming, *Bound for Freedom*, 296–97.

39. Flamming, *Bound for Freedom*, 331–68.

40. See Cloward and Ohlin, *Delinquency and Opportunity*.

41. Sánchez, *Becoming Mexican American*, 201, 213, 215–16.

42. Historian Robin D. G. Kelley describes the growth of Black leftist and class activism in the 1920s and 1930s. See Kelley, *Race Rebels*, 103–21.

43. Hawkins interview, tape no. 1, side B, transcript 56.

44. Sides, *L.A. City Limits*, 27–28.

45. Vargas, *Labor Rights*, 83–89; Sánchez, *Becoming Mexican American*, 229, 234.

46. Brinkley, "New Deal," 85–88.

47. Ferguson, "Industrial Conflict," 4. See Cohen, *Making a New Deal*.

48. Hawkins interview, tape no. 1, side B, transcript 43–54.

49. Hawkins interview, tape no. 1, side B, transcript 41.

50. Flamming, "Becoming Democrats," 286–87.

51. Roybal interview, transcript 1–2, 4, 8, 10–12; Joe Holley, "Calif. Rep. Edward R. Roybal, 89, Dies," *WP*, October 27, 2005; Bernstein, *Bridges of Reform*, 35–36.

52. Sides, *L.A. City Limits*, 37, 58.

53. Several scholars have explored how the relationship between African Americans and Mexican Americans has developed since World War II. See Bernstein, *Bridges of Reform*; Brilliant, *Color of America*; Rosas, *South Central Is Home*; Bauman, *Race and the War*; Krochmal, *Blue Texas*; Araiza, *To March for Others*.

54. The category "Spanish-Surname Population" was a term used in US census records to represent residents of Latina/o descent. In Los Angeles, Mexican Americans made up the majority of the "Spanish-Surname Population" in the decades immediately following World War II.

55. See Gregory, *Southern Diaspora*, 5.

56. For further reading about Great Migrations, see Moore, *To Place Our Deeds*; Trotter, *Great Migration*; Grossman, *Land of Hope*; Painter, *Exodusters*; Sandoval-Strausz, *Barrio America*; Wilkerson, *Warmth of Other Suns*.

57. Camarillo, "Cities of Color," 9.

58. Sides, *L.A. City Limits*, 110; Flamming, *Bound For Freedom*, 369; Nicolaides, *My Blue Heaven*, 211. For further insight into how Los Angeles communities like Compton changed over the course of the twentieth century as a result of immigration from Mexico and Central America, see Camarillo, "Cities of Color."

59. See Arredondo, *Mexican Chicago*; Fernández, *Brown in the Windy City*.

60. For further reading about Mexican American population statistics and the census, see Grebler, Moore, and Guzmán, *Mexican-American People*.

61. Sides, *L.A. City Limits*, 2, 38; Camarillo, *Chicanos in California*, 76–78; US Census of Population and Housing, 1960.

62. Gregory, *Southern Diaspora*, 34, 330, 332; Sánchez interview, session one; "Negroes and Mexican Americans," 10–12, 24.

63. See Brooks, *Alien Neighbors, Foreign Friends*; Kurashige, *Shifting Grounds of Race*.

64. Pagán, *Murder at Sleepy Lagoon*, 156–58, 168–70; Ngai, *Impossible Subjects*, 175.

65. Sides, *L.A. City Limits*, 95, 101, 106–8, 118.

66. Sides, *L.A. City Limits*, 81–82.

Chapter Two

1. Scholar Tricia Rose uses the framing "Black noise" to describe the development of rap music and how it allows African Americans to articulate their experiences within the United States. I use this term to symbolize the surprising nature of the Watts Rebellion. Because Los Angeles was outside of the Jim Crow South, policymakers assumed that Black life was substantially better in California. I use the term "Black noise" to articulate the ways in which the uprising helped lay bare decades of injustice that was overshadowed by assumptions that Los Angeles was devoid of racism. See Rose, *Black Noise*, xii-xvi.

2. For an early analysis of how US federal policy shaped Black-Brown interactions during the New Deal, see Daniel, *Chicano Workers*.

3. Pycior, *LBJ and Mexican Americans*, 115–20.

4. Rubén Salazar, "Youth Drive May Skip Mexican-Americans, Over-Publicized Negro Groups May Get $2 Million Fund, Welfare Official Says," *LAT*, February 4, 1963, LACA, Yorty Papers, Youth Matters (Newspaper Clippings, etc.) 1961–63, Box C-1007.

5. EOA, 1964, p. 508.

6. Orleck, "Introduction: The War on Poverty," 9.

7. EOA, 1964, p. 516.

8. EOA, 1964, p. 516.

9. See Sanders, *A Chance for Change*, 5–6.

10. See Bernstein, *Bridges of Reform*, 4.

11. See Brilliant, *Color of America*; Kurashige, *Shifting Grounds of Race*; Varzally, *Making a Non-White America*; Wild, *Street Meeting*; Leonard, *Battle for Los Angeles*; Johnson, "Constellations of Struggle," 155–72.

12. Since the late nineteenth century, African Americans attempted to develop relationships with Africa, its diaspora, and other colonized groups around the globe. Like the civil rights movement more broadly, the Watts Rebellion received international attention. See Dudziak, *Cold War Civil Rights*.

13. See Bauman, *Race and the War*, 5; Germany, "Politics of Poverty," 745–47; Phelps, *People's War on Poverty*, 4–5.

14. Sides, *L.A. City Limits*, 157.

15. Augustus F. Hawkins, "Inside on Washington," *LAS*, August 13, 1964; "Area Development, Jobs Moving Ahead—Hawkins," *LAS*, June 18, 1964; "Hawkins Program Two Years Ahead of LBJ," *LAS*, April 16, 1964.

16. "Congressmen War on Poverty," *LAS*, April 9, 1964.

17. For an analysis of how academia and the public have used civil rights history, see Hall, "Long Civil Rights Movement," 1233–63.

18. Clayson, *Freedom Is Not Enough*, 7, 14; Orleck, *Storming Caesar's Palace*, 128.

19. "Four Congressmen Attack Poverty," *LAS*, April 9, 1964.

20. Senate Report, Economic Opportunity Act of 1964, p. 7.

21. "Committee to Urge Poverty War Merger," *LAT*, May 28, 1965; Bauman, *Race and the War*, 21–22.

22. Bauman, *Race and the War*, 22–25; Paul Weeks, "Poverty Agency Adopts Sweeping New Policy," *LAT*, October 26, 1965.

23. Ruiz to Hawkins, March 30, 1965, Green, Ruiz Papers, M0295, Box 10, Folder 13.

24. Hawkins to Ruiz, April 5, 1965, Green, Ruiz Papers, M0295, Box 10, Folder 13.

25. Paul Weeks, "Congressmen Back New Anti-Poverty Agency: Four Democrats Ask Washington to Bypass Youth Opportunities Board on Programs," *LAT*, June 5, 1965.

26. Weeks, "Congressmen Back New Anti-Poverty Agency."

27. *Violence in the City*, Governor's Commission, 10; Valerie Reitman and Mitchell Landsberg, "Watts Riots, 40 Years Later," *LAT*, August 11, 2005.

28. Horne, *Fire This Time*, 54.

29. Katzenbach to the President, Memo, August 17, 1965, LBJL, Ex HU 2, WHCF, "HU 2/ST 5 11/22/63–8/23/65," Box 25; Reitman and Landsberg, "Watts Riots."

30. Katzenbach to the President; Myrna Oliver, "Former Lt. Gov., Congressman Glenn M. Anderson Dies at 81: Politician: Longtime South Bay Figure Leaves Legacy of Public Works Projects," *LAT*, December 14, 1994; Reitman and Landsberg, "Watts Riots"; Kathy Williamson, "Tommy Jacquette: Legendary L.A. Activist Succumbs," *LAS*, November 19, 2009.

31. See Felker-Kantor, *Policing Los Angeles*, 20–22.

32. Mexican American Angelenos challenged police violence for several decades. See Escobar, *Race, Police*.

33. Crump, *Black Riot in Los Angeles*, 27, 30; Sonenshein, "Coalition Building in Los Angeles," 452–53.

34. Califano to the President, Memo, September 11, 1965, LBJL, Ex HU 2, WHCF, "HU 2/ST 5 8/24/65–9/11/–65," Box 25; *Violence in the City*, 1.

35. Glenn Fowler, "Ex-Gov. LeRoy Collins Dies at 82: Floridian Led Way in 'New South,'" *NYT*, March 13, 1991; "LeRoy Collins; Former Florida Governor Battled

Discrimination," *LAT*, March 14, 1991; Carter to Moyers, Memo, August 20, 1965, LBJL, Ex HU 2, WHCF, "HU/ST5 8/24/65-9/11/65," Box 25.

36. Collins to the President, Memo, LBJL, Ex HU 2, WHCF, "HU2/ST5 8/24/65-9/11/65," Box 25.

37. Collins to the President.

38. Mayor to Humphrey, LACA, Yorty Papers, "Correspondence, July-August 1965," Box C-1005; Collins to the President.

39. Collins to the President.

40. Bauman, *Race and the War*, 42-48; Collins to the President.

41. Collins to the President.

42. Collins to the President.

43. Shriver to Collins, Telegraph, August 23, 1966, LBJL, Ex HU 2, WHCF, "HU2/ST5 8/24/65-9/11/65," Box 25; Shriver to Murphy, LACA, Yorty Papers, "General: United States Government Economic Opportunity, 1965," Box D-25; Long to O'Brien, Memo, August 30, 1966, LBJL, Ex HU 2, WHCF, "HU2/ST5 8/24/65-9/11/65," Box 25.

44. Shriver to Collins; Shriver to Murphy; Long to O'Brien; Collins to the President.

45. Since the early twentieth century, local governments have often compiled studies in the aftermath of race riots, uprisings, and unrest that ended in violence. See Chicago Commission on Race Relations, *Negro in Chicago*; National Advisory Commission on Civil Disorders, *Report of the National Commission*; Oklahoma Commission to Study the Tulsa Race Riot of 1921, *Report by the Oklahoma Commission*; Special Committee on the Los Angeles Crisis, *To Rebuild Is Not Enough*; Moynihan, *Negro Family*, 29-34.

46. *Violence in the City*.

47. Art Berman, "Riot Inquiry: McCone to Head Commission Brown Appointees Will Seek Causes, Recommend Cures," *LAT*, August 20, 1965; Glenn Fowler, "John A. McCone, Head of C.I.A. in Cuban Missile Crisis, Dies at 89," *NYT*, February 16, 1991; Myrna Oliver, "John A. McCone, 89; Helped Establish CIA," *LAT*, February 16, 1991.

48. *Violence in the City*, "Letter to Governor Brown."

49. For further reading about Mexican American and LAPD relations, see Escobar, "Dialectics of Repression."

50. *Violence in the City*, 27-28, 36.

51. Sandoval-Strausz, *Barrio America*, 146.

52. Sandoval-Strauz, *Barrio America*, 147.

53. Hernández, *City of Inmates*, 138-39.

54. *Violence in the City*, 41.

55. *Violence in the City*, 38-41; Galarza, "La Mula No Nacio Arisca," 199-206.

56. Booker Griffin, "Black-Chicano Cooperation Termed One-Sided Ripoff," *LAS*, October 31, 1974.

57. See, Sides, *L.A. City Limits*, 108-12; Self, *American Babylon*, 97-99. The rise of studies that examine suburbanization have helped historians understand the importance of race and urban space since World War II. See Lassiter, *Silent Majority*, 4-5.

58. *Violence in the City*, 49-56, 60-61.

59. "Hawkins Likens Riot in L.A. to Selma Marches," *LAT*, August 19, 1965; Dick West and Paul Weeks, "Dr. King Hears Watts Protests Over Heckling," *LAT*, August 19, 1965.

60. Helen Rowan, "A Minority Nobody Knows," *Atlantic Monthly*, 1967, 47–52.

61. Curtis J. Sitomer, "Mexican-Americans, A Minority's Plight," *Christian Science Monitor*, November 5, 1965.

Chapter Three

1. Johnson, "Executive Order 11330," American Presidency Project.
2. See Murch, *Living for the City*, 4. See also Horne, *Fire This Time*, 187.
3. Escobedo, *From Coveralls to Zoot Suits*, 18, 21.
4. Hinton, *War on Poverty*, 12.
5. Hinton, *War on Poverty*, 29, 33.
6. "Los Angeles City Laws For Youth," 1, LACA, Yorty Papers, "Youth Matters (Newspaper Clippings, etc.) 1961–1963," Box C-1007; "Yorty Asks Aid to Halt Teen Riots," *Los Angeles Examiner*, October 11, 1961; Bauman, *Race and the War*, 19.
7. EOA, 1964, p. 508.
8. "(1954) Brown v. Board of Education," Blackpast.
9. Ransby, *Ella Baker*, 66.
10. "Future Plan and Program of the N.A.A.C.P.," 254–55.
11. "About," LAS, https://lasentinel.net/about; Sides, *L.A. City Limits*, 30–32.
12. Hawkins interview, audio recording, tape no. 1, side B, transcript 43.
13. See Murch, *Living for the City*, 58–60.
14. See Hine, "Rape and the Inner Lives," 914.
15. See Gregory, *Southern Diaspora*, 18–19.
16. Sánchez interview, audio recording, session one.
17. Pagán, *Murder at the Sleepy Lagoon*, 94–101; Escobedo, *From Coveralls to Zoot Suits*, 17–18.
18. Pulido, *Black, Brown, Yellow, and Left*, 61–76.
19. Pulido, *Black, Brown, Yellow, and Left*, 59.
20. Johnson, "To Fulfill These Rights," LBJL website.
21. Johnson, "To Fulfill These Rights."
22. Murch, *Living for the City*, 97–98.
23. Brown, *Fighting for US*, 9; Moreno, "Understanding the Role of Conflict," 182–83.
24. Brown, *Fighting for US*, 38.
25. Mayes, *Kwanzaa*, 63–65; Horne, *Fire This Time*, 187; Karenga, "Karenga, Maulana (1941–)."
26. Mayes, *Kwanzaa*, 68; Correspondence, May and Slonager Inspection Reports, Office of Economic Opportunity Inspection Division, 1964–67, California (Alameda–Los Angeles), NACP, Box 6, Folder: Los Angeles (EYOA) Sept.–Dec. 1967, REOLS, RG 381.
27. Jacquette interview, audio recording, session 1.
28. Mayes, *Kwanzaa*, 68; Fullmer to May, Memorandum, March 14, 1966, NACP, Inspection Reports, 1964–67, Office of Economic Opportunity Inspection Division, CAP, (Los Angeles, CA), Box 7, Folder: Los Angeles (EYOA) March 1966, REOLS,

RG 381; Jacquette interview, audio recording, session 1B; Stannard to May, September 15, 1967, NACP, Inspection Reports, 1964–67, Office of Economic Opportunity Inspection Division, California (Alameda-Los Angeles), Box 6, Folder: Los Angeles (EYOA) Sept.–Dec. 1967, REOLS, RG 381.

29. Fullmer to May, Memorandum.
30. Fullmer to May, Memorandum; Flamming, *Bound For Freedom*, 243–44.
31. See Taylor, *Promise of Patriarchy*, 5–6; Blain, *Set the World on Fire*, 28–30.
32. Fullmer to May, Memorandum.
33. Jacquette interview, audio recording, session 1.
34. Jacquette interview, audio recording, session 1B.
35. Weeks to May, Memorandum; Brown, *Fighting for US*, 40.
36. Weeks to May, Memorandum.
37. Jacquette interview, audio recording, session 1B.
38. Chávez, *My People First! "¡Mi Raza Primero!,"* 44.
39. Castro interview audio recording, session 2.
40. "A Summary of Economic Opportunity Act of 1964," CSA, SOEO, F3751:1; Ogbar, "Brown Power to Brown People," 254–55; Sánchez interview, audio recording, session 1.
41. Sánchez interview, audio recording, session 1.
42. Chavez, *¡Mi Raza Primero!*, 47–48.
43. Sánchez interview, audio recording, session 1.
44. Sánchez interview, audio recording, session 1.
45. Sánchez interview, audio recording, session 1.
46. Sánchez interview, audio recording, session 1.
47. Sánchez interview, audio recording, session 1.
48. Pulido, *Black, Brown, Yellow, and Left*, 116.
49. Chávez, *¡Mi Raza Primero!*, 49.
50. Rosas, *South Central Is Home*, 77.
51. Arellanes interview, audio recording, session 3.
52. Arellanes interview, audio recording, session 3.
53. "Who We Are," Los Angeles County HRC website.
54. Bill Robertson, "Mexican-American Leaders Urge Unity," *LAS*, March 24, 1966.
55. Robertson, "Mexican-American Leaders."
56. Castro interview, audio recording, session 2.
57. Wing to May, Memorandum, February 28, 1966, NACP, Inspection Reports, 1964–67, Office of Economic Opportunity Inspection Division, CAP (Los Angeles, CA), Box 7, Folder: Los Angeles (EYOA), Jan. 1966–Feb. 1966, REOLS, RG 381.
58. Peter Barts, "Negro Gains Vex Coast Mexicans: Rising Aide After Los Angeles Riots Stirs Resentment," *NYT*, October 17, 1965.
59. See Carrigan and Webb, "The Lynching of Persons," 411–38; Hernández, *City of Inmates*; Camarillo, *Chicanos in a Changing Society*.
60. Ken Fanucchi, "Mexicans, Negroes Deny Racial Friction," *LAT*, March 28, 1966.
61. Fullmer to May, Memorandum.
62. Fullmer to May, Memorandum.

63. Program Proposal for Job Placement of Deprived Teens for Summer Work, Huntington, Hahn Papers, Box 2.26.1, Folder 14.

64. Pete Petersen to Paul Zimmer, Memorandum, August 20, 1968, F3751:5, Folder: State of California, Gubernatorial Records—Press Releases, Governor's Office, 1964–65, 67, CSA.

Chapter Four

1. Johnson, "Radio and Television Remarks," LBJL website.
2. Ellis, *Freedom's Pragmatist*, 14.
3. "Biography, Lyndon B. Johnson," LBJL website.
4. For *Mendez v. Westminster* (1946) and *Cisneros v. Corpus Christi Independent School District* (1970), two important cases in Mexican Americans' struggle against school segregation, see Valencia, *Chicano Students and the Courts*.
5. Pycior, *LBJ and Mexican Americans*, xiii, 14, 22; Lerner, "To Be Shot," 253.
6. Vargas, *Labor Rights*, 65; Sides, *L.A. City Limits*, 30; Blain, *Set the World on Fire*, 47–48.
7. Lerner, "To Be Shot," 246–51; Pycior, *LBJ and Mexican Americans*, 30.
8. Billington, "Lyndon B. Johnson and Blacks," 29; Lerner, "To Be Shot," 271–73.
9. "Biography, Lyndon B. Johnson," LBJL website; Billington, "Lyndon B. Johnson and Blacks," 36, 41; Berry, *And Justice for All*, 21, 26–37.
10. "Civil Rights Act of 1957," Blackpast; Brauer, "Kennedy, Johnson," 101–10.
11. See Harrington, *Other America*; Lewis, *La Vida*; Clark, *Dark Ghetto*; Moynihan, *Negro Family*.
12. Katz, *Undeserving Poor*, 17–24.
13. Katz, *Price of Citizenship*, 58–65.
14. Brauer, "Kennedy, Johnson," 101–10; Orleck, "Introduction: The War on Poverty," 6.
15. "(1963) Lyndon B. Johnson, 'Address,'" Blackpast.
16. "(1963) Lyndon B. Johnson, 'Address.'"
17. Orleck, "Introduction: The War on Poverty," 3.
18. Johnson, "Annual Message to the Congress," American Presidency Project.
19. Johnson, "Annual Message to the Congress."
20. Johnson, "Annual Message to the Congress."
21. Pycior, *LBJ and Mexican Americans*, 148–51.
22. Johnson, "To Fulfill These Rights," LBJL website.
23. "Recommendation No. 15. Discrimination Against Mexican-Americans, Indians and Other Minority Groups from White House Conference and other Federal Programs," TFTRS, "Other Minority Groups," Box 49, LBJL.
24. The metaphor of the "sleeping giant" has greatly shaped discourse about Mexican Americans' partisan participation for decades. Otto Santa Ana offers insight into the historical development of the metaphor. See Santa Ana, *Brown Tide Rising*, 2, 54–56.
25. Daniel, *Chicano Workers*, 2–3, 5–6, 11–12.
26. Sylvester to Alexander, Memo, May 3, 1966, LBJL, Ex HU2/MC, WHCF, Box 22, "HU 2/ MC 4 (4/14/66–5/24/66)."

27. Bernhard to Kuchel, Letter, April 22, 1966, LBJL, TFTRS, Box 67, "Mexican-Americans,"; Booker to Staff Directors, Memo, April 6, 1966, LBJL, TFTRS, Box 49, "Other Minority Groups."

28. Farmer and Wiley to Abram and Coleman, October 21, 1965, LBJL, TFTRS, Box 67, "Civil Rights Leadership."

29. To the President, Memo, November 17, 1965, LBJL, Ex HU2/MC, WHCF, Box 22.

30. Booker, Press Release (date unknown), TFTRS; Box 3, "Press Releases," LBJL.

31. Biographical Sketches, TFTRS, Box 3, "Press Releases," LBJL; "A. Philip Randolph Is Dead; Pioneer in Rights and Labor," NYT, May 17, 1979.

32. For research on African American segregation in Los Angeles and the West, see Jefferson, Living the California Dream; Hudson, West of Jim Crow.

33. Booker, Press Release, April 11, 1966, LBJL, TFTRS, Box 3, "Press Releases."

34. Eric Pace, "Bayard Rustin Is Dead at 75; Pacifist and a Rights Activist," NYT, August 25, 1987.

35. Minutes, March 5, 1966, LBJL, TFTRS, Box 4, "Council Meeting 3/5/66."

36. Transcript, November 17, 1965, Opening General Session, 1965, LBJL, TFTRS, Box 22.

37. Booker to Staff Directors, Memo, April 22, 1966, LBJL, Ex HU2/MC, WHCF, Box 22, "HU 2/MC 1/5/66–4/13/66"; "Militants May Picket White House Rights Confab," Jet Magazine, Vol. XXX, No. 2, April 21, 1966, 3.

38. Transcript of Press Conference on the White House Conference to Fulfill These Rights, May 24, 1966, LBJL, Ex HU2/MC, WHCF, Box 22, "HU 2/MC 4/14/66–5/24/66."

39. "Fannie Lou Hamer (1917–1977)," Blackpast; "Hamer, Fannie Lou," Martin Luther King Institute; Ellis, Freedom's Pragmatist, 185–86; "Fannie's Speech to the DNC 1964," Hamer Civil Rights Museum website.

40. Draft of Council's Report to the Conference, May 6–8, 1966, LBJL, Ex HU2/MC, WHCF, Box 22, "HU2/MC 4/14/66–5/24/66"; Hopkins to McKenzie, Memo, April 14, 1966, LBJL, Ex HU2/MC, WHCF, Box 22, "HU2/MC 4/14/66–5/24/66"; "Opal Jones Heads D.C. Delegation," LAS, May 26, 1966.

41. Report of the White House Conference, 44–45, 47–48.

42. Report of the White House Conference, 46.

43. General Resolutions, Other Minorities, TFTRS, Box 52, LBJL; Report of the White House Conference, 40.

44. General Resolutions, LBJL; Mexican American: A New Focus, 23, 56–57.

45. Califano to Hernandez, et al., letter, May 24, 1966, LBJL, Ex HU2/MC, WHCF, Box 22, "HU2/MC 4/14/66–5/24/66."

46. North to Califano, October 19, 1966, LBJL, Gen HU, WHCF, Box 24, "HU2/MC 8/1/66–12/31/66"; Invitation, White House Staff Meeting, October 11, 1966, LBJL, Ex HU, WHCF, Box 23, "HU2/MC 6/7/66–10/12/66"; "Proposed Timetable: Equality of Opportunity, A Conference on The Civil Rights of the Spanish Surname Communities" (working title), October 11, 1966, LBJL, Ex HU, WHCF, Box 23, "HU2/MC 6/7/66–10/12/66." For further reading about the Bracero Program, see Gutiérrez, Walls and Mirrors, 133–46.

47. George Ramos, "Bert Corona, Labor Activist Backed Rights for Undocumented Workers," *LAT*, January 17, 2001. For further reading about Corona's life and activism, see Garcia, *Memories of Chicano History*.

48. Rubén Salazar, "Humphrey Asks Action By Mexican-Americans: Vice President Addresses," *LAT*, October 28, 1967.

49. North to Califano, Proposal, September 29, 1966, LBJL, Ex HU, WHCF, Box 23, "HU2/MC 6/7/66–10/12/66"; *Civil Rights Digest*, 9, "Urban Unrest-General-Booklets, Magazines, and Newspaper Clippings, 1966-1971," LACA, Snyder Papers, Box C-0202.

50. Vice President to Califano, Memo, September 5, 1966, LBJL, Ex HU, WHCF, Box 23, "HU2/MC 6/7/66–10/12/66."

51. To the President, Telegram, January 11, 1967, LBJL, Gen HU, WHCF, Box 24, "HU2/MC 1/1/67."

52. Brown to Mr. President, Letter, January 23, 1967, LBJL, Gen HU, WHCF, Box 24, "HU2/MC 1/1/67"; David Stout, "George E. Brown Jr., 79, Dies; A Congressman for 18 Terms," *NYT*, July 17, 1999.

53. Ximenes interview.

54. North to Sprague, Memo, June 9, 1967, LBJL, Ex FG 686/A, WHCF, Box 386, "FG 687 Interagency Committee on Mexican American Affairs (11/22/63–12/31/67)."

55. The Mexican American: A New Focus, xi–xiii.

56. The Mexican American: A New Focus, 145–46.

57. The Mexican American: A New Focus, 197.

58. The Mexican American: A New Focus, 26–28, 53–54.

59. The Mexican American: A New Focus, 26–28, 53–54.

60. The Mexican American: A New Focus, 199.

61. The Mexican American: A New Focus, 203–4.

62. *Civil Rights Digest*, 9–13, "Urban Unrest-General-Booklets, Magazines, and Newspaper Clippings, 1966-1971," LACA, Snyder Papers, Box C-0202.

63. "Victory Claimed at El Paso Meet," *East Los Angeles Tribune*, November 2, 1967, LBJL, Ex FG 686/A, Box 386, "FG 687 Interagency Committee on Mexican American Affairs (11/22/63–12/31/67)."

64. Johnson, "Statement by the President," American Presidency Project.

Chapter Five

1. Rubén Salazar, "Abernathy Leads Grape Strike Marchers, Then Meets Chavez: Leaders Symbolically Set Seal on 'Black and Brown Coalition of the Poor' at Conference in Calexico," *LAT*, May 18, 1969.

2. Historian Laura Araiza's recent work examines relationships between the UFW and African American civil rights organizations. For further reading about this history, see Lauren Araiza, *To March for Others: The Black Freedom Struggle and the United Farm Workers* (Philadelphia: University of Pennsylvania Press, 2014), 106–39.

3. Rubén Salazar, "Abernathy Leads Grape Strike Marchers, Then Meets Chavez: Leaders Symbolically Set Seal on 'Black and Brown Coalition of the Poor' at Conference in Calexico," *LAT*, May 18, 1969.

4. Research in Mexican American urban history has grown over the past two decades. See for example, Amezcua, *Making Mexican Chicago*; Arredondo, *Mexican Chicago*; Fernández, *Brown in the Windy City*; Sandoval-Strausz, *Barrio America*.

5. While Puerto Ricans, Indigenous peoples, and other ethnic groups have historically used "Brown" as a form of racial identification, this study of Black-Brown relations specifically refers to African Americans and Mexican Americans.

6. Mantler, *Power to the Poor*, 90; Clayson, *Freedom Is Not Enough*, 85; Bauman, *Race and the War*, 8-9.

7. Honey, *To The Promised Land*, 99, 103, 105.

8. Orleck, "Introduction: The War on Poverty," 2.

9. Young, "Introductory Remarks to the Departments of Government," Delivered to the American Jewish Congress, May 15, 1968, RSCLC, Part 2, Subseries 2, Reel 7, Frame 00855-00856.

10. Los Angeles became a central location for Chicano movement organizations and protests, but movements thrived in other key locations as well. For further analyses of the Chicano movement, see, for example, Gómez-Quiñones and Vásquez, *Making Aztlán*; Montejano, *Quixote's Soldiers*; Patiño, *Raza Sí, Migra No*; San Miguel, *In the Midst of Radicalism*.

11. For further reading about multiracial challenges to racial discrimination in the courts, see Brilliant, *Color of America*, 5-9.

12. See Honey, *To The Promised Land*, 2, 110.

13. For further reading about the civil rights movement, see Marable, *Race, Reform, and Rebellion*; Ransby, *Ella Baker*; Cole, *Campus Color Line*.

14. For further reading about Rosa Parks, see Theoharis, *Rebellious Life*.

15. "Introduction," King Institute; Garrow, *Bearing the Cross*; 77-78, 82.

16. Carson, *Autobiography of King Jr.*, 305.

17. Carson, *Autobiography of King Jr.*, 328.

18. Carson, *Autobiography of King Jr.*, 330.

19. King, "Casualties of the War."

20. Dick West and Paul Weeks, "Dr. King Hears Watts Protests Over Heckling," LAT, August 19, 1965; "Introduction," King Institute.

21. Mantler, *Power to the Poor*, 90-93.

22. King, Statement, n.d., RSCLC, Part 4, Series VIII, Reel 27, Frame 00705-00709.

23. "Indians, Poor Whites, Blacks Ready For 'Poor March,'" CD, March 23, 1968.

24. "Indians, Poor Whites, Blacks.'"

25. Mantler, *Power to the Poor*, 91.

26. "Dr. King Announces Assignment to 15 Acres for 'Poor' Campaign," AW, January 21, 1968.

27. Robert Farrell, "Angelenos Join MLK in Planning 'Poor People's March,' April 22," LAS, March 21, 1968; "3 Buses Take L.A. Poor to 'March on Washington,'" LAS, May 16, 1968; Thomas Kilgore interview, January 7, 1987, audio recording, tape V, side one.

28. SCLC Los Angeles Itinerary, n.d., RSCLC, Part 4, Series VIII, Reel 27, Frame 00082-00083.

29. "The Poor People's Campaign: What Local Citizens Think," LAS, May 9, 1968.

30. "Poor People's Campaign."

31. "Statements of Demands for Rights of the Poor Presented to Agencies of the U.S. Government by the Poor People's Campaign and its Committee of 100," April 29–30, May 1, 1968, RSCLC, Part 4, Series VIII, Reel 26, Frame 00706, 00756–00762; "Committee of 100," RSCLC, Part 4, Series VIII, Reel 26, Frame 00756–00762; Mantler, *Power to the Poor*, 111.

32. "Statements of Demands," Frame 00707–00708; Mantler, *Power to the Poor*, 129.

33. "Statements of Demands," Frame 00714–00715.

34. "Statements of Demands," Frame 00721–00724.

35. "Statements of Demands," Frame 00721–00724.

36. Barnes to Young, Letter, April 16, 1968, RSCLC, Part 2, Records of the Executive Director and Treasurer, Subgroup II, Series IV, Reel 6, Frame 00461–00462.

37. "King Murdered," *CD*, April 6, 1968; Mantler, *Power to the Poor*, 121–22, 127–28.

38. Henry Leifermann, "Poor People's March Leaves Memphis Hotel," *BA*, May 4, 1968.

39. Leifermann, "Poor People's March."

40. "Poor People's Campaign"; Faith Berry, "The Anger and Problems and Sickness of the Poor of the Whole Nation Were in This One Shantytown," *NYT*, July 7, 1968.

41. "Poor People's Campaign"; Memo Number 2, n.d., RSCLC, Western Poor People's Campaign, Part 4, Series VIII, Reel 27, Frame 00468–00470; Memo Number 1, n.d., RSCLC, Western Poor People's Campaign, Part 4, Series VIII, Reel 27, Frame 00475; Mantler, *Power to the Poor*, 134–35.

42. "3 Buses Take L.A. Poor to 'March on Washington,'" *LAS*, May 16, 1968; Mantler, *Power to the Poor*, 142.

43. Arellanes interview, audio recording, session 3, October 11, 2011.

44. Freedman, *Old News*, 17, 19, 25.

45. Berry, "Anger and Problems"; "Poor March in Capital Protests L.A. Arrests: Leaders Claim Mexican-Americans Were Indicted Unfairly for Walkout at Schools," *LAT*, June 4, 1968.

46. Mantler, *Power to the Poor*, 157–58.

47. Foley, *Quest for Equality*, 140.

48. Paul Valentine, "Too Many Factions Sap Poor People's Unity," *WP*, July 16, 1968; Mantler, *Power to the Poor*, 156; Henry Leifermann, "Poor People's March a Giant Step: Civil Rights movement Gets Itself Together," *CD*, June 22, 1968.

49. Abernathy, Address, Washington, DC, June 14, 1968, RSCLC, Part 4, Series VIII, Reel 26, Frame 00413–00420.

50. "Solidarity Day, 1968," *WP*, June 20, 1968; Freedman, *Old News*, 34, 35, 86; Mantler, *Power to the Poor*, 173.

51. "Highlights From Speeches at 'Solidarity Day' Day Rally," *WP*, June 20, 1968.

52. Ethel L. Payne, "Women Set the Tone of the Poor March," *CD*, June 22, 1968; Mantler, *Power to the Poor*, 172.

53. Wiley to Young, Letter, March 25, 1968, Records of the Executive Director and Treasurer, Part 2, Subgroup II, Series IV, Reel 6, Frame 00358–00359, RSCLC.

54. The East Los Angeles "Blowouts" were a foundational protest of the Chicano movement. For details about how law enforcement responded to the protests, see, Haney López, *Racism on Trial*, 9.

55. For Immediate Release, n.d., Part 4, Series VIII, Reel 27, Frame 01002, RSCLC.
56. "Poor March in Capital."
57. Press Release, June 11, 1968, RSCLC, Poor People's Campaign, Mexican-American Contingent, Part 4, Series VIII, Reel 27, Frame 01001.
58. Leifermann, "Poor People's March a Giant Step."
59. Oropeza, *King of Adobe*, 6–7.
60. Paul Valentine, "Rift Mended; Poor Stage New Protests: Rifts Mended as Marches Stage New Protests at Agriculture," *WP*, May 28, 1968.
61. Valentine, "Rift Mended."
62. "Resurrection City Shut, Abernathy, Others Seized," *CD*, June 25, 1968; Paul Valentine, "Tijerina Charges Poor Were Betrayed: Mexican-American Assails SCLC Leaders," *WP*, July 12, 1968.
63. Paul Valentine, "Poor March Betrayed Goals, Tijerina Charges: Mexican Leader Says Interests of Non-Negro Contingents Were Slighted," *WP*, July 12, 1968.
64. "Ethnic Groups Form Coalition," *CD*, July 2, 1968.
65. Mantler, *Power to the Poor*, 183.

Chapter Six

1. "Improving the Quality of Urban Life, Model Neighborhoods Under the Demonstration Cities Act," Office of Demonstrations and Intergovernmental Relations, November 16, 1966, CSA, SOEO, F375:2 Folder: OEO, Federal General-Memoranda.
2. Scholars define civil unrest initiated by white supremacist practices, policies, and institutions against a marginalized group as riots. Uprisings and rebellions typically refer to civil unrest in response to a single incident of white supremacist violence, such as police brutality. The Chicano moratorium police riots are an example of police descending on groups of Mexican Americans. See, for example, Hinton, *America on Fire*, 6–7.
3. "Walter Reuther," AFL-CIO. For a comprehensive account of Reuther's life and career, see Lichtenstein, *Most Dangerous Man*.
4. Reuther to Johnson, Memo, May 13, 1965, LBJL, "Report of the Wood-Haar Task Force-III," Legislative Background, Model Cities, Box 1.
5. Gooding-Williams, "On Being Stuck," 6.
6. Katz, *Undeserving Poor*, 16.
7. Spector to Weaver, Memo, May 24, 1966, LBJL, Legislative Background, Model Cities 1966, "The Legislative Struggle," Box 2; Nicoll to Califano Jr., Memo, June 29, 1966, LBJL, Legislative Struggle, Model Cities 1966, "The Legislative Struggle-II," Box 2.
8. Weber and Wallace, "Revealing the Empowerment Revolution," 174.
9. DCMD Act, Public Law 87-754, November 3, 1966, 1258.
10. DCMD Act.
11. "Improving the Quality."
12. Historian Thomas Sugrue has closely examined the political, economic, and spatial factors that shaped the "urban crisis" in Detroit. See, for example, Sugrue, *Origins of the Urban Crisis*, 1–6.

13. Robert Weaver was part of a small cohort of African Americans who entered politics through the New Deal. See, Pritchett, *Robert Clifton Weaver*. Weaver wrote widely about urban conditions and the experiences of African American urbanites more specifically. See Weaver, *Negro Labor*; Weaver, *Negro Ghetto*; Weaver, *Urban Complex*; Weaver, *Dilemmas in Urban America*.

14. Pritchett, "Which Urban Crisis?" 269–71.

15. Lyndon Johnson began his political career in the New Deal and worked to expand social programs rooted in the New Deal during his presidency. See Lerner, "'To Be Shot,'" 273.

16. Remarks of the President at the Signing Ceremony of S.3497, The Housing and Urban Development Act of 1968, n.d., LBJL, Reports on Enrolled Legislation, "P.L. 90-448 S3497 (I) 8/1/68," Box 46.

17. Weaver to Rommel, Letter, October 25, 1966, LBJL, Reports on Enrolled Legislation, P.L. 89-744 to P.L. 89-756, "P.L. 89-754, 3708, 11/3/66," Box 46.

18. Horne, "'Riot' and 'Revolt,'" 393; Davis, *City of Quartz*, 17–18.

19. Weaver to Yorty, Telegram, November 1967, LACA, Yorty Papers, "Housing: General, 1967," Box D-16.

20. "Improving the Quality of Urban Life, Model Neighborhoods Under the Demonstration Cities Act," November 1966, Office of Demonstrations and Intergovernmental Relations, CSA, SOEO, F375:2, Folder: OEO, Federal General-Memoranda.

21. Ray Hebert, "L.A.'s Model Cities Bid Has Two Goals: L.A. Has Dual Purpose in Model Cities Entry," *LAT*, June 18, 1967.

22. Ray Hebert, "L.A. Loses Out in Bid for Model Cities Funds: No Surprise Expressed," *LAT*, November 17, 1967; Vincent J. Burke, "63 Cities Selected for Model Program of Slum Renovation: Model Program," *LAT*, November 17, 1967.

23. The Chicano movement gained momentum in 1968 after a series of youth-led demonstrations in Los Angeles and other cities of the Southwest. For further research on the Chicano movement, see Chávez, *My People First! "¡Mi Raza Primero!"*; Gómez-Quiñones and Vásquez, *Making Aztlán*; Garcia, *Chicano Movement*.

24. Yorty to Mogulof, April 12, 1968, LACA, Yorty Papers, "Housing and Urban Development/Model Cities Program, 1968," Box D-15.

25. Sonenshein, *Politics in Black and White*, 85–86, 89–94.

26. Ximenes to Yorty, July 15, 1968, LACA, Yorty Papers, "Housing and Urban Development/Model Cities Program, 1968," Box D-15.

27. President Lyndon Johnson selected Vicente Ximenes to the Office of Economic Opportunity and to lead the Inter-Agency Cabinet Committee on Mexican American Affairs in response to Mexican Americans' call for federal recognition. See Kells, *Vicente Ximenes*. For a close analysis of Lyndon Johnson's relationship with Mexican Americans, see Pycior, *LBJ and Mexican Americans*.

28. Sánchez, *Boyle Heights*, 159–60.

29. Ray Hebert, "Boyle Heights Boils over Federal Grant: Some Don't Want it," *LAT*, May 26, 1968.

30. The CSO had an early history of multiracial organizing. For further reading, see Bernstein, *Bridges of Reform*, 141–45.

31. Program, Mexican American Opportunity Foundation 1978 Annual Aztec Awards Banquet, Huntington, Edelman Papers, Folder 47.8: "Civic Service Organizations," Box 47.

32. Morales to Yorty, May 6, 1968, LACA, Yorty Papers, "Housing and Urban Development/Model Cities Program, 1968," Box D-15.

33. Several scholars have chronicled multiracial relations in Los Angeles prior to 1960. See Bernstein, *Bridges of Reform*; Wild, *Street Meeting*; Varzally, *Making a Non-White America*; Kurashige, *Shifting Grounds of Race*. For research that examines post-1960 multiracial relations, see Brilliant, *Color of America*; Araiza, *To March for Others*; Pulido, *Black, Brown, Yellow, and Left*; Sánchez, "Why Are Multiracial Communities," 153-70.

34. "Minorities Forming a National Coalition," *San Francisco Chronicle*, March 9, 1968, LACA, Snyder Papers, "Urban Unrest-General-Booklets, Magazines, and Newspaper Clippings: 1966-1971," Box C-0202.

35. Sides, *L.A. City Limits*, 155-57.

36. Dymally to Yorty, May 15, 1968, LACA, Yorty Papers, "General: Calif., State of General Correspondence 1968," Box D-21.

37. Avila, *Popular Culture*, 156-61.

38. Hebert, "Boyle Heights Boils."

39. "Five Year Print Out for 147 Model Cities Under the Administration's Proposed 'Better Communities Act,'" 1973, Huntington, Hahn Papers, Folder 1, Box 120.

40. County of Los Angeles Model Neighborhood Program, 1969-75, pp. 3-4, Huntington, Hahn Papers, Folder: Urban Affairs, 1973, Box 120.

41. Marcia Madison, *Report on the Progress of Los Angeles Model Cities Program in Relation to other Model Cities Programs*, February 10, 1972, UCLA-YRL, Bradley Papers, Folder 3: Model Cities Program, 1972, Box 1917.

42. "Office of Los Angeles Mayor Sam Yorty," April 14, 1971, LACA, Yorty Papers, "Housing: Model Cities Program/General, 1971," Box D-15.

43. See Pulido, *Black, Brown, Yellow and Left*, 73-74.

44. Sanchez interview, December 20, 2012, audio recording, session four; Chávez, *¡Mi Raza Primero!*, 63.

45. Richard Vasquez, "Polls Reflect Diversity of Views: Outsiders Fomented Riot: Barrio Residents Describe Riot Reactions," *LAT*, September 6, 1970.

46. "Were Deputies Mousetrapped?" KNBC Editorial, September 2, 1970, LACA, Snyder Papers, "Urban Unrest—East L.A. Disturbance, 1970-1971," Box C-202; Chávez, *¡Mi Raza Primero!*, 65, 70; Bermúdez, "Alicia Escalante," 100-103.

47. Vasquez, "Polls Reflect Diversity."

48. Gómez-Quiñones and Vásquez, *Making Aztlán*, xxv.

49. Chávez, *¡Mi Raza Primero!*, 72. For a compilation of Salazar's work, see *Salazar: A Selection of Columns*.

50. Whaley to Yorty, Memo, January 25, 1971, LACA, Snyder Papers, "Urban Unrest—East L.A. Disturbance, 1970-1971," Box C-202; Whaley to Yorty, Memo, January 19, 1971, LACA, Snyder Papers, "Urban Unrest—East L.A. Disturbance, 1970-1971," Box C-202; "Mexican-American Judge Feted by Forum," *LAT*, January 29, 1961.

51. "Moratorium Aftermath," KABC-TV Editorial E14-71, February 1-2, 1971, LACA, Snyder Papers, "Urban Unrest—East L.A. Disturbance, 1970-1971," Box C-202;

"Moratorium March," KHJ-TV Editorial 111, February 14–16, 1971, LACA, Snyder Papers, "Urban Unrest—East L.A. Disturbance, 1970–1971," Box C-202; Chávez, ¡Mi Raza Primero!, 75.

52. Tlalocán Commercial Center, E/NE Community Development Corporation, August 1, 1972, LACA, Snyder Papers, "Model Cities, July–December 1972," Box C-0159.

53. City of Los Angeles Model Cities Program Executed Contracts, 1971–72, UCLA-YRL, Bradley Papers, Folder 2: Model Cities Program 1971–72, Box 1917.

54. "Blacks Asked to Come to 'Latin Nites' Fest," LAS, June 8, 1972.

55. Pamphlet, Own Recognizance Assistance and Rehabilitation Project, n.d., LACA, Snyder Papers, "Model Cities, July–December 1972," Box C-0159.

56. The national headquarters of the BPP used antipoverty funding to help build survival programs and to challenge local officials. See Self, American Babylon, 242–55.

57. Nelson, Body and Soul, 10–12.

58. County of Los Angeles Model Neighborhood Program, 1969–75, p. 13, Huntington, Hahn Papers, Folder: 1, Box 120.

59. Bauman, "Watts Summer Festival, 1966–," Blackpast.

60. "Greater Watts Model Neighborhood," UCLA-YRL, Bradley Papers, Folder 2: Model Cities Program, 1971–72, Box 1917.

61. "Greater Watts Model Neighborhood"; "Watts Writers Work on 'Soul,'" LAS, August 1, 1968; "Watts Workshop Writes Plays for Caesars Palace," LAS, October 30, 1969.

62. The East L.A. "Blowouts" helped demonstrate the organizing power among a younger generation of Mexican American activists. See Haney López, Racism on Trial, 16–21.

63. Gómez-Quiñones and Vásquez, Making Aztlán, XXV.

64. "Major Model Cities Grant Awarded to Cal State L.A.," Press Release, August 17, 1971, UCLA-YRL, Bradley Papers, Folder 14: E/NE Model Cities Neighborhood School, 1971, Box 1407.

65. City of Los Angeles Model Cities Executed Contracts.

66. Historian Edward Escobar has written widely about the relationship between Mexican Americans and the LAPD. See Escobar, "Unintended Consequences," 1483–514.

67. Proposed Agreement with Mexican-American Legal Center, 1971, UCLA-YRL, Bradley Papers, Folder 5: Model Neighborhood Legal Center, 1971, Box 1407.

68. Richard Nixon's campaign for president galvanized a contingent of white suburban voters known as the Silent Majority, who increasingly understood strong centralized government as an impingement on their freedom. Several scholars have examined the rise of the Silent Majority starting in the 1960s. See Nicolaides, My Blue Heaven, 326.

69. Lassiter, Silent Majority, 1–5.

70. Romney to Yorty, February 24, 1971, LACA, Yorty Papers, Folder: "Housing: Model Cities/General, 1971," Box D-15.

71. Orleck, "Conclusion: The War on Poverty," 439–40; Orleck, Storming Caesar's Palace, 121–24.

72. Hawkins, Letter, March 13, 1973, UCLA-YRL, Hawkins Papers, Folder: H. Con Res 174, Box 1.

73. Baida to Yorty, Letter, February 6, 1973, UCLA-YRL, Bradley Papers, Folder 5: HUD: Chrono File, 1973, Box 1463; Hyde to Yorty, Letter, February 23, 1973, ULCA-YRL, Bradley Papers, Folder 6: HUD: Housing and Urban Development, 1973, Box 1463; Clayson, *Freedom Is Not Enough*, 149.

Epilogue

1. Katz, *Undeserving Poor*, 126; O'Connor, *Poverty Knowledge*, 242–43; Feldstein, *Motherhood in Black and White*, 2–3; Felker-Kantor, *Policing Los Angeles*, 1.

2. Horne, *Fire This Time*, 355.

3. "The L.A. Riots: 15 Years After Rodney King," *Time Magazine*, https://content.time.com/time/specials/2007/la_riot/0,28757,1614117,00.html; Los Angeles Times Staff, "L.A. Riots 20 Years Later, 1992 Riots Timeline," *LAT*, April 20, 2012, https://timelines.latimes.com/los-angeles-riots/.

4. See Butler, "Endangered/Endangering," 15–17.

5. Horne, *Fire This Time*, 355–56; "L.A. Riots: 15 Years After"; "L.A. Riots 20 Years Later"; Special Committee on the Los Angeles Crisis, *To Rebuild Is Not Enough*, 1.

6. *To Rebuild Is Not Enough*, 14–15.

7. Felker-Kantor, *Policing Los Angeles*, 233.

8. *To Rebuild Is Not Enough*, 12.

9. *To Rebuild Is Not Enough*, 1, 11.

10. Felker-Kantor, *Policing Los Angeles*, 233.

11. Terms, including "Hispanic-Origin," reflect changes in terminology used by the US census in the 1980s and 1990s. The term Latina/o is used to describe how immigration from Latin America also shaped demographics in the 1980s and 1990s Los Angeles.

12. For an analysis how Latinas/os and immigration from Central and South America have shaped US cities since the late twentieth century, see Davis, *Magical Urbanism*; Sandoval-Strausz, *Barrio America*.

13. *To Rebuild Is Not Enough*, 1.

14. *To Rebuild Is Not Enough*, 2.

15. *To Rebuild Is Not Enough*, 13.

16. Historian Brenda Stevenson describes some of the interracial conflict between African Americans and Asian Americans that surfaced in the 1992 uprising. See Stevenson, *Contested Murder of Latasha Harlins*, 72–75.

17. Yussuf J. Simmonds, "Villaraigosa Commits to Black-Brown Unity: Candidate Addresses Recent High Schools Campus Unrest," *LAS*, April 28, 2005. See Camarillo, "Cities of Color," 1–2.

Bibliography

Oral Histories

Arellanes, Gloria. Interview conducted in 2011 by Virginia Espino. Center for Oral History Research, Young Research Library, University of California, Los Angeles.
Castro, Vickie. Interview conducted in 2013 by Virginia Espino. Center for Oral History Research, Young Research Library, University of California, Los Angeles.
Hawkins, Augustus F. Interview conducted in 1998 by Carlos Vasquez. Center for Oral History Research, Young Research Library, University of California, Los Angeles.
Jacquette, Tommy. Interview conducted in 2006 by Alva Moore Stevenson. Center for Oral History Research, Young Research Library, University of California, Los Angeles.
Kilgore, Thomas. Interview conducted in 1986–87 by Robin D. G. Kelley. Center for Oral History Research, Young Research Library, University of California, Los Angeles.
Roybal, Edward. Interview no. 184 conducted in 1975 by Oscar J. Martínez. Institute of Oral History, University of Texas, El Paso.
Sanchez, David. Interview conducted in 2012 by Virginia Espino. Center for Oral History Research, Young Research Library, University of California, Los Angeles.
Ximenes, Vicente. Interview conducted on October 10, 2001, by Jim Morrison. Accessed November 1, 2022. https://voces.lib.utexas.edu/collections/stories/vicente-ximenes. Voces Oral History Center, Moody College of Communication, University of Texas, Austin.

Manuscript Collections

California State Archives, Sacramento, CA
    Inventory of the State Office of Economic Opportunity
Cecil H. Green Library, Department of Special Collection, Stanford University, Stanford, CA
    Papers of Bert Corona
    Papers of Manuel Ruiz
Charles E. Young Research Library, Department of Special Collections, University of California, Los Angeles, CA
    Papers of Augustus F. Hawkins, 1935–90
    Thomas Bradley Administrative Papers
Henry E. Huntington Library, Manuscript Collections, San Marino, CA
    Papers of Edmund Edelman
    Papers of Kenneth Hahn

King Library and Archive, Martin Luther King Jr. Center for Nonviolent Social Change, Atlanta, GA
    Records of the Southern Christian Leadership Conference, 1954–70
Los Angeles City Archives, Erwin Piper Technical Center, Los Angeles, CA
    Papers of Councilman Arthur Snyder
    Papers of Mayor Samuel Yorty
Lyndon Baines Johnson Presidential Library and Museum, University of Texas at Austin, TX
    Papers of the White House Conference To Fulfill These Rights
    White House Central Files
    White House Public Opinion Mail—Civil Rights
United States National Archives at College Park, College Park, MD
    Records of Agencies for Economic Opportunity and Legal Services
    Records of the Community Services Administration

Newspapers and Periodicals

Atlanta Daily World
Baltimore Afro-American
Black Law Journal
Chicago Defender
Christian Science Monitor
Crisis
Jet Magazine
Los Angeles Examiner
Los Angeles Sentinel
Los Angeles Times
New York Times
Time Magazine
Washington Post

Government Documents, Reports, and Laws

Chicago Commission on Race Relations. *The Negro in Chicago*. New York: Arno Press, 1968.

Civil Rights Act of 1964. Public Law 88-352, Eighty-Eighth Congress. Session 2, July 2, 1964.

Demonstration Cities and Metropolitan Development Act. Public Law 87-754. November 3, 1966.

Economic Opportunity Act of 1964. Public Law 88-452. August 20, 1964.

Mexican American, The: A New Focus on Opportunity: Testimony Presented at the Cabinet Committee Hearings on Mexican American Affairs. El Paso, Texas, October 26–28, 1967.

Moynihan, Daniel. *The Negro Family: The Case for National Action*. Office of Policy Planning and Research. United States Department of Labor, March 1965.

Munden, Kenneth. *The Office of Economic Opportunity in the Kennedy Administration*, 1973.

National Advisory Committee on Civil Disorders. *Report of the National Commission on Civil Disorders*. Washington, DC: US Government Printing Office, 1968.

Negroes and Mexican Americans in South Central and East Los Angeles. Division of Labor Statistics and Research, Department of Industrial Relations. San Francisco, California, 1966.

Oklahoma Commission to Study the Tulsa Race Riot of 1921. *A Report by the Oklahoma Commission to Study the Tulsa Race Riot of 1921*. February 21, 2001.

Report of the White House Conference to Fulfill These Rights. Washington, DC: US Government Printing Office, 1966.

Senate Report. Economic Opportunity Act of 1964. Report No. 1218. Eighty-Eighth Congress, 1964.

Special Committee on the Los Angeles Crisis. *To Rebuild Is Not Enough: Final Report and Recommendations of the Assembly Special Committee on the Los Angeles Crisis*. Sacramento, CA: Assembly Publications Office, September 28, 1992.

Treaty of Guadalupe Hidalgo, February 2, 1848, https://avalon.law.yale.edu/19th_century/guadhida.asp#art8n. Accessed July 14, 2023.

US Bureau of the Census. *Census of Population and Housing, 1960: General Characteristics of the Population: By Census Tracts: Las Vegas, Nevada–Los Angeles/Long Beach, CA*. Washington, DC: Government Printing Office, 1961.

US Bureau of the Census. *1970 Census of Population: General Social and Economic Characteristics, California*. Washington, DC: Government Printing Office, 1972.

US Bureau of the Census. *1980 Census of Population and Housing: Summary Characteristics for Governmental Units and Standard Metropolitan Statistical Areas, California*. Washington, DC: Government Printing Office, 1982.

US Bureau of the Census. *1990 Census of Population: General Population Characteristics, California*, vol. 1. Washington, DC: Government Printing Office, July 1992.

Violence in the City—An End or a Beginning. A Report by the Governor's Commission on the Los Angeles Riots, December 2, 1965.

Secondary Sources

Acuña, Rodolfo. *Occupied America: A History of Chicanos*. New York: Pearson Longman Publishing Group, 2007.

Amezcua, Mike. *Mexican Chicago: From Postwar Settlement to the Age of Gentrification*. Chicago: University of Chicago Press, 2022.

Anderson, Carol. *White Rage: The Unspoken Truth of Our Racial Divide*. New York: Bloomsbury Publishing, 2017. ProQuest e-book.

Araiza, Lauren. *To March for Others: The Black Freedom Struggle and the United Farm Workers*. Philadelphia: University of Pennsylvania Press, 2014.

Arredondo, Gabriela F. *Chicago: Race, Identity, and Nation, 1916–39*. Champaign: University of Illinois Press, 2008.

Ashmore Youngblood, Susann. *Carry It On: The War on Poverty and the Civil Rights Movement in Alabama, 1964–1972*. Athens: University of Georgia Press, 2008.

Avila, Eric. *Popular Culture in the Age of White Flight: Fear and Fantasy in Suburban Los Angeles*. Berkeley: University of California Press, 2006.

Bauman, Robert. *Race and the War on Poverty: From Watts to East L.A.* Norman: University of Oklahoma Press, 2008.

Behnken, Brian. *Fighting Their Own Battles: Mexican Americans, African Americans, and the Struggle for Civil Rights in Texas*. Chapel Hill: University of North Carolina Press, 2011.

———. *The Struggle in Black and Brown: African American and Mexican American Relations During the Civil Rights Era*. Lincoln: University of Nebraska Press, 2011.

Bermúdez, Roise. "Alicia Escalante, The Chicana Welfare Rights Organization, and the Chicano Movement." In *The Chicano Movement: Perspectives from the Twenty-First Century*, edited by Mario T. Garcia, 95–116. New York: Routledge, 2014. ProQuest e-book.

Bernstein, Shana. *Bridges of Reform: Interracial Civil Rights Activism in Twentieth-Century Los Angeles*. New York: Oxford University Press, 2011.

Berry, Mary Frances. *And Justice for All: The United States Commission on Civil Rights and the Continuing Struggle for Freedom in America*. New York: Alfred A. Knopf, 2009.

Billington, Monroe. "Lyndon B. Johnson and Blacks: The Early Years." *The Journal of Negro History* 62 (1977): 26–42.

Blain, Keisha. *Set the World on Fire: Black Nationalist Women and the Global Struggle for Freedom*. Pennsylvania: University of Pennsylvania Press, 2018.

Bollens, John C., and Grant B. Geyer. *Yorty: Politics of a Constant Candidate*. Pacific Palisades, CA: Palisades Publishers, 1973.

Brauer, Carl M. "Kennedy, Johnson, and the War on Poverty." *Journal of American History* 69, no. 1 (1982): 98–110.

Brilliant, Mark. *The Color of America Has Changed: How Racial Diversity Shaped Civil Rights Reform in California, 1941–1978*. New York: Oxford University Press, 2010.

Brinkley, Alan. "The New Deal and the Idea of the State." In *The Rise and Fall of the New Deal Order, 1930–1980*, edited by Steve Fraser and Gary Gerstle, 85–121. Princeton, NJ: Princeton University Press, 1989.

Brooks, Charlotte. *Alien Neighbors, Foreign Friends: Asian Americans, Housing, and the Transformation of Urban California*. Chicago: University of Chicago Press, 2009.

Broussard, Albert. *Black San Francisco: The Struggle for Racial Equality in the West*. Lawrence: University of Kansas Press, 1993.

Brown, Scot. *Fighting for US: Maulana Karenga, the US Organization, and Black Cultural Nationalism*. New York: New York University Press, 2003.

Bunch, Lonnie. "'The Greatest State for the Negro': Jefferson L. Edmonds, Black Propagandist of the California Dream." In *Seeking El Dorado: African Americans in California*, edited by Lawrence B. De Graaf, Kevin Mulroy, and Quintard Taylor, 129–48. Seattle: University of Washington Press, 2001.

Busto, Rudy V. *King Tiger: The Religious Vision of Reis López Tijerina*. Albuquerque: University of New Mexico Press, 2005.

Butler, Judith. "Endangered/Endangering: Schematic Racism and White Paranoia." In *Reading Rodney King/Reading Urban Uprising*, edited by Robert Gooding-Williams, 15–22. New York: Routledge, 1993.

Camarillo, Albert. *Chicanos in a Changing Society: From Mexican Pueblos to American Barrios In Santa Barbara and Southern California, 1848–1930*. Cambridge, MA: Harvard University Press, 1979.

———. *Racial Borderhoods of America: Mexican Americans and the Changing Ethnic/Racial Landscapes of Cities, 1850–2000*. New York: forthcoming.

———. *Chicanos in California: A History of Mexican Americans in California*. San Francisco: Boyd & Fraser Publishing Co., 1984.

———. "Cities of Color: The New Racial Frontier in California's Minority-Majority Cities." *Pacific Historical Review* 76, no. 1 (2007): 1–28.

———. "Navigating Segregated Life in America's Racial Borderhoods, 1910–1950s." *Journal of American History* 100, no. 3 (December 2013): 645–62.

Campbell, Marne. *Making Black Los Angeles: Class, Gender, and Community, 1850–1917*. Chapel Hill: University of North Carolina Press, 2016.

Carrigan, William D., and Clive Webb. "The Lynching of Persons of Mexican Origin or Descent in the United States, 1848 to 1928." *Journal of Social History* 37, no. 2 (December 1, 2003): 411–38.

Carson, Clayborne, ed. *The Autobiography of Martin Luther King, Jr*. New York: Grand Central Publishing, 1998.

Chávez, Ernesto. *My People First! "¡Mi Raza Primero!": Nationalism, Identity, and Insurgency in the Chicano Movement in Los Angeles, 1966–1978*. Berkeley: University of California Press, 2002.

Clark, Kenneth B. *Dark Ghetto: Dilemmas of Social Power*. New York: Harper and Row, 1965.

Clayson, William S. *Freedom Is Not Enough: The War on Poverty and the Civil Rights Movement in Texas*. Austin: University of Texas Press, 2010.

Cloward, Richard A., and Lloyd E. Ohlin. *Delinquency and Opportunity: A Theory of Delinquent Gangs*. Glencoe, MN: Free Press, 1960.

Cohen, Lizabeth. *Making a New Deal: Industrial Workers in Chicago, 1919–1939*. New York: Cambridge University Press, 1990.

Cole, Eddie. *The Campus Color Line: College Presidents and the Struggle for Black Freedom*. Princeton, NJ: Princeton University Press, 2022.

Crump, Spencer. *Black Riot in Los Angeles: The Story of the Watts Tragedy*. Los Angeles: Trans-Anglo Books, 1966.

Daniel, Cletus E. *Chicano Workers and the Politics of Fairness: The FEPC in the Southwest, 1941–1945*. Austin: University of Texas Press, 1991.

Davis, Mike. *City of Quartz: Excavating the Future in Los Angeles*. New York: Vintage Books, 1992.

———. *Magical Urbanism: Latinos Reinvent the US City*. New York: Verso Books, 2000.

Deverell, William. *Whitewashed Adobe: The Rise of Los Angeles and the Remaking of the American Past*. Berkeley: University of California Press, 2004.

Du Bois, W.E.B. "Colored California." *Crisis*, August 1913.

Dudziak, Mary L. *Cold War Civil Rights: Race and the Image of American Democracy*. Princeton, NJ: Princeton University Press, 2000.

Ellis, Sylvia. *Freedom's Pragmatist: Lyndon Johnson and Civil Rights*. Gainesville: University of Florida Press, 2013.

Escobar, Edward J. "The Dialectics of Repression: The Los Angeles Police Department and the Chicano Movement, 1968–1971." *Journal of American History* 79, no. 4 (1993): 1483–514.

———. *Race, Police, and the Making of a Political Identity: Mexican Americans and the Los Angeles Police Department, 1900–1945*. Berkeley: University of California Press, 1999.

———. "The Unintended Consequences of the Carceral State: Chicana/o Political Mobilization in Post-World War II America." *Journal of American History* (2015): 174–84.

Escobedo, Elizabeth R. *From Coveralls to Zoot Suits: The Lives of Mexican American Women on the World War II Home Front*. Chapel Hill: University of North Carolina Press, 2013.

Feldstein, Ruth. *Motherhood in Black and White: Race and Sex in American Liberalism, 1930–1965*. Ithaca, NY: Cornell University Press, 2000.

Felker-Kantor, Max. *Policing Los Angeles: Race, Resistance, and the Rise of the LAPD*. Chapel Hill: University of North Carolina Press, 2018.

Ferguson, Thomas. "Industrial Conflict and the Coming of the New Deal: The Triumph of Multinational Liberalism in America." In *The Rise and Fall of the New Deal Order, 1930–1980*, edited by Steve Fraser and Gary Gerstle, 3–31. Princeton, NJ: Princeton University Press, 1989.

Fernández, Johanna. *The Young Lords: A Radical History*. Chapel Hill: University of North Carolina Press, 2020.

Fernández, Lilia. *Brown in the Windy City: Mexicans and Puerto Ricans in Postwar Chicago*. Chicago: University of Chicago Press, 2014.

Flamming, Douglas. "Becoming Democrats: Liberal Politics and the African American Community in Los Angeles, 1930–1965." In *Seeking El Dorado: African Americans in California*, edited by Lawrence B. De Graaf, Kevin Mulroy, and Quintard Taylor, 279–308. Seattle: University of Washington Press, 2001.

———. *Bound for Freedom: Black Los Angeles in Jim Crow America*. Berkeley: University of California Press, 2005.

Foley, Neil. *Quest for Equality: The Failed Promise of Black-Brown Solidarity*. Cambridge, MA: Harvard University Press, 2010. JSTOR e-book.

Freedman, Jill. *Old News: Resurrection City*. New York: Grossman Publishers, 1970.

"Future Plan and Program of the N.A.A.C.P." Report of the Committee on Future Plan and Program of the National Association for the Advancement of Colored People. In *Major Problems in African-American History: Documents and Essays*, edited by Thomas Holt and Elsa Barkley Brown, 254–55. Boston: Houghton Mifflin, 2000.

Galarza, Ernesto. "La Mula No Nacio Arisca." In *Mexican-Americans in the United States: A Reader*, edited by John Burma, 199–206. Cambridge, MA: Schenkman Publishing Company, Inc., 1970.

García, Mario T. *The Chicano Generation: Testimonios of the Movement*. Oakland: University of California Press, 2015.

———. *Memories of Chicano History: The Life and Narrative of Bert Corona*. Berkeley: University of California Press, 1994.

———. *Mexican Americans: Leadership, Ideology, and Identity, 1930–1960*. New Haven, CT: Yale University Press, 1989.

Garrow, David J. *Bearing The Cross: Martin Luther King, Jr. and the Southern Christian Leadership Conference*. New York: Perennial, 2004.

Germany, Kent. *New Orleans After the Promises: Poverty, Citizenship, and the Search for the Great Society*. Athens: University of Georgia Press, 2007.

———. "The Politics of Poverty and History: Racial Inequality and the Long Prelude to Katrina." *Journal of American History* 94, no. 3 (2007): 743-51.
Gómez, Laura. *Manifest Destinies: The Making of the Mexican American Race*. New York: New York University Press, 2018.
Gómez-Quiñones, Juan, and Irene Vásquez. *Making Aztlán: Ideology and Culture of the Chicana and Chicano Movement, 1966-1977*. Albuquerque: University of New Mexico Press, 2014.
Gooding-Williams, Robert. "On Being Stuck." In *Reading Rodney King/Reading Urban Uprising*, edited by Robert Gooding-Williams, 1-12. New York: Routledge, 1993.
Grebler, Leo, Joan W. Moore, and Ralph C. Guzman. *The Mexican-American People, the Nation's Second Largest Minority Group*. New York: Free Press, 1970.
Gregory, James. *The Southern Diaspora: How the Great Migrations of Black and White Southerners Transformed America*. Chapel Hill: University of North Carolina Press, 2005.
Grossman, James. *Land of Hope: Chicago, Black Southerners, and the Great Migration*. Chicago: University of Chicago Press, 1991.
Gutiérrez, David. *Walls and Mirrors: Mexican Americans, Mexican Immigrants, and the Politics of Ethnicity*. Berkeley: University of California Press, 1995.
Hall Dowd, Jacqueline. "The Long Civil Rights Movement and the Political Uses of the Past." *Journal of American History* 91, no. 4 (2005): 1233-63.
Hämäläinen, Pekka, and Samuel Truett. "On Borderlands." *Journal of American History* 90, no. 2 (2011): 338-61.
Harrington, Michael. *The Other America: Poverty in the United States*. New York: Macmillan, 1962.
Haney López, Ian F. *Racism on Trial: The Chicano Fight for Justice*. Cambridge, MA: Belknap Press of Harvard University Press, 2003.
———. *White By Law: The Legal Construction of Race*. New York: New York University Press, 2006.
Hernández, Kelly Lytle. *City of Inmates: Conquest, Rebellion, and the Rise of Human Caging in Los Angeles, 1771-1965*. Chapel Hill: University of North Carolina Press, 2017.
Hine Clark, Darlene. "Rape and the Inner Lives of Black Women in the Middle West." *Signs* 14, no. 4 (Summer 1989): 912-20.
Hinton, Elizabeth. *America on Fire: The Untold History of Police Violence and Black Rebellion Since the 1960s*. New York: Liveright Publishing Co., 2021.
———. *From the War on Poverty to the War on Crime: The Making of Mass Incarceration in America*. Cambridge, MA: Harvard University Press, 2016.
Hirsch, Arnold. *Making the Second Ghetto: Race and Housing in Chicago, 1940-1960*. Chicago: University of Chicago Press, 1998.
Holt, Thomas C. *The Movement: The African American Struggle for Civil Rights*. New York: Oxford University Press, 2021.
Honey, Michael K. *To The Promised Land: Martin Luther King and the Fight For Economic Justice*. New York: W. W. Norton & Co., 2018.
Horne, Gerald. *Fire This Time: The Watts Uprising and the 1960's*. New York: Da Capo Press, 1997.

———. "'Riot' and 'Revolt' in Los Angeles, 1965 and 1992." In *Seeking El Dorado: African Americans in California*, edited by Lawrence B. De Graaf, Kevin Mulroy, and Quintard Taylor, 377–404. Seattle: University of Washington Press, 2015.

Hudson, Lynn. *West of Jim Crow: The Fight Against California's Color Line*. Urbana: University of Illinois Press, 2020.

Hunter, Tera. *To 'Joy My Freedom: Southern Black Women's Lives and Labors After the Civil War*. Cambridge, MA: Harvard University Press, 1998.

Jackson, Kenneth. *Crabgrass Frontier: The Suburbanization of the United States*. New York: Oxford University Press, 1985.

Jefferson, Alison Rose. *Living the California Dream: African American Leisure Sites During the Jim Crow Era*. Lincoln: University of Nebraska Press, 2020.

Johnson, Gaye Theresa. "Constellations of Struggle: Luisa Moreno, Charlotta Bass, and the Legacy for Ethnic Studies." *Aztlán: A Journal of Chicano Studies* 33, no. 1 (2008): 155–72.

———. *Spaces of Conflict, Sounds of Solidarity: Music, Race, and Spatial Entitlement in Los Angeles*. Berkeley: University of California Press, 2013.

Jones, Martha S. *Vanguard: How Black Women Broke Barriers, Won the Vote, and Insisted on Equality for All*. New York: Basic Books, 2020.

Katz, Michael B. *The Price of Citizenship: Redefining the American Welfare State*. Philadelphia: University of Pennsylvania Press, 2008.

———. *The Undeserving Poor: From the War on Poverty to the War on Welfare*. New York: Pantheon Books, 1989.

Kelley, Robin D. G. *Hammer and Hoe: Alabama Communists During the Great Depression*. Chapel Hill: University of North Carolina Press, 1990.

———. *Race Rebels: Culture, Politics, and the Black Working Class*. New York: The Free Press, 1994.

Kells, Michelle Hall. *Vicente Ximenes, LBJ's Great Society, and Mexican American Civil Rights Rhetoric*. Carbondale: Southern Illinois University Press, 2018.

Kiffmeyer, Thomas. *Reformers to Radicals: The Appalachian Volunteers and the War on Poverty*. Lexington: University of Kentucky Press, 2008.

Krochmal, Max. *Blue Texas: The Making of a Multiracial Democratic Coalition in the Civil Rights Era*. Chapel Hill: University of North Carolina Press, 2016.

Kruse, Kevin. *White Flight: Atlanta and the Making of Modern Conservatism*. Princeton, NJ: Princeton University Press, 2005.

Kun, Josh, and Laura Pulido, eds. *Black and Brown in Los Angeles: Beyond Conflict and Coalition*. Berkeley: University of California Press, 2013.

Kurashige, Scott. *Shifting Grounds of Race Black and Japanese Americans in the Making of Multiethnic Los Angeles*. Princeton, NJ: Princeton University Press, 2007.

Lassiter, Matthew D. *The Silent Majority: Suburban Politics in the Sunbelt South*. Princeton, NJ: Princeton University Press, 2007.

Leonard, Kevin. *The Battle for Los Angeles: Racial Ideology and World War II*. Albuquerque: University of New Mexico Press, 2006.

Lerner, Mitchell. "'To Be Shot at by the Whites and Dodged by the Negroes': Lyndon Johnson and the Texas NYA." *Presidential Studies Quarterly* 39, no. 2 (2009): 245–74.

Levenstein, Lisa. *A Movement Without Marches: African American Women and the Politics of Poverty in Postwar Philadelphia*. Chapel Hill: University of North Carolina Press, 2009.

Lewis, Oscar. *La Vida; A Puerto Rican Family in the Culture of Poverty From San Juan to New York*. New York: First Vintage Books, 1968.

Lichtenstein, Nelson. *The Most Dangerous Man in Detroit: Walter Reuther and the Fate of American Labor*. New York: Basic Books, 1995.

Lipsitz, George, George Sánchez, Kelly Lytle Hernández, Daniel HoSang, and Natalia Molina. "Race As A Relational Theory: A Roundtable Discussion." In *Relational Formations of Race: Theory, Method, and Practice*, edited by Natalia Molina, Daniel Martinez HoSang, and Ramón A. Gutiérrez, 22–42. Berkeley: University of California Press, 2019. JSTOR e-book.

MacLean, Nancy. *Freedom Is Not Enough: The Opening of the American Workplace*. Cambridge, MA: Harvard University Press, 2006.

Mantler, Gordon. *Power to the Poor: Black-Brown Coalition and the Fight for Economic Justice, 1960-1974*. Chapel Hill: University of North Carolina Press, 2013.

Marable, Manning. *Race, Reform, and Rebellion: The Second Reconstruction in Black America, 1945-1990*. Jackson: University Press of Mississippi, 2007.

Márquez, John D. *Black-Brown Solidarity: Racial Politics in the New Gulf South*. Austin: University of Texas Press, 2013.

Martinez, Monica. *The Injustice Never Leaves You: Anti-Mexican Violence in Texas*. Cambridge, MA: Harvard University Press, 2020.

Matusow, Allen. *The Unraveling of America: A History of Liberalism in the 1960s*. New York: Harper and Row, 1984.

Mayes, Keith A. *Kwanzaa: Black Power and the Making of the African-American Holiday Tradition*. New York: Routledge, 2009.

Mitchell, Koritha. *From Slave Cabins to the White House: Homemade Citizenship in African American Culture*. Champaign: University of Illinois Press, 2020. JSTOR e-book.

Molina, Natalia. *How Race Is Made in America: Immigration, Citizenship, and the Historical Power of Racial Scripts*. Berkeley: University of California Press, 2014.

Montejano, David. *Quixote's Soldiers: A Local History of the Chicano Movement, 1966-1981*. Austin: University of Texas Press, 2010.

Moore Wilson, Shirley Ann. *To Place Our Deeds: The African American Community in Richmond, California, 1910-1963*. Berkeley: University of California Press, 2000.

Moreno, Marisol. "Understanding the Role of Conflict, Factionalism, and Schism in the Development of the Chicano Student Movement: The Mexican American Student Association and La Vida Nueva at East Los Angeles College, 1967-1969." In *The Chicano Movement: Perspectives from the Twenty-First Century*, edited by Mario T. Garcia, 173–200. New York: Routledge, 2014. ProQuest e-book.

Murch, Donna. *Living for the City: Migration, Education, and the Rise of the Black Panther Party in Oakland, California*. Chapel Hill: University of North Carolina Press, 2010.

Nadasen, Premilla. *Welfare Warriors: The Welfare Rights Movement in the United States*. New York: Routledge, 2005.

Nelson, Alondra. *Body and Soul: The Black Panther Party and the Fight against Medical Discrimination.* Minneapolis: University of Minnesota Press, 2013.

Ngai, Mae. *Impossible Subjects: Illegal Aliens and the Making of Modern America.* Princeton, NJ: Princeton University Press, 2004.

Nichols, Casey D. "'The Magna Carta to Liberate Our Cities': African Americans, Mexican Americans, and the Model Cities Program in Los Angeles." *Pacific Historical Review* 90, no. 3 (August 2021): 377-98.

Nicolaides, Becky M. *My Blue Heaven: Life and Politics in the Working-Class Suburbs of Los Angeles, 1920-1965.* Chicago: University of Chicago Press, 2002.

Ogbar, Jeffrey O. G. "Brown Power to Brown People: Radical Ethnic Nationalism, the Black Panthers, and Latino Radicalism, 1967-1973." In *In Search of the Black Panther Party: New Perspectives on a Revolutionary Movement,* edited by Jama Lazerow and Yohuru Williams, 252-86. Durham, NC: Duke University Press, 2006.

Orleck, Annelise. "Conclusion: The War on Poverty and American Politics Since the 1960s." In *The War on Poverty: A New Grassroots History,* edited by Annelise Orleck and Lisa Hazirjian, 437-61. Athens: University of Georgia Press, 2011.

———. "Introduction: The War on Poverty from the Grassroots Up." In *The War on Poverty: A New Grassroots History, 1964-1980,* edited by Annelise Orleck and Lisa Gayle Hazirjian, 1-28. Athens: University of Georgia Press, 2011.

———. *Storming Caesars Palace: How Black Mothers Fought Their Own War on Poverty.* Boston: Beacon Press, 2006.

Oropeza, Lorena. *The King of Adobe: Reies López Tijerina: Lost Prophet of the Chicano Movement.* Chapel Hill: University of North Carolina Press, 2019.

———. *¡RazaSí! ¡Guerro No!: Chicano Protest and Patriotism During the Vietnam War Era.* Berkeley: University of California Press, 2005.

Pagán Obregón, Eduardo. *Murder at Sleepy Lagoon: Zoot Suits, Race, and Riot in Wartime L.A.* Chapel Hill: University of North Carolina Press, 2003. ProQuest e-book.

Painter, Nell Irvin. *Exodusters: Black Migration to Kansas After Reconstruction.* New York: W. W. Norton and Company, 1992.

Pascoe, Peggy. *What Comes Naturally: Miscegenation Law and the Making of Race in America.* Oxford, UK: Oxford University Press, 2009.

Patiño, Jimmy. *Raza Sí, Migra No, Chicano Movement Struggles for Immigrant Rights in San Diego.* Chapel Hill: University of North Carolina Press, 2017.

Phelps, Wesley. *A People's War on Poverty: Urban Politics and Grassroots Activists in Houston.* Athens: University of Georgia Press, 2014.

Pritchett, Wendell E. *Robert Clifton Weaver and the American City: The Life and Times of An Urban Reformer.* Chicago: University of Chicago Press, 2014.

———. "Which Urban Crisis? Regionalism, Race, and Urban Policy, 1960-1974." *Journal of Urban History* 32, no. 2 (2008): 266-86.

Pulido, Laura. *Black, Brown, Yellow, and Left: Radical Activism in Los Angeles.* Berkeley: University of California Press, 2006.

Pycior, Julie. *LBJ and Mexican Americans: The Paradox of Power.* Austin: University of Texas Press, 1997.

Quadagno, Jill. *The Color of Welfare: How Racism Undermined the War on Poverty*. New York: Oxford University Press, 1996.

Ransby, Barbara. *Ella Baker and the Black Freedom Movement*. Chapel Hill: University of North Carolina Press, 2000.

Robinson, Cedric J. *Black Marxism: The Making of the Black Radical Tradition*. Chapel Hill: University of North Carolina Press, 1983.

Roediger, David. *The Wages of Whiteness: Race and the Making of the American Working Class*. New York: Verso Press, 1991.

Romo, Ricardo. *East Los Angeles: History of a Barrio*. Austin: University of Texas Press, 1983.

Rosas, Abigail. *South Central Is Home: Race and the Power of Community Investment in Los Angeles*. Stanford, CA: Stanford University Press, 2019.

Rose, Tricia. *Black Noise: Rap Music and Black Culture in Contemporary America*. Hanover, PA: Wesleyan University Press, 1994.

Rothstein, Richard. *The Color of Law: A Forgotten History of How Our Government Segregated America*. New York: Liveright Publishing, 2017.

Salazar, Ruben. *A Selection of Columns Reprinted from the* Los Angeles Times. Los Angeles: Los Angeles Times, 1970.

Sánchez, George J. *Becoming Mexican American: Ethnicity, Culture, and Identity in Chicano Los Angeles, 1900–1945*. New York: Oxford University Press, 1995.

———. *Boyle Heights: How a Los Angeles Neighborhood Became the Future of American Democracy*. Oakland: University of California Press, 2021.

———. "Edward Roybal and the Politics of Multiracialism." *Southern California Quarterly* 92, no. 1 (April 2010): 51–73.

———. "'What's Good for Boyle Heights Is Good for the Jews': Creating Multiracialism on the Eastside during the 1950s.'" *American Quarterly* 56, no. 3 (September 2004): 663–69.

———. "Why Are Multiracial Communities So Dangerous: A Comparative Look at Hawai'i; Cape Town, South Africa, and Boyle Heights, California." *Pacific Historical Review* 86, no. 1 (2017): 153–70.

Sanders, Crystal R. *A Chance for Change: Head Start and Mississippi's Black Freedom Struggle*. Chapel Hill: University of North Carolina Press, 2016. JSTOR e-book.

Sandoval-Strausz, A. K. *Barrio America: How Latino Immigrants Saved the American City*. New York: Basic Books, 2019.

San Miguel, Guadalupe, Jr. *In the Midst of Radicalism: Mexican American Moderates during the Chicano Movement, 1960–1978*. New York: Oxford University Press, 2021.

Santa Ana, Otto. *Brown Tide Rising: Metaphors of Latinos in Contemporary American Public Discourse*. Austin: University of Texas Press, 2002.

Self, Robert O. *American Babylon: Race and the Struggle for Postwar Oakland*. Princeton, NJ: Princeton University Press, 2003.

Sides, Josh. *L.A. City Limits: African American Los Angeles from the Great Depression to the Present*. Berkeley: University of California Press, 2006.

Slocum, Karla. *Black Towns, Black Futures: The Enduring Allure of a Black Place in the American West*. Chapel Hill: University of North Carolina Press, 2019.

Sonenshein, Raphael. "Coalition Building in Los Angeles: The Bradley Years and Beyond." In *Seeking El Dorado: African Americans in California*, edited by Lawrence B. De Graaf, Kevin Mulroy, and Quintard Taylor, 450–73. Seattle: University of Washington Press, 2015.

———. *Politics in Black and White: Race and Power in Los Angeles*. Princeton, NJ: Princeton University Press, 1993. JSTOR e-book.

Stevenson, Brenda. *The Contested Murder of Latasha Harlins: Justice, Gender, and the Origins of the LA Riots*. New York: Oxford University Press, 2015.

Sugrue, Thomas. *The Origins of the Urban Crisis: Race and Inequality in Postwar Detroit*. Princeton, NJ: Princeton University Press, 1996.

Sullivan, Patricia. *Days of Hope: Race and Democracy in the New Deal Era*. Chapel Hill: University of North Carolina Press, 1996.

Taylor, Keeanga-Yamahtta. *Race For Profit: How Banks and the Real Estate Industry Undermined Black Homeownership*. Chapel Hill: University of North Carolina Press, 2021.

Taylor, Quintard. *The Forging of a Black Community: Seattle's Central District from 1870 through the Civil Rights Era*. Seattle: University of Washington Press, 1994.

———. *In Search of a Racial Frontier: African Americans in the American West, 1528–1990*. New York: W. W. Norton and Company, 1999.

Taylor, Ula Y. *The Promise of Patriarchy: Women and the Nation of Islam*. Chapel Hill: University of North Carolina Press, 2017.

Theoharis, Jeanne. *The Rebellious Life of Mrs. Rosa Parks*. Boston: Beacon Press, 2015.

Trotter, Joe, Jr., ed. *The Great Migration in Historical Perspective: New Dimensions of Race, Class, and Gender*. Bloomington: Indiana University Press, 1991.

Vaca, Nicolás C. *Presumed Alliance: The Unspoken Conflict Between Latinos and Blacks and What It Means for America*. New York: Rayo Press, 2004.

Valenica, Richard R. *Chicano Students and the Courts: The Mexican American Legal Struggle for Educational Equality*. New York: New York University Press, 2008.

Vargas, Zaragosa. *Labor Rights Are Civil Rights: Mexican American Workers in Twentieth Century America*. Princeton, NJ: Princeton University Press, 2005.

Varzally, Allison. *Coloring Outside Ethnic Lines: Making a Non-White America in California, 1925–1955*. Berkeley: University of California Press, 2007.

Villanueva, Nicholas, Jr. *The Lynching of Mexicans in the Texas Borderlands*. Albuquerque: University of New Mexico Press, 2018.

Weaver, Robert Clifton. *Dilemmas in Urban America*. Cambridge, MA: Harvard University Press, 1965.

———. *The Negro Ghetto*. New York: Russell and Russell, 1948.

———. *Negro Labor: A National Problem*. Port Washington, NY: Kennikat Press, 1946.

———. *The Urban Complex: Human Values in Urban Life*. Garden City, NY: Doubleday, 1964.

Weber, Bret, and Amanda Wallace. "Revealing the Empowerment Revolution: A Literature Review of the Model Cities Program." *Journal of Urban History* 38, no. 1 (2012): 173–92.

Wild, Mark. *Street Meeting: Multiethnic Neighborhoods in Early Twentieth Century Los Angeles*. Berkeley: University of California Press, 2005.

Wilkerson, Isabel. *The Warmth of Other Suns: The Epic Story of America's Great Migration*. New York: Random House, 2010.

Williams, Rhonda. *The Politics of Housing: Black Women's Struggles Against Urban Inequality*. New York: Oxford University Press, 2005.

Online Sources

"(1954) Brown V. Board of Education." Primary Documents. Blackpast. Accessed January 26, 2022. www.blackpast.org/african-american-history/brown-v-board-education-1954/.

"(1957) Civil Rights Act of 1957." Blackpast. Accessed October 31, 2022. www.blackpast.org/african-american-history/civil-rights-act-1957/.

"(1963) Lyndon B. Johnson. 'Address Before a Joint Session of Congress.'" Blackpast. Accessed October 31, 2022. www.blackpast.org/african-american-history/1963-lyndon-b-johnson-address-joint-session-congress/.

"About." *Los Angeles Sentinel*. Accessed April 6, 2022. https://lasentinel.net/about.

Bauman, Robert. "Watts Summer Festival, 1966–." Blackpast. Accessed March 1, 2024. www.blackpast.org/african-american-history/watts-summer-festival-1966/.

"Biography, Lyndon B. Johnson." Lyndon Baines Johnson Presidential Library and Museum. Accessed September 16, 2022. www.lbjlibrary.org/life-and-legacy/the-man-himself/biography.

Bond de Pérez, Zanice. "Fannie Lou (1917–1977)." Blackpast. Accessed September 16, 2022. www.blackpast.org/african-american-history/hamer-fannie-lou-1917-1977/.

"Fannie's Speech to the DNC 1964." Fannie Lou Hamer Civil Rights Museum. Accessed September 16, 2022. www.thefannielouhamercivilrightsmuseum.com/fannie-lou-hamers-speech-to-the-dnc.html.

"Hamer, Fannie Lou (October 6, 1917–March 14, 1977)." Martin Luther King Jr. Research and Education Institute, Stanford University. Accessed September 16, 2022. https://kinginstitute.stanford.edu/encyclopedia/hamer-fannie-lou.

"Introduction." Martin Luther King Jr. Research and Education Institute, Stanford University. Accessed September 16, 2022. https://kinginstitute.stanford.edu/introduction.

Johnson, Lyndon B. "Annual Message to Congress on the State of the Union." January 8, 1964. The American Presidency Project, University of California at Santa Barbara. Accessed November 1, 2022. www.presidency.ucsb.edu/documents/annual-message-the-congress-the-state-the-union-25.

———. "Executive Order 11330-Providing for the Coordination of Youth Opportunity by Programs." March 5, 1967. The American Presidency Project, University of California at Santa Barbara. Accessed January 19, 2022. www.presidency.ucsb.edu/documents/executive-order-11330-providing-for-the-coordination-youth-opportunity-programs.

———. "Special Message to Congress Recommending a Program for Cities and Metropolitan Areas." January 26, 1966. The American Presidency Project, University of California at Santa Barbara. Accessed September 16, 2022.

www.presidency.ucsb.edu/documents/special-message-the-congress-recommending-program-for-cities-and-metropolitan-areas.

———. "Statement by the President Summarizing Actions on the Recommendations of the Inter-Agency Committee on Mexican American Affairs." February 23, 1968. Accessed October 31, 2022. https://www.presidency.ucsb.edu/documents/statement-the-president-summarizing-actions-the-recommendations-the-inter-agency-committee. The American Presidency Project, University of California at Santa Barbara.

Johnson, Lyndon Baines. "Radio and Television Remarks Upon Signing the Civil Rights Bill," July 2, 1964. Lyndon Baines Johnson Presidential Library and Museum. Accessed September 16, 2022. www.lbjlibrary.net/collections/selected-speeches/november-1963-1964/07-02-1964.html.

Karenga, Tiamoyo. "Karenga, Maulana (1941–)." Blackpast. Accessed September 16, 2022. www.blackpast.org/african-american-history/karenga-maulana-c-1943/.

"Walter Reuther." AFL-CIO-America's Unions. Accessed October 14, 2022. https://aflcio.org/about/history/labor-history-people/walter-reuther.

"Who We Are." County of Los Angeles Commission on Human Relations. Accessed September 16, 2022. https://hrc.lacounty.gov/.

Index

Italic page numbers refer to illustrations.

Abernathy, Ralph, 107–8, 116, 118, 120–21, 123–24
activism: class activism and economic justice, 24, 95, 113–14, 115–16, 126; collaborative power, 39–40, 74–79, 106; diversity within movements, 4–5, 8, 15–16, 35, 41–42, 110–11; and mass protests, 116, 123, 127, 141, 143; militant, 69–70, 81; moderate vs. militant, 71–72; terminology used, 11; youth activists, 6, 60–66, 68–69, 71–72, 119. *See also* Black Freedom movement; Chicano movement; Poor People's Campaign (PPC); student-led demonstrations
Ad Hoc Committee for Better Community Understanding, 143
aerospace industry, 31
African Americans: Black Freedom movement, 2, 5, 6, 34–36, 39, 69, 94, 107–8; Democratic Party engagement, 25–26, 27; labor movement, 24–25; migration to Los Angeles, 12–13, 17; migration to urban centers (1940–70), 28–29; politicization of Black youth, 63–66; "To Fulfill These Rights" conference, 92–97; unemployment and labor during Depression, 23–24; unemployment and poverty, 54–55; upward mobility of, 21. *See also* Black-Brown relations
Agricultural Adjustment Act, 25
Aid to Families with Dependent Children, 154
American Federation of Labor, 24

American Federation of Labor-Congress of Industrial Organizations (AFL-CIO), 49, 93
American GI Forum, 6, 15, 97, 101
Anderson, Glenn, 45, 46
Anguiano, Lupe, 78, 99
antipoverty programs: antipoverty activism, 4–5; challenges to, 117, 128–29; federal funding for, 1, 51, 85; health care, 75–76; in Los Angeles, 38–39, 41–42, 49–50, 68, 71; women's roles in, 121–22; youth-oriented, 60, 69, 78. *See also* Economic Opportunity Act (EOA); Model Cities initiative
Anti-War movement, 68
Appalachia, 85
Area Program for Enrichment Exchange, 148–49
Arellanes, Gloria, 76, 119
arts programs, 129, 145, 147–48
Asian Americans, 12, 16, 35, 157, 178n16
Assembly Special Committee, 155–58
author's methodology, 3–4, 8–11; Los Angeles as case study, 5–8; terminology used, 10–11
Avalon neighborhood, 29

Baker, Ella, 63
Baldwin Hills neighborhood, 29
Banking Act, 25
Barcero Program, 97
Barnes, Albert, 117–18
Barrio Free Clinic, 76
Barrows v. Jackson, 29
Bass, Charlotta, 17
Beasley, Harriet, 115

193

Bernhard, Berl, 91
Bernstein, Shana, 15
Black-Brown relations: coalitions, 39; coalitions in Los Angeles, 137–38; and economic justice, 126–27; frameworks of collaboration, 77–80; history of, 12–17, 160n4; Los Angeles as case study, 5–8; during 1960s, 88–92; overview, 2–5; after Poor People's Campaign, 123–26; in twenty-first century, 158. *See also* multiracial coalitions and collaborations
Black Freedom movement, 2, 5, 6, 34–36, 39, 69, 94, 107–8
"Black noise," 33, 52, 157, 164n1
Black Panther Party for Self-Defense (BPP), 61, 64, 71, 75, 147
Black Power movement, 68, 111–12; impact of on SCLC, 112–13
"blowout" schools, 148, 177n62
Bontemps, Arna, 17
Booker, James, 91
borderlands: Los Angeles, 161–62n1; status of, 14–15
Boyle Heights neighborhood, 21–22, 30, 74, 136
Bradley, Thomas, 135, 140, 156
Brazier, Wesley, 72
Bremond, Walter, 119
Brinkley, Alan, 25
Brookins, H. Hartford, 20
Brotherhood of Sleeping Car Porters, 24, 26, 90, 93
Brown, Edmund "Pat," 45, 51, 53
Brown, George E., Jr., 36, 100
Brown, Willie, 155
Brown Berets (Young Citizens for Community Action), 15, 60, 61, 73–74, 75, 80
Brown v. Board of Education of Topeka (1954), 4, 58, 62–63

Califano, Joseph, 97, 98–99
California: restrictive real estate covenants, 18; statehood and racial classifications, 14; university-level education, 68
California Master Plan for Education, 68
California National Guard, 154–55; Watts Rebellion, 47
California State University, Los Angeles, 148
Camarillo, Albert, 13, 161n15
Carmichael, Stokely, 111
Castillo, Leonel J., 104
Castro, Vickie, 73–74, 78
Catholic Youth Organization, 71
Central Avenue District, 19, 29
Chale con el Draft, 140
Chávez, César, 98, 107
Chávez, Ernesto, 74
Chavez Ravine neighborhood, 138
Chicago Freedom movement, 109
Chicano moratorium (Los Angeles), 140–46, 142, 143, 152, 174n2
Chicano movement: background and growth of, 6–8; and Black-Brown coalitions, 107–8, 110; "blowout" schools, 148; culturally relevant teaching materials, 123; and federal policy, 34, 73; in Los Angeles, 172n10; and Model Cities funding, 135; in urban areas, 108, 134–35; youth involvement in, 68, 104, 175n23
Christopher, Warren, 93
Citizens' Crusade Against Poverty, 90
civil disobedience, 4–5
Civil Rights Acts (1957 and 1964), 2, 66, 85, 86; and economic legislation, 116–17; legacy of, 82–83; limitations of, 126–27, 129–30
Clark, Kenneth, 85
Clark, Ramsey, 122–23
class stratification, 110; class activism and economic justice, 24, 95, 113–14, 115–16, 126; intersections of with race, 27; and multiracial coalitions, 113–14. *See also* Poor People's Campaign (PPC)

194 Index

Clayson, William, 37
Collins, H. H., 22
Collins, LeRoy, 47–49, 50–51
colonialism: legacy of, 13–14; settler-colonial frameworks, 13, 16–17, 32; Vietnam War as, 112
Committee of 100 (PPC), 115–17
Communist Party USA, 24
Community Action Programs (CAPs), 34–35, 48, 103; Head Start, 35, 56, 102, 126
Community Development Revenue Sharing, 151
Community on Juvenile Delinquency and Youth Crime, 38
Community Relations Service, 47
Community Service Organization (CSO), 136
Community War on Poverty Committee (CWPC), 36–37, 41–42, 100
Compton neighborhood, 29
Congress of Industrial Organizations, 24
Congress of Racial Equality (CORE), 39, 91, 92
Connolly, John, 37
Corona, Bert, 82, 97–98, 99, 101, 115
Council on Mexican-American Affairs, 90
Crawford, John, 71
criminal justice system, 13, 149
cross-racial organizing, 8, 35
Crusade for Justice, 115
"culture of poverty," 55

Democratic Party: Black and Brown shift to, 1, 26–27; complex identity of, 38; New Deal Democrats, 4, 25–26
Demonstration Cities and Metropolitan Development, 128, 131, 151. *See also* Model Cities initiative
Department of Housing and Urban Development (HUD), 101, 128, 132
Deverell, William, 13
Diamond, Stan, 45

Díaz, José, 15
discrimination: criminal justice system, 13, 149; defense industry, 90; employment, 31; housing, 29, 56
Domínguez, Emilio, 118–19
Downey neighborhood, 30
Du Bois, W. E. B., 12, 19
Dymally, Mervyn, 137–38

East Los Angeles, 56, 57, 73, 74; California State University, Los Angeles, 148; high schools in, 148–49
Economic and Youth Opportunities Agency (EYOA), 39–40, 49, 50, 77
"Economic Bill of Rights for All Americans," 111
Economic Development Agency, 36
economic justice, 3–4
Economic Opportunity Act (EOA): background of, 1, 34, 59, 86–88, 87; and Black-Brown relations, 51, 87–88; challenges to, 153; and civil rights legislation, 116; community involvement focus of, 37–38; impact of, 36; Title II, 34–35, 38–39; and youth engagement, 66–76; youth-oriented programming, 61–62
Economic Opportunity Foundation (EOF), 39
Egas, Victor, 90
Eisenhower, Dwight D., 52
Elizondo, Roy, 99
El Paso, TX, 17; civil rights hearings in (1967), 101, 136
employment discrimination, 31
Equal Employment Opportunity Commission (EEOC), 83, 89, 90
Escobar, Edward, 141, 177n66
Escobedo, Elizabeth, 61
Esparza, Moctesuma, 73
ethnic studies, 65, 68
Everett, Ronald, 68. *See also* Karenga, Maulana "Ron"

Fair Employment Practices Committee (FEPC), 89–90
Farmer, James, 91
farm workers, 107
Federal Housing Authority, 31
Felker-Kantor, Max, 45–46
Fernandez, Daniel, 90
Fernández, Johanna, 16
Flamming, Douglas, 14, 20
Florence-Firestone neighborhood, 139
Florence neighborhood, 29
Flores, Augustine A., 97, 99, 101–2
Foley, Neil, 120
Frazier, E. Franklin, 85
"Freedom Budget," 6, 94, 111
Frye, Marquette, 43, 43–44
Frye, Rena, 43, 43–44
Frye, Ronald, 43, 43–44

Galarza, Ernesto, 55, 98, 101
Gallegos, Herman, 57
Garcia, Hector, 99, 101
Garcia, Louis, 79
GI Forum, 6, 15, 97, 101
Goldwater, Barry, 88
Gómez, Laura, 14
Gonzales, Corky, 98, 115, 119, 120, 122–23, 124
Governor's Commission on the Los Angeles Riots, 33, 52. *See also* McCone Commission
Gray, Jesse, 95
Great Depression, 23–24; New Deal programs, 25–26; racism and xenophobia during, 24
Greater Watts Model Neighborhood, 139–40
Great Migration, 17, 28–29; Second, 63–64
Great Society reforms, 86
Green Meadows neighborhood, 134
Greenwood neighborhood (Tulsa), 19
Gregory, James, 21, 28
Gutiérrez, José Angel, 104
Guzmán, Ralph, 99, 101, 104

Hämäläinen, Pekka, 14
Hamer, Fannie Lou, 95
Hargett, James, 114
Harrington, Michael, 85
Hawkins, Augustus F.: background in Los Angeles, 12, 19–20; and coalition-building, 50–51, 57; commitment to collaboration, 40–41; and Community War on Poverty Committee (CWPC), 37, 39, 41–42; family's migration, 20–21; and growing Black political power, 36; and Inter-Agency Cabinet Committee on Mexican American Affairs (I-AC), 97; on labor movement, 25; and *Los Angeles Sentinel*, 63; and Model Cities initiative, 130, 140; outreach to youth activists, 72–73; photo of, 20; shift from Republican to Democratic Party, 26; support for Office of Economic Opportunity, 150–51; and War on Poverty, 1, 4, 15–16
Hawthorne School, 125
Head Start program, 35, 56, 102, 126
health clinics, 76
Height, Dorothy, 92, 97, 108, 121–22
Hernández, Alfred J., 89, 97, 99, 101
Hernández, Kelly Lytle, 13, 18
Higginbotham, Leon, 93
Hine, Darlene Clark, 64
Hinton, Elizabeth, 61
Holland, Lacine, 44–45
Holliday, George, 154
Home Owners' Loan Corporation, 18, 31
Horne, Gerald, 133, 161n15
Housing and Urban Development Act (1965), 132–33
housing discrimination, 29, 56. *See also* segregation
Howard University, 66–68, 67, 88–89
Humphrey, Hubert, 48, 59, 93, 98–99
Huntington Park neighborhood, 30
hypersegregation, 5, 8, 17, 30, 32, 77, 111, 120, 134, 139

identity formation (racial), 14, 80, 145
Immigration and Nationality Act (1965), 54
individual responsibility, 1, 81, 85
Industrial Workers of the World, 25
Inglewood neighborhood, 30
Inter-Agency Cabinet Committee on Mexican American Affairs, 83, 97–105
International Ladies Garment Workers Union, 25, 26

Jackson, Jesse, 115, 118
Jacquette, Tommy, 45, 69–73, 70, 80
Japanese Americans, 30
Jet Magazine, 95
Jim Crow laws, 111
Job Corps, 102
job discrimination, 31
Johnson, Gaye Theresa, 160n4
Johnson, Lyndon B., 33, 93, 99; background and beliefs on race, 83–88; Civil Rights Act (1964), 2, 16, 82; Economic Opportunity Act (EOA), 2, 34, 86–88, 87; Inter-Agency Cabinet Committee on Mexican American Affairs, 135–36; and Mexican Americans, 82–83, 104–5; President's Council on Youth Opportunity, 59; and SCLC, 118; Task Force on Urban Problems, 129; and US West, 105–6; War on Poverty, 1; Watts Rebellion, 47; youth engagement, 61–62, 66–68, 67, 88–89
Joint Ventures, 79
juvenile delinquency, 5, 15, 65, 74, 146

Karenga, Maulana "Ron," 68–69
Kaslow, Audrey, 98, 99
Katz, Michael, 130
Kennedy, John F., 33–34, 52, 85, 132; antipoverty initiatives, 85–86; Committee on Juvenile Delinquency, 38
Kerner Commission Report, 33, 157, 158
Kilgore, Thomas, Jr., 114
King, Coretta Scott, 118, 121–22

King, Martin Luther, Jr., 4, 35, 82, 92, 107, 111; death of, 117; and Poor People's Campaign, 112–13
King, Rodney, 133, 154–55, 158
Korea Town, 157
Kovner, Joseph, 138
Ku Klux Klan, 13
Kun, Josh, 161n15

labor unions, 24–25; recruitment and immigration, 17–18; United Farm Workers, 107
land rights of Mexican Americans, 124
La Raza Unida Conference, 104
Latin American Civic Association, 89
law enforcement and hypersegregation, 30–31
League of United Latin American Citizens (LULAC), 34, 84, 89, 97, 101
Lerner, Mitchell, 84
Lewis, Oscar, 55, 85
Lincoln Heights neighborhood, 73
Lipsitz, George, 161n15
Little Tokyo, 28
looting, 44–45
Lopez, Daniel, 102
López, Frank, 145–46
López, Ian Haney, 6–7, 145, 162n3
López, J. Robert, 77–78
Lorraine Hotel (Memphis, TN), 118
Los Angeles: aerospace industry, 31; African American migration to, 16–17; Assembly Special Committee, 155–58; Black and Brown political power, 36–42; as case study, 1, 5–8; Chicano moratorium, 140–46, 142; Chicano movement in, 172n10; County Human Relations Commission, 77; demographics, 18, 28, 156–57; demographic shifts post–World War II, 130–31; economic justice in, 23–27; Greater Watts Model Neighborhood, 139–40; history of race relations in, 162n7; map of, 7; Mexican American activism in, 110; Mexican American

Index   197

Los Angeles (cont.)
    migration to, 30; Mexican city to US city transition, 14, 18, 23; migration to and community development of, 12, 17–23, 32, 64; Model Cities initiative, 133–40; neighborhoods, 16, 18; Poor People's Campaign recruitment, 114; residential segregation, in, 21; school districts, 139–40; segregation post–World War II, 5, 8; as settler-colonial city, 13; as US-Mexico borderland city, 161–62n1; and War on Poverty, 36–37; World War II-era, 27–31. See also names of individual neighborhoods
Los Angeles Board of Education, 73
Los Angeles City Laws for Youth (booklet), 62
Los Angeles Crisis, 158
Los Angeles Police Department (LAPD), 45–46, 141; Black Panther raid, 147; Rodney King incident, 154–55
Los Angeles Sentinel (newspaper), 63
Los Angeles Youth Council, 74–75

Mantler, Gordon, 113
Marcha por Justicia, 144
march on Selma, 47
Marshall, Thurgood, 93
mass incarceration, 13
McCone, John A., 52
McCone Commission, 51–57, 158
McCullom, Donald, 82
McKissick, Floyd, 92
mestizo identities, 14
Mexican-American Lawyers Club, 149
Mexican American Opportunity Foundation (MAOF), 137–38
Mexican American Political Association (MAPA), 6, 15, 34, 40, 77, 88, 90, 104
Mexican Americans: "Brownness" and identity, 145; Chicano moratorium (Los Angeles), 140–46, 142, 143; civil rights movement, 39; conflict in Los Angeles Model Cities initiative, 138–39; Democratic Party engagement, 25–26, 27; and deportation, 24; as forgotten population, 102–4; Inter-Agency Cabinet Committee on Mexican American Affairs, 97–105; and Jim Crow, 83; labor movement, 21, 25; land rights, 124; legal status of, 13; and McCone Commission, 52–53; migration of, 29–30, 54; politicization of Brown youth, 63–66; unemployment and poverty, 54–55; youth activism, 73–74; youth culture, 61; zoot suit culture, 64–65, 71–72. See also Black-Brown relations; Chicano movement
Mexican-American Unity Conference, 90
Mexican American Youth Organization, 104
Mexico-US border, 17–18
Miller, Loren, 29
Minikus, Lee W., 43
Mississippi Freedom Democratic Party, 95
Mitchell, Clarence, Jr., 93
Model Cities initiative, 6, 104, 128–29; decline of, 146–51; history and overview of, 129–33; legacy of, 151–52; in Los Angeles, 133–40; in Los Angeles school districts, 139–40; Plaza de la Raza community center, 145–46; restructuring of under Nixon, 149–51; riot prevention, 143
Model Neighborhood Legal Center, 149
Molina, Natalia, 20
Montes, Miguel, 79, 89, 98, 99, 101
Montgomery Improvement Association, 111
Montoya, Arthur, 138
Morales, Dionicio, 137
moratorium demonstrations, 141. See also Chicano moratorium (Los Angeles)
Movimiento Estudiantil Chicanx de Aztlán, 15

Moynihan, Daniel Patrick, 55, 85
mulatto identities, 14
multiracial children, 13–14
multiracial coalitions and collaborations, 35; barriers to, 16–17; Black-Brown coalitions, 39, 137–38; Black-Brown coalitions in Los Angeles, 15–16; economic justice, 126–27; Poor People's Campaign (PPC) planning, 109–117; Southern Christian Leadership Conference (SCLC), 107–8. *See also* Black-Brown relations
multiracial neighborhoods, 16
Muñoz, Rosalio, 140, 144
Murch, Donna, 63–64, 68

NAACP (National Association for the Advancement of Colored People), 15, 39, 63, 92, 121
National Advisory Commission on Civil Disorders (Kerner Commission), 33, 157, 158
National Association of Colored Women's Clubs, 15
National Council of Negro Women, 92
National Industrial Recovery Act, 25
National Poor People's Steering Committee, 113
National Urban League, 15, 39, 71, 92, 117
National Welfare Rights Organization (NWRO), 115, 121, 122
National Youth Authority (NYA), 84
Nation Institute, 112
Neighborhood Youth Corps, 102
Nelson, Alondra, 147
New Deal Democrats, 4, 25–26
New Mexico, 14
Nickerson Gardens Community Development Project, 71
Nixon, Richard, 149–51, 177n68
nonviolence: adherence to, 111–12; militant, 112–13
North, David, 98

O'Connor, Alice, 85
Office of Economic Opportunity (OEO), 39, 49, 51; and Black-Brown violence as concern, 79–80; challenges to, 150–51; and Committee of 100, 117; and youth activists, 73
Olivares, Graciela, 90
Operation Breadbasket, 115
Operation SER, 102
Organization US, 68–69, 72
Orneles, Robert, 99
Oropeza, Lorena, 124
The Other America (Harrington), 85
outdoor education, 79–80
Own Recognizance Assistance and Rehabilitation Project, 146

Pachuca and Pachuco culture, 61
Pagán, Eduardo, 64
pardo identities, 14
Parker, William H., 44, 45–47
Parks, Rosa, 111
Peña, Albert, 90
Peters, A. A., 114
Pico-Union neighborhood, 157
Plaza de la Raza community center, 145–46
Poblano, Ralph, 77
police harassment and brutality, 53–54, 149; death of Rubén Salazar, 143; Marcha por Justicia, 144; policing and hypersegregation, 30–31; Young Chicanos for Community Action (Brown Berets), 64, 73–74, 75
Political Association of Spanish-Speaking Organizations, 6, 15, 34, 88, 90
political power of Black and Brown people, 36–42
Poor People's Campaign (PPC), 106, 107–8; Committee of 100, 115–17; government agency hearings, 115–16; after King's death, 117–23; planning, 109–117; Resurrection City, 119–20;

Index 199

Poor People's Campaign (PPC) (cont.) SCLC-Mexican American conflict, 123–24, 125; Solidarity Day, 121; women's roles in, 121–22
Poor People's Coalition, 125
poverty: and activism, 110; culture of, 55; cycle of, 54–55; "poverty knowledge," 85; research on, 85; and stereotypes, 85–86; terminology, 10–11. *See also* Poor People"s Campaign (PPC)
President's Council on Youth Opportunity, 59–60
prison rehabilitation projects, 146
Pulido, Laura, 65–66, 161n15
Pycior, Julie, 33, 83

Quevedo, Eduardo, 90, 98, 99
"Quiet Riot," 78–79

racism: racial hierarchies, 13–14; "rainbow racism," 161n15; Rodney King incident, 154–55; *sistema de castas*, 13–14; structural and institutional, 15–16, 73. *See also* Watts Rebellion (1965)
Randolph, A. Philip, 6, 90, 93, 94, 108, 111
Ransby, Barbara, 63
Reagan, Ronald, 151, 153
real estate development, 31
Rebuild L.A. campaign (Bradley), 156
Red Cap Station Porters, 24
redlining, 31, 155
Republican Party, 26–27
residential segregation, 29, 56
Resurrection City (PPC), 119–20, 125. *See also* Poor People's Campaign (PPC)
Reuther, Walter, 121, 129–30, 151
Ríos, Anthony, 136–37
Robinson, Frances, 115
Rodriguez, Linda, 1
Roosevelt, Franklin Delano, 84, 89–90, 132; Executive Order 8802, 90

Roosevelt, James, 36
Rosas, Abigail, 75–76
Rose, Tricia, 164n1
Roybal, Edward R.: background in Los Angeles, 12, 22; early political career, 26–27; family's migration, 21–23; and growing Brown political power, 36; legacy of, 136; photo of, 22; and police reform, 149; and War on Poverty, 4, 15–16
Roybal, George, 102–3
Ruiz, Manuel, 40, 90
Rustin, Bayard, 4, 63, 93, 94, 108

Salazar, Rubén, 34, 143
Sánchez, David, 64, 73, 74–75
Sánchez, Leopold, 143
Sanders, Crystal, 35
Sandoval-Strausz, A. K., 54
San Francisco State University, 65
schools: "blowout," 148; Model Cities initiative in, 139–40; and socioeconomic stratification, 56; tutoring centers, 149
Scott King, Coretta, 118, 121–22
Second Great Migration, 63–64
segregation: and overpolicing, 30–31; hypersegregation, 5, 8, 30, 32, 77, 111, 120, 134, 139; Los Angeles post–World War II, 5, 8; at neighborhood level, 18; in Poor People's Campaign, 120–21
Self, Robert, 16
Self Leadership for all Nationalists Today, 72
settler-colonial frameworks, 13, 16–17, 32
Shelley v. Kraemer, 29
Shriver, Sargent, 49, 50, 147
Sickle Cell Anemia Education and Detection Program, 147
Sides, Josh, 27
"silent majority" rhetoric, 149–50, 177n68
sistema de castas, 13–14

Sleepy Lagoon Defense Committee (SLDC), 15
Social Action Training Center (SATC), 69
Social Security Act, 76
Solidarity Day, 121
Sonenshein, Raphael, 135
Sons of Watts, 146
South Central Los Angeles, 32, 44, 45, 56, 134, 140, 147, 156, 157. *See also* Watts Rebellion (1965)
Southern Christian Leadership Conference (SCLC), 92, 107; and Black Power, 112–13; foundation of, 111; outreach to new cities, 114
South Los Angeles, 29, 30
Special Committee on the Los Angeles Crisis, 153
Stevenson, Brenda, 178n16
student-led demonstrations, 140–46, 142, 143. *See also* youth
Student Nonviolent Coordinating Committee, 111
Sugrue, Thomas, 174n12
Sullivan, Leon, 93

Taylor, Christopher, 20
Taylor, Keeanga-Yamahtta, 18
Teen Post, 78, 80
Téllez, Louis, 101
Third World Liberation Front, 65–66
Thomas, Ernest, 95
Tijerina, Reies López, 118, 120, 121, 123, 124
Title II (EOA), 34–35, 38–39. *See also* Economic Opportunity Act (EOA)
"To Fulfill These Rights" conference (1966), 83, 92–97; class differences, 95; exclusion of Mexican Americans from, 90, 91–92, 96–97; legacy of, 110–11
To Rebuild Is Not Enough (report), 153, 155–56, 157
Treaty of Guadalupe Hidalgo (1848), 12–13, 123

Truan, Carlos, 103–4
Truett, Samuel, 14
Truman, Harry S., 52
Tucker, Curtis, Jr., 155
Tulsa, OK, 19

unemployment and poverty, 54–55
United Auto Workers, 130
United Farm Workers, 98, 107
United Mexican American Students, 15
United Presbyterian Church, 70
United Steel Workers, 26
United Way, 49
university-level education, 68
"urban crisis," 131–32, 161n18
urban renewal, 101–2, 133, 138
US Agency for International Development, 100
US-Mexico War, 12, 13

Veterans Administration, 31
Vietnam War, 112
Villaraigosa, Antonio, 158
violence: racialized, 13; youth culture and, 61–62
Volunteers in Service to America (VISTA), 73–74
Voting Rights Act (1965), 86

War on Poverty, 34; extension and reform (1970s), 1; legacy of, 153–54; Los Angeles's role in, 36–37; at neighborhood level, 19; and youth activism, 68; youth-oriented programming, 59–63
War on Poverty Incorporated, 98
Warren, Earl, 59, 62
Washington, Dorothy, 79
Washington, Leon, Jr., 63
Watts neighborhood, 29
Watts Rebellion (1965), 4, 6, 33, 35–36, 42–51, 46; impact of, 95–96; legacy of, 57–58, 109, 140; McCone Commission, 51–57
Watts Summer Festival, 147–48

Index   201

Weaver, Robert C., *93*, 101, 128, 132, 133–34, 136, 175n13
Welcome to Los Angeles: April 29, 1992 (video), 155
welfare: stereotypes of recipients, 154; rights movement, 161n17
Welfare Planning Council, 49
Westminster Neighborhood Association (WNA), 70–71
white supremacy, 20, 30, 38, 49, 79, 146, 174n2; Ku Klux Klan, 13. *See also* racism
Wiley, George, 91, 122
Wilkerson, Isabel, 17
Wilkins, Roy, 92, 93, 94, 97, 121
Williams, Annabelle, 71
Williams, Hosea, 114, 122
Willowbrook neighborhood, 29, 139
Wilson, Charles, 36
Wirin, A. L., *43*
Women Strike for Peace, 115

Ximenes, Vicente T., 83, 100–101, 135–36, 175n27

Yorty, Sam: Economic Opportunity Act (EOA), 37–38; EOF (Economic Opportunity Foundation) vs. YOB (Youth Opportunities Board), 39–40; Los Angeles Youth Council, 74–75; Model Cities initiative, 134, 135–36, 137–38; and municipal power conflicts, 4, 34, 35, 41–42; Watts Rebellion, 47, 48; youth-oriented programs, 62
Young, Andrew, 110, 117–18, 122
Young, Whitney, 92, 93, 94, 97
Young Chicanos for Community Action (YCCA), 75, 78
Young Citizens for Community Action (YCCA), 73–75
youth: in Chicano movement, 68, 104, 175n23; politicization of, 63–66; activism, 6, 60–66, 68–69, 71–72, 119; centers, 78; culture and violence, 61–62; youth-led organizations, 15, 175n23; youth-oriented antipoverty programming, 59–63. *See also* student-led demonstrations
Youth Opportunities Board (YOB), 38; and EOF, 39

zoot suit culture, 64–65, 71–72
Zoot Suit Riots (1943), 30, 61, 64, 77